Lecture Notes in Artificial Intelligence 3012

Edited by J. G. Carbonell and J. Siekmann

Subseries of Lecture Notes in Computer Science

Springer
Berlin
Heidelberg
New York
Hong Kong
London
Milan
Paris
Tokyo

Koichi Kurumatani   Shu-Heng Chen
Azuma Ohuchi (Eds.)

Multi-Agent for Mass User Support

International Workshop, MAMUS 2003
Acapulco, Mexico, August 10, 2003
Revised and Invited Papers

 Springer

Series Editors

Jaime G. Carbonell, Carnegie Mellon University, Pittsburgh, PA, USA
Jörg Siekmann, University of Saarland, Saarbrücken, Germany

Volume Editors

Koichi Kurumatani
National Institute of Advanced Industrial Science and Technology (AIST)
Aomi 2-41-6, Koto-ku, Tokyo 135-0064, Japan
E-mail: k.kurumatani@aist.go.jp

Shu-Heng Chen
National Chengchi University, Department of Economics
Taipei, Taiwan, 11623, R.O.C.
E-mail: chchen@nccu.edu.tw

Azuma Ohuchi
Hokkaido University, Graduate School of Engineering
N13, W8 Kita-Ku, Sapporo, 060-8628, Japan
E-mail: ohuchi@complex.eng.hokudai.ac.jp

Library of Congress Control Number: 2004104314

CR Subject Classification (1998): I.2.11, C.2.4, I.2, I.6

ISSN 0302-9743
ISBN 3-540-21940-4 Springer-Verlag Berlin Heidelberg New York

Springer-Verlag is a part of Springer Science+Business Media

springeronline.com

© Springer-Verlag Berlin Heidelberg 2004
Printed in Germany

Typesetting: Camera-ready by author, data conversion by DA-TeX Gerd Blumenstein
Printed on acid-free paper   SPIN: 10997727   06/3142   5 4 3 2 1 0

Preface

This volume is the postproceedings of the Workshop on Multiagent for Mass User Support 2003 (MAMUS 2003). It consists of revised papers presented at the meeting and invited ones based on the program committee's recommendation. The workshop was organized in association with the 18th International Joint Conference on Artificial Intelligence (IJCAI 2003), August 10, 2003, Acapulco, Mexico. The aim of the workshop was to investigate new directions of multiagent technology and its applications to support mass users and society by using social coordination mechanisms in both the artificial intelligence and social science senses.

Multiagent and agent-based simulations have been providing new methodologies and viewpoints for studying societies. They are becoming effective tools for modeling and simulating social systems. On the other hand, the rapid progress of IT (information technology) such as ubiquitous or pervasive computing is bringing changes to communications, decision-making processes, and even possibly to how people conduct themselves in their daily lives. People in a ubiquitous computing environment would be able to access information networks, communicate with each other, exchange information, and obtain sensing data on an everywhere, anytime basis. Such an information environment is expected to open up a new application field where each user's utility is increased and the efficiency of the whole system (society) is also improved. This is the objective of mass user support. In order to realize mass user support systems, we need to investigate the problem from the two viewpoints of social systems and information technology. By social coordination we mean analysis of social systems from the viewpoint of balancing the utilities provided to individuals and the whole system.

Papers included in this volume are categorized as follows. The *theoretical background* section includes two papers that characterize mass user support and social coordination. Kurumatani discusses the characteristics of the problem and gives its formalization and analysis. Chen proposes CE Lab, a platform where both human and software agents work together, especially to integrate experimental economics, behavioral economics, and agent-based computational economics.

The *resource allocation algorithms* section has three papers. Cheng proposes a market-based resource allocation algorithm for information collection in emergency scenario. Kawamura discusses the Theme Park Problem, in which he analyzes the effect of information provision on many users. Matsuo proposes story-based planning that generates visiting plans according to users' intentions and preferences.

Traffic systems is an important area of applications for mass user support. In the *Mass User Support in Traffic Systems* section, Yamashita proposes an algorithm for large numbers of users to exchange their driving plans in order to increase the utilities for individuals and the whole system. Shinoda analyzes the usability of dial-a-ride buses, especially their efficiency in large-scale towns.

Because mass user support essentially requires resource allocation among users, the problem can be formalized in the game theoretic sense as the simplest edge problem. The *game theoretic analysis* section includes two papers: Suzuki discusses role changes in the social dilemma game to manage limited common resources; Yamashita formalizes the dynamics of group formation mechanisms from the game theoretic viewpoint.

From the engineering viewpoint, it is crucial that we design large-scale systems that handle many communication and computation tasks in order to realize mass user support. In the section titled *Architectures for Social Coordination Mechanisms*, Amamiya and Pitt propose a multiagent system called KODAMA for managing individual digital rights for information trading. Murakami proposes Fairy Wing, which is a user profile accumulation system that works with RF-ID tags. Sashima proposes a multiagent architecture called CONSORTS for service coordination in a ubiquitous computing environment.

As the editors of this volume, we would like to thank the members of the program committee and the anonymous reviewers for their important contributions. We would also like to thank Akio Sashima for his typesetting of this volume.

Tokyo, February 2004   Koichi Kurumatani
                                                                Shu-Heng Chen
                                                                Azuma Ohuchi

Program Committee Members

Robert L. Axtell (The Brookings Institution)
Shu-Heng Chen (National Chengchi University)
Hidenori Kawamura (Hokkaido University)
Koichi Kurumatani (National Institute of Advanced Industrial Science and Technology, Japan)
Kazuo Miyashita (National Institute of Advanced Industrial Science and Technology, Japan)
Itsuki Noda (National Institute of Advanced Industrial Science and Technology, Japan)
Azuma Ohuchi (Hokkaido University)
Keiji Suzuki (Future University – Hakodate)
Michael P. Wellman (University of Michigan)

Table of Contents

Architectures for Social Coordination Mechanisms

Mass User Support by Social Coordination among Citizens in a Real Environment

Koichi Kurumatani

Multiagent Team (MA), Cyber Assist Research Center (CARC)
National Institute of Advanced Industrial Science and Technology (AIST)
Aomi 2-41-6, Koto-ku, Tokyo 135-0064, Japan
k.kurumatani@aist.go.jp
http://www.kurumatani.org

Abstract. We propose the concept of mass user support realized by social coordination among citizens in a real environment. By real environment, we mean an environment integrating a world of abstract information such as the Internet with the physical world. Rapid progress in IT, especially ubiquitous or pervasive computing, is helping to bring about an environment where direct communication among citizens and realtime delivery of sensory information becomes possible not only within buildings but also in cities or in a driving environment. In the real environment, we can expect a new information service called mass user support that can be achieved by social coordination among users. An example of social coordination is dynamic resource allocation of spatio-temporal resources, i.e., traffic control for vehicles and pedestrians, by which the utility provided to both individuals and the whole system can be increased. In this paper, we first illustrate the concept of mass user support by giving several examples and then introduce a new kind of multiagent architecture called CONSORTS that is expected to be an infrastructure for social coordination. We analyze the characteristics of social coordination, compared with the conventional methods, and propose a course of software implementation to realize mass user support by coordinating users' intentions and preferences.

1 Introduction

We propose the concept of mass user support realized by social coordination among users in a real environment. By real environment, we mean an environment integrating an abstract information world such as the Internet with the real physical and spatio-temporal world where humans and physical objects exist. Rapid progress in IT, especially ubiquitous computing [1] or pervasive computing [2], is helping to bring about an environment where direct communication and delivery of sensory information can be done over wide areas, i.e., in buildings, cities, on roads, or nation-wide, rather than in a proximate environment shared by individuals.

In a real environment, we can expect a new kind of information service called mass user support that cannot be achieved by a simple combination of separate personal information services. For instance, let us consider a service to simultaneously help many vehicles and pedestrians to navigate. These days, many

K. Kurumatani et al. (Eds.): MAMUS 2003, LNAI 3012, pp. 1–17, 2004.

vehicles are equipped with car navigation systems that automatically make driving plans for the driver by using the current position of a vehicle and road maps in the car navigation system, and the system provides navigation service such as telling tuning direction at crossings to drivers during the trip. Some car navigation systems provide more sophisticated planning by using congestion information provided by VICS (Vehicle Information and Communication System) [3], i.e., these make plans to avoid congestion and to save total trip time.

We have, however, a question on the utility of such sophisticated services. What would happen when all drivers use such a congestion-avoiding planning strategy simultaneously? The answer is likely that many drivers would select roads that seem to be less crowded but in doing so make the roads crowded, which would in turn cause an oscillation in road traffic congestion that never converges. We can imagine the same situation in navigating many pedestrians in a building, theme park, or cities. It is quite possible that oscillation of congestion might occur if information about the current status of congestion were to be provided directly to pedestrians via information devices such as cellular phones or PDAs and then letting them choose the shortest path independently.

We need, therefore, some kind of coordination mechanism among users in order to provide good services under such situations, that is, we need to coordinate users' intentions and preferences socially. Mass user support is an information service that realizes such social coordination among users in daily lives by using cooperating software agents in a real environment. By social coordination, we mean automatic negotiation by software agents that work as proxies for users rather than explicit and verbal communication directly done by the human users themselves. The rapid progress of information network technology is expected to bring about a ubiquitous or pervasive network that will provide anytime, everywhere connectivity to information networks. In addition, we expect that mass user support will become one of the key services of the ubiquitous or pervasive network, besides the conventional information service images.

We have to pay attention to the difference between social coordination and collaboration. Collaboration is a highly organized activity done by human users in order to achieve goals, which usually needs long time before obtaining a solution. In contrast, social coordination requires realtime responses, e.g., drivers have to react rapidly to give a traffic lane to others. On the other hand, the best solution is not necessary in social coordination. If the best solution is unobtainable, the benefit may still be obvious; e.g., if we could reduce by only one percent of the total losses caused by a traffic jam in a city or in a country, it would bring much benefit to the economy and natural environment. Reflecting on the nature of the problem, social coordination requires different approaches from the ones developed for collaboration, e.g., CSCW (Computer-Supported Cooperative Work) [4], Collaborative Multiagent [5], conventional web-based meeting, and so on.

From the engineering viewpoint, we also introduce a multiagent architecture called CONSORTS, which is an infrastructure for electronic social coordination in a ubiquitous computing environment, by which software agents can trace users' movement histories, understand their intentions and preferences, construct user models, and negotiate with each other while protecting the users' privacy by using temporal identifiers. The functionality of mass user support is realized as a service agent in the architecture. The key functionality is realized by coordination of software agents, i.e., personal agents that serve as proxies for users, a service agent as the social coordinator, and a spatio-temporal reasoner.

After describing examples of mass user support and the CONSORTS architecture, we will analyze the characteristics of mass user support that cannot be formalized as a simple combination of personal services for individual users, and which consequently require coordination among users. We then compare various computational methods to realize the coordination. It seems useful to prepare some kind of standard problem in order to compare the methods in different environments.

2   Examples of Mass User Support

We can find many situations where social coordination is essential and a mass user support service would improve the efficiency and utility. In particular, mass user support is effective when we need to coordinate resources in a realtime manner, that is, realtime resource allocation is required. The aim of mass user support is to increase the efficiency of both individual users and the whole system simultaneously. Examples of application areas where social coordination is effective and mass user support is useful are as follows (Fig. 1):

1. Facility Usage and Layout Design:
    For pedestrian users, social coordination is expected to reduce waiting time in private or public facilities (e.g., at theme park attractions, or in stores, government offices, etc.), and also to increase the utility that each user may be seeking, e.g., fun, interest, or education. This kind of problem is called the Theme Park Problem [6][7].
2. Road Traffic:
    In the road traffic context, social coordination is expected to reduce traffic congestion and to shorten each driver's trip time, by coordinating users' driving plans according to their destinations and road constraints. The aim is not only to reduce congestion but also to increase each user's convenience and comfort. The problem is called the Car Navigation Problem [8]. Social coordination would also be effective to dynamically control driving plans of public transportation vehicles such as dial-a-ride buses [9].
3. Global Traffic Control:
    In addition to services for each driver and passenger, social coordination is also expected to control the global traffic system, e.g., to dynamically control intervals and durations of traffic signals, to change the direction of one-way streets, and to temporarily stop inflow to streets.
4. Supply Chain:
    Social coordination is useful to increase the efficiency of the supply chain by adapting it in a realtime manner to dynamically changing environments such as road traffic and whether, in contrast with conventional off-line scheduling.

Mass user support has different characteristics from conventional information services. The main difference is that mass user support is not just a combination of personal services for individual users. For instance, individually minimizing the waiting time for attractions in a theme park can result in an oscillation in queue length and waiting time, which consequently decreases total utility provided to each user. We should notice that utility means not only time efficiency but also convenience, comfort, fun, and so on. Methods to generate plans with several evaluation functions such as story-based planning [10] can be combined with dynamic resource allocation to generate several kinds of user utility for theme park, road traffic, and so on.

An example of mass user support for the Theme Park Problem is shown in Fig. 2 [6]. People tend to make reservations to a popular attraction regardless of the crowd in front of it, and they might forget attractions that are not crowded and yet ones that they are fairly interested in. By coordinating users' intentions and preferences about attractions, there is a possibility of controlling resource coordination while keeping user satisfaction.

3   CONSORTS – Architecture for Ubiquitous Agents

CONSORTS (Coordination System of Realworld Transaction Service) is a multiagent architecture for a ubiquitous computing environment, which is designed to 1) coordinate several kinds of services and 2) support social coordination by introducing mass user support services. The key concepts of CONSORTS are semantic grounding and cognitive resources. By using sensory information brought by the ubiquitous computing environment, agents have a grounding in the physical world and are conscious of physical resources (especially spatio-temporal resources) in a cognitive way, i.e., they can recognize, reorganize, and operate raw physical resources as cognitive resources. The services made possible by CONSORTS include 1) extension of conventional personal services using information about the physical world such as position and 2) forms of information provision and social coordination that go beyond personal support.

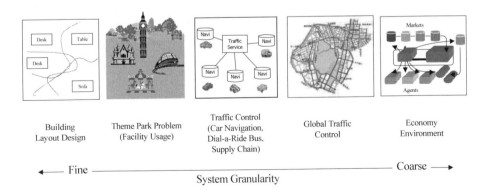

		Traffic Control		
Building	Theme Park Problem	(Car Navigation,	Global Traffic	Economy
Layout Design	(Facility Usage)	Dial-a-Ride Bus,	Control	Environment
		Supply Chain)		

◄─── Fine ── Coarse ──►
System Granularity

Fig. 1. Examples of Mass User Support

Realtime Resource Allocation

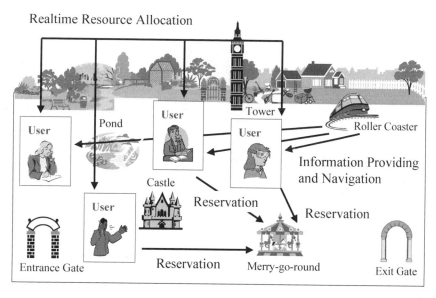

Fig. 2. Theme Park Problem

In the architecture, we assume that users have mobile information devices such as PDAs, cellular phones, and so on. We also assume that the users' positions are captured by sensors such as GPS, RF-ID tags, or wireless LAN and their tracks of moving history are also sensed and registered in the spatio-temporal reasoner. Service agents provide situation-based services that use information about a user's position and movement history. One such situation-based service is information provision according to the user's position. For instance, when a user is near an attraction that s/he might be interested in, a navigation agent tells the user about the way to get there (Fig. 3) [11, 12, 13, 14]. In version 1 of the architecture [14], all modules are designed and implemented as FIPA-Agents [15].

As an example of mass user support, let us again consider user navigation in a theme park, this time, one which coordinates many users' intentions and preferences about attractions. The service is implemented as follows. The first part is a personal service, which navigates users to their favorite places according to their intentions and preferences, i.e., maximizing the number of places they want to visit and minimizing moving distance and time, while obtaining the needed guidance information. The second one is a social coordination service, which tries to decrease the congestion degree and total movement distance and time of all users, by making plans for all the users while coordinating their intentions and preferences.

Another important part of this architecture is the model for describing the user, i.e., 1) intentions: goals that the user should be achieved during a period such as a day, 2) preferences: goals that the user expects achieve during the period, and 3) attributes: a static description about the user that can be used to retrieve suitable information.

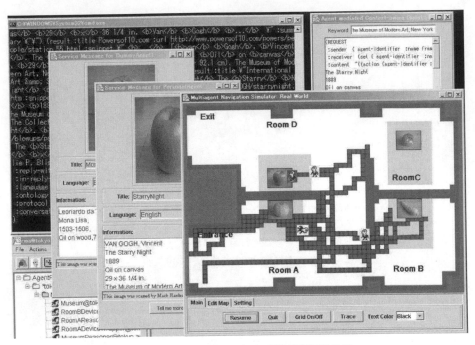

Fig. 3. Museum Scenario in CONSORTS [14]

We are now designing CONSORTS version 3 (Fig. 4). To summarize the functionality of CONSORTS ver.3, it works as an infrastructure to provide the following mechanisms (Fig. 5):

1. Service Adaptation:
    It provides suitable services by adjusting and invoking related software according to the situation where users exist. Providing information according to user's position as illustrated in the museum scenario is an example of service adaptation.
2. Service Combination:
    It provides common languages for services that are implemented in different contexts. This can be done by introducing an ontology for the semantic web [16], especially a semantic gateway or WebSLIT [14].
3. Service Composition:
    It composes new services from available ones. Typically, it is a solution to connect the output of an available service with the input of another service, and so on, i.e., to construct a pipeline of services. This functionality requires a service combination in order to connect an output with an input. One example is a navigation service for drivers or pedestrians that reflects situation (weather, and the aim of driving), preference (reducing time, or enjoying the landscape), and congestion degree obtained from other services (e.g., by VICS).

4. Social Coordination:

    It achieves social coordination and provides mass user support, including dynamic resource allocation (especially, spatio-temporal resources) to many users simultaneously. The functionality is realized as a social coordinator service and information provision service for each user. A simple mass user support is an appointment service to mass users such as groups, which coordinates users' plans, determines meeting points, and shows the meeting points and the directions on how to get there.

5. Agent Security:

    It provides a basic framework to ensure the order of agent society and security of agents in the architecture. The order is mainly assured by dynamic allocation of computational resources to the software agents (not for users). Security is mainly kept by introducing a mechanism for eliminating agents that act strangely, i.e., the architecture prevents agents that show strange or illegal behaviors from using computational resources.

As an example of service images, the design of the vehicle navigation system on CONSORTS is shown in Fig. 6. There are two main functionalities in the system. One is a scenario generator for the future, and the other is an experience archive for the past.

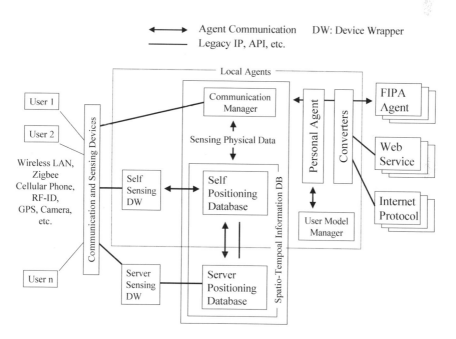

Fig. 4. CONSORTS Version 3 – Architecture for Ubiquitous Agents

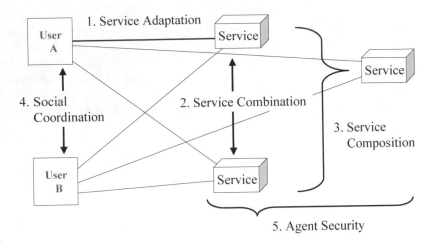

Fig. 5. Service Coordination Mechanism in CONSORTS

Regarding the scenario generation, by referring to the user's personal goal and driving preferences and by using dynamic resource allocation, the system provides a route-planning functionality. The route planner generates drive plans that are customized to the user, e.g., a scenic route is generated if the user's aim is leisure, and timesaving plan is generated if the aim is work. Along with personalized planning, the system communicates with the dynamic resource allocater that is executed on an external server. The dynamic resource allocater produces plans that better fit the user's aim and preferences yet also increase the whole traffic system's efficiency.

The experience archiver stores realtime sensing data, camera images, domestic information, and personal impressions as the record of driving history that is called transforming panoramic experience. The archived data becomes a travel memory or realtime diary that can be used for planning in the future. The experience archive can be exchanged with others via P2P or an external archive server. This exchange mechanism provides other kinds of services, such as generating graphical road maps, detecting the possibility of natural disasters (disaster prediction), and so on.

4   Formalization of Social Coordination

In this section, we analyze the characteristics of mass user support as an engineering problem and also formalize social coordination as a general problem.

4.1 Decentralization of Coordination Mechanism

As an engineering problem, mass user support can be regarded as a problem for information technology to provide suitable information to many users simultaneously, by analyzing the status of the whole system, by coordinating users' intentions and preferences, and by generating messages specific to each user. It can be designed and implemented as plug-in modules to conventional services that assume no coordination among users.   In the no coordination situation, users make their own decisions independently. If there are enough and to spare of resources, they do not need mass user support. However, because there are conflicts among resources in many real situations, some kind of coordination and mass user support would be of benefit. We seek such criteria to characterize and analyze social coordination in this section.

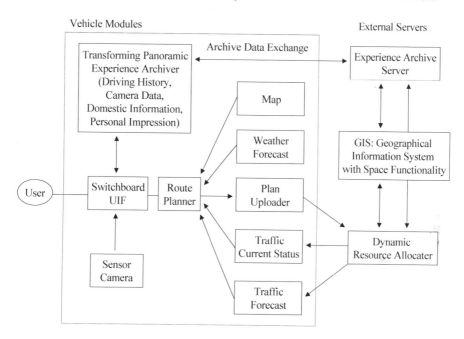

Fig. 6. Design of Vehicle Navigation System on CONSORTS

One should notice the necessity of decentralizing the coordination mechanism, which cannot be handled by conventional centralized algorithms. In other words, social coordination requires approaches beyond the conventional ones to ensure suitable resource allocation. The differences between centralized and decentralized coordination are as follows.

1. Centralized Coordination
    Full plans and schedules for all users are determined at a central server with realtime responses given in an open environment. Although such full coordination can be solved by realtime planning or scheduling, it is unrealistic in large-scale systems such as road traffic or whole city, because we cannot expect to receive or send the entire realtime information because of communication restrictions and the need to ensure the users' privacy. In small-scale systems, e.g. in a supply chain system that might exist in a company, full coordination could be achieved by gathering all relevant information.
2. Decentralized Coordination
    Rough plans and outline of schedules are determined by the server and are delivered to users. The recipient users (or their agents) determine the details.

As mentioned above, we do not have enough communication capacity or computation power to draw up complete plans at the server in many real situations.   Although such decentralized coordination can be seem as a distributed version of centrally controlled planning, decentralized coordination cannot be achieved by conventional planning or scheduling because of communication and computational restrictions.

4.2 Category of Information Provision

It is useful to categorize information types that are provided to users from the viewpoint of 1) how the provided information should be handled by the users and 2) for what time-span the information is generated.

1.   Obligation or Reference
Information provided to users is categorized as either obligation type or reference type. An example of the obligation type is a traffic signal. Drivers should obey traffic lamps at a crossing, or they will be legally punished. An example of the reference type is the information provided by car navigation systems. Drivers do not necessarily follow the information, i.e., they have options to accept or neglect the recommendations provided by the system.
2.   Current or Forecast Data
Basically, users are provided with raw data about current status, e.g., VICS could provide a bulletin board showing information about traffic congestion [3]. We can expect, however, short-time forecasts about the relatively near future will become possible by 1) gathering users' intentions (e.g., destinations) and by 2) mining data about the past status of the whole system. Information provided to users should be associated with this kind of time-span information (current or forecast).

Even when we design a simple service of providing reference information with a short-term forecast, we need to pay attention to social coordination. The reason is that the utility (effectiveness) of reference-type information depends on other users' utilities. For instance, imagine a situation where you are running information services of 1) realtime on-line car navigation, or 2) short-time traffic forecasting. When the percentage of your customers (users) is relatively small, you don't have to consider the influence of your customers' behaviors on the whole system. However, as the number of customers increases, their behaviors begin to influence the whole system, which means that you need to take the effect into consideration and you need some kind of mass user support to coordinate their intentions and preferences.

4.3 Resource Space, Plan, Utility

In this section, we formalize the theme park problem as an example of social coordination in order to use computational methods to deal with it. The formalization is as follows. The symbol U denotes the set of all users, while u denotes each user, i.e.:

$$U = \{u_i \mid i \in [1, n_u]\}, \; n_u = \mid U \mid. \; T = \{t_i \mid i \in [1, n_t]\}, \; n_t = \mid T \mid.$$
$$S = \{s_i \mid i \in [1, n_s]\}, \; n_s = \mid S \mid. \; R = T \times S = \{r_{ij} = (t_i, s_j)\}.$$

The set T is given as temporal segments in the form of a simple discrete representation of time, and the set S is given as spatial segments in the form of qualitative representations of space [17, 18], e.g., a region corresponding to neighborhood of an attraction in a theme park or a region in which users can access a specific wireless LAN access point. The social resource set R is defined as the direct product of the temporal segments and spatial segments, and the resource capacity is represented as a numeric function: $cap(r): R \rightarrow \Re$.

A plan for a certain user is a sequence of points in the resource set R in time, where there is no identical spatial segment at any temporal segment in any plan, which means that the user cannot consume two or more spatial segments at a time. More than one plan can be connected to become a longer one when there is no common temporal segment that belongs to a pair of plans selected from the original ones, i.e.:

$$plan_{new} = connect(plan_1, \ldots, plan_n) = \cup \; plan_i, \quad i \in [1, n],$$
$$\text{if} \quad \forall \, plan_i \, (\forall \, plan_j \, (\neg \exists t_k \, (plan_i = (t_k, *) \wedge plan_j = (t_k, *)))), \quad i \neq j,$$
$$* \text{ is any of spatial segments.}$$

This connection process is mainly used to generate a new candidate plan from simple short ones. From the viewpoint of searching or planning in artificial intelligence, the search space has the complexity of the number of S to the number of T: $O(Plan) = \mid S \mid^{\mid T \mid}$ where $Plan$ is the set of all possible plans.

The resource space where plans are generated and verified is shown in Fig. 7. The vertical axis shows the time flow represented by temporal segments, and the horizontal axis shows the spatial segments. A plan for an individual user is shown as a broken line, and congestion (resource conflict) occurs on the places indicated by the circles. If the resource capacity is less than the number of total plans crossing at these places, congestion occurs.

Another important element in the formalization is the utility of plans, which is used to measure their effectiveness for individual users and society. Basically, both of the utilities can be defined arbitrarily to control the coordination process. As a utility for individuals, it is a way to use 1) the sum of the evaluation of each resource and 2) the evaluation of special sequences appearing in the plan. The problem of how a utility is evaluated is related with intention, preference, interest, fun, etc., of users. Planning methods that put an emphasis on personal aspects can be also used in this process, e.g., story-based planning [10].

As utility for society, we use macro-attributes of the society, e.g., degree of congestion, usage ratio of resource, environment pollution, and so on. Another problem is to balance the individual and society utilities. The criteria for balance are related with the policy of what kind of social coordination is required.

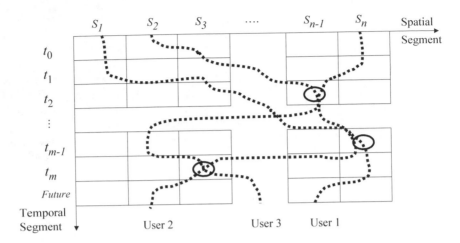

Fig. 7. Plans and Congestion in Resource Space

5   Algorithms for Mass User Support

5.1 Comparison of Conventional Methods

We can take various approaches to the social coordination problem. At first sight, it seems to be a kind of planning or scheduling problem in the artificial intelligence sense. Although a plan can be drawn up for an individual user, conventional planning and scheduling techniques cannot handle social coordination very well, because they are incapable of realtime response and they cannot handle mass user interaction.

Combinatorial optimization methods such as the genetic algorithm (GA) or reinforcement learning work well because of their ability of generating a range of solution candidates, but they are also incapable of realtime response. Stochastic distribution, e.g., CSMA/CD used in Ethernet (IEEE802.3) for packet collision avoidance, works quickly, but it cannot generate good plans because it doesn't take the user's intention or preferences into consideration.

Another approach is to introduce some kind of market or auction mechanism, e.g., preparing a bulletin board where a part of plans linked to users' intentions and preferences can be exchanged among users. The market and auction mechanisms reflect individual intentions and preferences well and can generate good plans quicker than planning, GA, or reinforcement learning, but they are slower than stochastic distribution.

In summary, the candidate mechanisms for social coordination have the following merits and demerits.

1.   Combinatorial Optimization
      In many cases, the coordination problem can be formalized as a combinatorial optimization problem [19], which can be generally solved by using the genetic

algorithm [20]. This approach can give the most optimal solution, but realtime response is nearly impossible.

2. Stochastic Distribution
    Stochastically distributing resources among users is time efficient (e.g., [21]) and can be analyzed by a queueing network (e.g., [22]). The solution obtained by this approach usually lacks accuracy, i.e., its solutions are far from optimal ones.
3. Market Mechanism
    Methods based on a market mechanism [23, 24] can reflect users' motivations and intentions, and they work faster than planning or scheduling. Basically though, fluctuations are observed in market mechanisms, by which the behavior of the whole system becomes unstable.
4. Planning and Scheduling
    Conventional AI planning and scheduling (e.g., [25]) can control spatial and/or temporal complexity and the accuracy of the solution by using heuristics. Unfortunately, preparing good heuristics valid for any kind of problem is nearly impossible.

5.2 Approaches to Social Coordination Algorithm

We are designing social coordination algorithms for mass user support, especially for dealing with the theme park problem and car navigation problem. In the following sections, we use the phrases **user agent** and (dynamic resource) **allocater**. A user agent is a software agent that works as proxy for a user. An allocater is a software agent that dynamically allocates resources to users. Usually resource allocaters exit their controlling area and are executed at servers embedded in the infrastructure. The basic design policy of the social coordination algorithms is as follows:

1. Micro-Macro Flow:
    Although planning for each user is made at the micro-level independently, social coordination is made at the macro-level. The basic idea of the algorithms is that 1) each user agent carries out planning independently, 2) the resource allocater analyzes the whole system at the macro-level, and 3) each user agent modifies its original plan (Fig. 8).
2. Decentralized Coordination:
    We assume decentralized coordination. There exist of several user agents and a couple of resource allocaters. The allocaters determine the rough coordination policy, and each user agent determines the detailed plan.
3. Coordination with Distance-based Focus:
    We can exploit the locality of the spatio-temporal space, i.e., we can bundle the influence from far regions when coordinating in local regions. This kind of distance-based focus can reduce the complexity of the coordination algorithms.

The first algorithm is called **stochastic planning**. In this method, the temporal complexity for the plan search is estimated in a realtime manner, and the accuracy of the solution (plans) is dynamically changed according to time restrictions. When there is no coordination service, each user agent makes plan independently. This status of no coordination gives the worst output, and the algorithm tries to improve the status within a given computation time. The process of stochastic planning is as follows.

1. Micro Planning:
    Each user agent generates a micro-level plan and forwards it to the responsible dynamic resource allocater. Even if the social coordination service is down, each user can use the plan generated by his/her agent; i.e., the design is fault tolerant.

2. Resource Distribution (1):
    The resource allocater receives the micro-plans from the user agents, analyzes the status of the whole system, and sends revised plans or a revision policy back to the user agents. When the number of user agents is relatively low, there is a possibility that the allocater can determine the detailed revisions for all user agents. However, when the number of user agent is large, the allocater can generate only a revision policy for each agent, i.e., that the original plan has no problem, or other candidates should be searched, and so on.

3. Resource Distribution (2):
    The process of generating a revised plan and revision policy is carried out by the combination of planning and stochastic distribution. Resource allocater carries out planning from the rough distribution for the whole system and gradually refines the plans as long as computation time remains. When the computation deadline reaches, the allocater terminates the planning and determines the revision policy by using stochastic distribution.

4. Micro Plan Revision:
    The user agent receives revised plans and uses them, or when it receives only a revision policy, the user agent revises its original plans according to the revision policy.

To put it simply, stochastic planning can be regarded as planning with a stochastic distribution.

The second method is called **plan exchange market**. In a plan exchange market, user agents can exchange resources directly. User agents are given virtual currency at fixed intervals of running time. Spatio-temporal resources and virtual currency are exchanged in a market by using a single or double auction mechanism. The user agent can exchange resources not only at the present but also in the future; i.e., exchanges can be made in the direction of the temporal axis. To stabilize the market mechanism, intervention by neutral agents can be introduced into the market. The plan exchange market can be linked to real currency, for example, a road pricing system in which road traffic is charged per passage of vehicle. To summarize the plan exchange market, introducing a market mechanism gives the incentive for resource distribution to each user and brings load balance to the whole system.

In order for social coordination algorithms to be accepted in real society, they can be evaluated by the following criteria.

-   From the viewpoint of equality, there should be an upper limit of variance on user utility (efficiency, effectiveness).
-   The average utility of each user should increase with repeated use of the service.
-   The efficiency of the total system (community, society) should increase.

In addition, we have to pay attention to the scalability of the system. The social coordination service can be designed as a plug-in extension to conventional services, which preserves the scalability of the conventional information devices and communications infrastructure such as cellular phone and car navigation system.

6   Conclusion

We proposed the concept of mass user support realized by social coordination among users in daily life. It is a mutual concession mechanism of social resources, e.g., space, time, reservations, and so on, that works by automatic negotiation among software agents rather than explicit and verbal communications exchanged by human users. We have also proposed a multiagent architecture CONSORTS in which mass user support services are provided in addition to conventional personal support.

As an example of social coordination, we outlined, formalized, and analyzed mass user navigation in a theme park. Although at first glance, the navigation seems to be a planning or scheduling problem, we showed that conventional problem-solving mechanisms such as planning, scheduling, GA, reinforcement learning, or stochastic distribution itself do not work well. To solve the problem, we proposed two ideas for social coordination. One is called stochastic planning, which estimates computational complexity in a realtime manner and switches two mechanisms of planning and stochastic distribution according to remained time. The other one is called plan exchange market, where plans are exchanged in a market with virtual currency.

Social coordination is not a part of social collaboration or computer-supported collaborative work. Social coordination requires a realtime response capability, although it does not necessarily generate the best solutions. Realtime response does not seem to be crucial in the theme park problem, but it is very important in other applications, such as social coordination in traffic control, because, for example, drivers do not have much time to make mutual concessions in traffic or to wait for navigation guidance. Moreover, even a one percent reduction in losses due to traffic problems in a city or country would be of great benefit to the economy and environment.

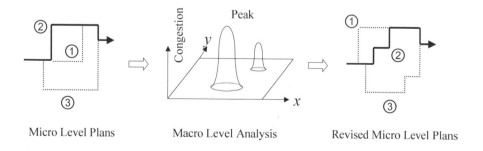

Micro Level Plans   Macro Level Analysis   Revised Micro Level Plans

Fig. 8. Micro Plan Revision through Macro Analysis

We analyzed the characteristics of mass user support, which is not simply the sum of services provided to individual users, and compared key technologies to realize mass user support. There are two issues that need to be resolved before putting mass user support in a real society. The first one is to develop coordination mechanisms that have a realtime response capability in an open environment. As analyzed in the previous section, each method has its merits and drawbacks. We think that it is useful to prepare some kind of standard problem to compare various approaches. The second one is to design the whole coordination system, i.e., mobile devices for users, communications and sensing methods between users and the environment, and coordination services that work in real situations.

Social coordination is an underlying mechanism in our daily lives. The intention of this research is to enhance mutual concession mechanisms in a sophisticated way by using software technologies embedded in a real environment. We will examine and refine the definition of the problems and the algorithms, first by multiagent simulation and later by applying them to real situations where agents are implemented in the CONSORTS architecture.

Acknowledgements

The author would like to thank Hidenori Kawamura, Tomohisa Yamashita, Akio Sashima, Kiyoshi Izumi, Yutaka Matsuo, Kousuke Shinoda, and Noriaki Izumi for their comments and suggestions on social coordination and the architecture for ubiquitous agents.

References

[1]   Weiser, M.: The Computer for the Twenty-First Century. Scientific American, vol. 265, September, 94-104 (1991).
[2]   Banavar, G., Beck, J., Gluzberg, E., Munson, J., Sussman, J.B., Zukowski, D.: Challenges: An Application Model for Pervasive Computing. In Mobile Computing and Networking, 266-274 (2000).
[3]   VICS (Vehicle Information and Communication System) is information service in ITS (Intelligent Transport Systems): http://www.its.go.jp/ITS/
[4]   Baecker, R., Readings in Groupware and Computer-Supported Cooperative Work. Morgan Kaufmann (1993).
[5]   Grosz, B., Kraus, S. Collaborative Plans for Complex Group Action. Artificial Intelligence. 86(2), 269-357 (1996).
[6]   Kurumatani, K.: User Intention Market for Multi-Agent Navigation - An Artificial Intelligent Problem in Engineering and Economic Context. Working Note of the AAAI-02 Workshop on Multi-Agent Modeling and Simulation of Economic Systems, MAMSES-02, Technical Report WS-02-10, AAAI Press. 1-4 (2002).
[7]   Kawamura, H., Kurumatani, K., Ohuchi, A.: Modeling of Theme Park Problem with Multiagent for Mass User Support. In this volume, Multiagent for Mass User Support, LNAI 3012, in printing (2004).
[8]   Yamashita, T., Kurumatani, K.: Effect of Using Route Information Sharing to Reduce Traffic Congestion. In this volume, Multiagent for Mass User Support, LNAI 3012, in printing (2004).

[9]   Shinoda, K., Noda, I., Ohta, M., Kumada, Y., Nakashima, H.: Is Dial-a-Ride Bus Reasonable in Large Scale Towns ? – Evaluation of Usability of Dial-a-Ride System by Simulation. In this volume, *Multiagent for Mass User Support,* LNAI 3012, in printing (2004).

[10]   Matsuo, Y., Hiratsuka, S., Yamashita, T., Takagi, A., Okazaki, N., Tokiwa, T., Kurumatani, K.: Story-based Planning in Theme Park. In this volume, *Multiagent for Mass User Support,* LNAI 3012, in printing (2004). http://www.consorts.org/

[11]   Sashima, A., Izumi, N., Kurumatani, K.: CONSORTS: A Multiagent Architecture for Service Coordination in Ubiquitous Computing. In this volume, *Multiagent for Mass User Support,* LNAI 3012, in printing (2004).

[12]   Sashima, A., Kurumatani, K., Izumi, N.: Physically-Grounding Agents in Ubiquitous Computing. In the Proc. of Joint Agent Workshop, JAWS-2002 (Hakodate). 196-203 (2002).

[13]   Sashima, A., Izumi, N., Kurumatani, K.: Location-Mediated Service Coordination in Ubiquitous Computing. In Proc. of the Third International Workshop on Ontologies in Agent Systems (OAS-03), AAMAS-03. 39-46 (2003).

[14]   The Foundation for Intelligent Physical Agents (FIPA). http://www.fipa.org/

[15]   Berners-Lee, T., Hendler, J., Lassila, O.: The Semantic Web. Scientific American (2001).

[16]   Kurumatani, K: Generating Causal Networks for Mobile Multi-Agent Systems with Qualitative Regions. In the Proc. of IJCAI'95 (Montreal), 1750-1756 (1995).

[17]   Kurumatani, K., Nakamura, M.: Qualitative Analysis of Causal Graphs with Equilibrium Type-Transition. In the Proc. of IJCAI'97 (Nagoya), 542-548 (1997).

[18]   Lawler, E.L, Lenstra, J.K., Rinnooy Kan, A.H.G., Shmoys, D.B. (eds.): The Traveling Salesman Problem: A Guided Tour of Combinatorial Optimization, John Wiley & Sons (1985).

[19]   Goldberg, D.E.: Genetic Algorithms in Search, Optimization and Machine Learning, Addison-Wesley (1989).

[20]   Floyd, S., Gummadi, R., Shenker, S: Adaptive RED: An Algorithm for Increasing the Robustness of RED. Technical Report, to appear, http://citeseer.nj.nec.com/floyd01adaptive.html (2001).

[21]   Chao, X., Miyazawa, M., Pinedo, M.: Queueing Networks, John Wiley & Sons (1999).

[22]   Wellman, M. P., Walsh, W. E., Wurman, P. R., MacKie-Mason, J.K.: Auction Protocols for Decentralized Scheduling. Games and Economic Behavior, 35, 271-303 (2001).

[23]   Prado, J. E., Wurman, P. R.: Non-Cooperative Planning in Multi-Agent, Resource-Constrained Environments with Markets for Reservations. Working Note of the AAAI-02 Workshop on Planning with and for Multiagent Systems, Technical Report WS-02-12, AAAI Press, 60-66 (2002).

[24]   Miyashita, K.: Learning Scheduling Control Knowledge through Reinforcements, International Transactions in Operational Research, 7(2), 125-138 (2000).

Toward a New Principle of Agent Engineering in Multiagent Systems: Computational Equivalence

Shu-Heng Chen and Chung-Ching Tai

AI-ECON Research Center
Department of Economics, National Chengchi University
Taipei, Taiwan
chchen@nccu.edu.tw
elliot@aiecon.org

Abstract. Agent-based Methodology (ABM) is becoming indispensable for the inter-disciplinary study of social and economic complex adaptive systems. The essence of ABM lies in the notion of autonomous agents whose behavior may evolve endogenously and can generate and mimic the corresponding complex system dynamics that the ABM is studying. Over the past decade, many computational intelligence (CI) methods have been applied to the design of autonomous agents, in particular, their adaptive scheme. This design issue is non-trivial since the chosen adaptive schemes usually have great impact on the generated system dynamics. Robert Lucas, one of the most influential modern economic theorists, has suggested using laboratories with human agents, also known as Experimental Economics, to help solving the design issue. While this is a promising approach, laboratories used in the current experimental economics is not computationally equipped to meet the demands of the task. This paper attempts to materialize Lucas' suggestion by establishing a laboratory where human subjects are equipped with the computational power that satisfies the *computational equivalence* conditions.

1 Introduction

The use of agent-based simulation to study complex adaptive systems has become increasingly popular. Its significance has been well demonstrated by a series of recent conferences and journals exclusively devoted to this subject. One of the major issues in agent-based simulation is *agent engineering*. In the agents literature, many have reported that the simulation results are highly dependent upon how agents are designed and how agents learn and adapt, i.e. *agent engineering does matter*. Hence, many work have been devoted to the research of agent engineering.

One important topic that agent engineering addresses is the *robustness* of agent-based simulation results. This is normally done by evaluating whether different learning algorithms used in the simulation would lead to different implications. While the famous *KISS principle*[1] has provided a simple approach, e.g.

---

[1] The KISS principle was first proposed in [ ]. It stands for *"Keep it simple, stupid."*

K. Kurumatani et al. (Eds.): MAMUS 2003, LNAI 3012, pp. 18–32, 2004.

reinforcement learning, for agent engineering, other sophisticated approaches, e.g., *genetic algorithms*, are also very popular in the agents literature. In fact, many techniques within the field of *computational intelligence* have been used for agent engineering. Given such a wide variety of techniques, there is a great need for a guideline on how to select an appropriate technique for agent engineering.

Recently, there is a guideline for techniques selection based on empirical observations. This guideline gives two possibilities. The first one uses data from field studies, surveys or census, while the second one uses data from laboratories with human subjects. In economics, laboratories data are becoming increasingly available from the study of *Experimental Economics* and *Behavioral Economics*. Since data from field studies, surveys or census are becoming difficult to obtain, it is inevitable for economists to use the second type of data to conduct research. This approach is known as *Lucas criterion* ([21,]). Lucas's criterion suggests that a comparison of the behavior of adaptive schemes with behavior observed in laboratory experiments involving human subjects can facilitate the choice of a particular adaptive scheme.

There are already many studies that grounded their agent engineering in the spirit of *Lucas's criterion*. For example, [ ] used two versions of genetic algorithm (*basic GA* and *augmented GA*) to implement agent engineering [ ]. She reported that the simulation results from basic GA give individual quantities and prices exhibited fluctuations over the entire duration and did not result in convergence to the rational expected equilibrium values, which was inconsistent with the experimental results involving human subjects. In contrast, the results of the augmented GA showed convergence to the rational expected equilibrium values, and were able to capture several features of the experimental behavior of human subjects better than other simple learning algorithms. According to Lucas criterion, the augmented GA was justified as an appropriate adaptive scheme. For more application of the Lucas criterion to justify the use of the GA or some of its specific versions, please refer to [2] and [ ].

In addition to Lucas criterion, empirical evidence from experiments has been used to examine if reinforcement learning adequately describes the way people behave. For example, [13] gives an evaluation of reinforcement learning versus some of its competitive alternatives, such as *direction learning* and *belief learning*, in experimental asymmetric-information games.

The purpose of this paper is to answer the following question:

To what extent experimental economics or behavioral economics can help build agent engineering? Does the proposed guideline really have a solid foundation?

Our hypothesis is that experimental economics and behavioral economics have their limits and can not solve the foundation issue of agent engineering. The published guideline therefore requires revision. In this paper, we shall argue that computational equivalence is the direction to go.

2   Computational Equivalence

Our hypothesis is based on the rationale that different learning algorithm requires different *computational resources* and that difference, to the best of our knowledge, has not been addressed in the experimental design including human subjects. As a result, the claim that an adaptive scheme (generated by one type of learning algorithm) is superior over others (generated by other types of learning algorithm), based on their simulation results, is not always valid. One scenario can be that the adaptive schemes become unavailable to human subjects due to the lack of high-performance computing facilities required by the adaptive schemes. Another scenario is for on-line transaction experiments where a very limited amount of time is allocated to the agents (human subjects) to process the data before making a decision. Such constraint makes it impossible for the human agents to carry out computationally-intensive adaptive schemes, such as *genetic programming* or *fuzzy neural networks*. Without considering the issue of computational resources, any comparative study based on experimental results is meaningless.

Let's take the *double-auction experiment* as an example. In this auction, both sellers and buyers submit bids which are then ranked from the highest to lowest to generate demand and supply profiles. Based on the profiles, the maximum quantity exchanged can be determined by matching selling offers (starting with the lowest price and moving up) with demand bids (starting with the highest price and moving down). Experiments based on double auction have a long history in experimental economics ([29]). While the experiments involving human subjects started 40 years ago, serious work on agent engineering is only just beginning. The zero-intelligence (ZI) trader was introduced by [15]. It was then extended into the zero-intelligence plus (ZIP) trader by [10]. More sophisticated agents based on human-written programs were considered by [26] and [27], which also motivated [7] to use genetic programming to make traders autonomous. Another related study is that by [12] who used the genetic algorithm to evolve traders. Given such a variety, can we answer which one provides better agent engineering in light of the experiments conducted by [29]? Can the experimental economics of the 1970s and 1980s resolve the selection issue?

Clearly not. ZIP, GA and GP differ in their required computational resources. Consequently, as mentioned above, in a computationally-poor environment, it is not surprising to see that the behavior of human subjects is quite similar to the agent-based simulation using simple heuristics, such as the *ZIP Plus* scheme, and may be quite distinctive from the one using genetic programming. However, that result alone cannot effectively lend support to the superiority of *ZIP Plus* over GP. Without knowing this critical relation, experiments involving human subjects would simply be too arbitrary to be a foundation of agent engineering. Unfortunately, this subtle point has not received sufficient attention on the part of either experimental economists or agent-based computational economists.

Experimental economics was developed in an age where decision supports provided by intensive computation was not available, whereas agent-based computational economics was cultivated in an era accompanied by increasing effi-

CE Lab

Fig. 1. A Web of the CE Lab

In the CE laboratory, each human participant will be connected to the "society" through a personal computer (client) and the server. The interactive dynamics of all participants then takes place through the web.

ciency in terms of both software and hardware. This sharp difference in computational background does not make the use of the former as the foundation of the latter as obvious as one might have thought initially. To address the pivotal questions, such as whether genetic algorithms (or any other CI tools) represent an essential learning process on the past of humans, the laboratory involving human subjects must be upgraded to such a degree that GA (or any other CI tool) can be effectively executed for human subjects. We shall call this condition *computational equivalence*. In other words, *unless the condition of computational equivalence is satisfied, experimental economics cannot serve as a way of defining a principle of agent engineering.* It is misleading to claim the superiority of one adaptive scheme over another simply by citing the experimental results observed in the laboratory which are not computationally equivalent.

Given this discussion, we propose a computer laboratory which is built in line with the condition of computational equivalence. In this laboratory, all human subjects can *choose* to follow any adaptive scheme (CI tool) which is already installed in the lab and is made available to the end users. Of course, they can also choose their own preferable ways of making decisions, e.g., relying on their simple heuristics, if they fail to see the benefits of using the sophisticated adaptive schemes. The whole idea is depicted in Figures 1 to 3.

The whole laboratory is webbed by a network as shown in Figure 1. This web provides the basic platform for running experiments involving human subjects. Each human subject (real agent) is connected to at least one computer (*client*). The participation of the real agents in the experiments, e.g., through submitting

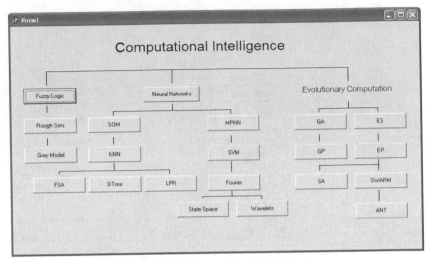

Fig. 2. Menu of Adaptive Schemes (CI Tools)

CI tools are made available for each human agent. From the computer screen, each human agent can choose his/her favorite adaptive scheme to learn from and adapt to the surrounding environment. The screen is presented to them in a very friendly manner. In this case, different classes of CI tools are grouped in an organization chart.

a limit order in a stock market experiment ([30]), proceeds via the client to the *server* and further to the whole web. Figure 2 is an expanding picture of what the human subject can see from his/her computer screen. Via this client machine, the real agent can acquire all the information pertinent to the experiment. The real agent may not have direct eye contact with other real agents since these clients are not necessarily located in the same room. Nonetheless, in the case where these clients are distributed in different places, real agents may still have eye contact with other participants via the attached camera.[2]

The idea of *computational equivalence* is exemplified in Figures 2 and 3. In addition to the basic information providing by the experiment, the client also provides real agents with a computationally-rich environment such that the agents are able to perform some non-trivial computation before they finalize their decision. Here, real agents can make their choice of the adaptation scheme that they would like to follow. For example, in the context of the double auction experiment, they can follow the GA to submit a bid or ask. If they *all* make such a choice, then the market dynamics will be pretty much similar to what [12] predicted. They can also follow the GP to learn a trading strategy first, and based on that strategy submit a bid or ask. Again, if they *all* make such a choice, then the market dynamics will be close to what [7] predicted. Of course, there

---

[2] To the best of our knowledge, experiments relying on eye contact are very limited. One of the examples is the famous *ultimatum game*.

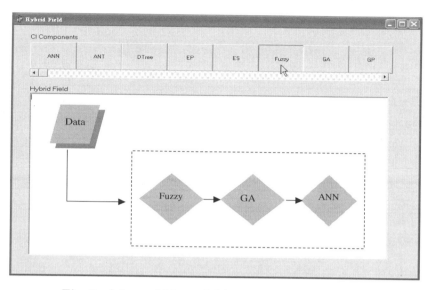

Fig. 3. Advanced Menu of Adaptive Schemes (CI Tools)

A human agent may combine several different CI tools into a hybrid system to learn and adapt. For example, a genetic neural fuzzy system is shown here.

is no reason why they should all choose the same adaptive scheme, as each can make a choice independently from the menu shown in Figure 2.

One recent research trend in computational intelligence involves the extensive use of hybrid systems, in which many tools work synergetically together as a *multi-agent system*. The CE lab also allows participants to organize their own hybrid systems from a set of CI tools. For example, a genetic neural fuzzy system ([24]) is shown in Figure 3.

Now, we can define what *computational equivalence* means. For an agent-based computational model, if each of the human agents behaves by *choosing exactly the same* form of agent engineering as the model suggests, then the experimental results, either individual or aggregate, will be the same as the agent-based simulation results, at least in a statistical sense. In other words, in a way quite different from the current directional relationship between experimental economics and agent-based computational economics, we are not only interested in replicating experimental results based on agent-based simulations, but what we have also said here is that agent-based simulation results can also be replicated by experiments if the "right" form of agent engineering is chosen by the human subjects in the experiment. This is the essence of *computational equivalence*.

The contributions of computational equivalence to complex adaptive economic systems are two-fold. *First*, it provides a *competing explanation* for the failure of some adaptive schemes to replicate the experimental results. In the past, such failures would usually be largely attributed to the irrelevancy of the chosen adaptive schemes. However, a competing explanation nowadays is that the laboratory is not well designed to satisfy the CE condition. Had it been so, those adaptive schemes might have proved their relevance in describing how humans behave. *Second*, through the CE lab, we can see that the agent-based computational economic model is no longer just a theoretical representation of the reality, but it can also serve as a blueprint for an economic system to be realized in the future. For example, [18] is not just an agent-based simulation of the fish market. If the fish market somehow becomes automated one day in the future and all market participants can get access to a computationally-rich environment to form their decisions, then [18] can be considered to be a blueprint of the real fish market.

Let us elaborate on the first point above using the example of *genetic programming*, one of the very popular CI tools. The following is a list of criticisms voiced by the journal referees on several of the authors' submissions. For the convenience of discussion, they are numbered as follows:

1. One can see why genetic programming (an extension of genetic algorithms) might work for computer problem-solving. However, genetic programming is not well grounded in considerations of human behavior.
2. There just isn't sufficient justification in the paper to support the view that what we have is a model for a population of agents learning over time (if they seriously wanted to push this view they would, for instance, need to tell readers how to interpret the cross-over operation).
3. The regular GP representation and presence of operators often lead to overly complex and unreliable solutions. Such solutions, comprised of complex combinations of functions and indicators, have often been difficult to understand and interpret. Deciphering the winning programs might be an impossible task in many applications. It might be impossible to use these rules in order to understand the process by which humans behave. The usefulness of the GP method for fundamental research thus seems quite restricted *a priori*.

As we shall argue here, none of these arguments is true when computational equivalence is imposed. Objection (1) is the most general type of criticism. It is true that, up to the present, genetic programming is not well grounded in considerations of human behavior, but the main reason for this is that we do not have a lab which can make it easier for human subjects to use GP in forming decisions. As was discussed before, GP is a highly computationally-demanding CI tool. How can we expect human subjects to seriously base their decisions on GP without first reducing their computational load to a reasonable degree? So, clearly, Objection (1) cannot be valid because it violates the computational equivalence condition.

Objection (2) is also similar to Objection (1), but is more technical-oriented. This kind of comment is frequently made in relation to other CI tools. In general, this means that a CI tool cannot be regarded as a sensible human learning and adaptation process if its major operator, e.g., the *cross-over operator* in GP, is empirically not analogous to human behavior. Without acknowledging computational equivalence, this argument is also misplaced. Whether or not a CI tool can be an effective description of human behavior has nothing to do with whether the society has an innate sense of that operator. On the other hand, managers who use GP to make predictions may not need to be convinced that its technical operators have empirical social meaning. As long as human behavior is concerned, the key issue is whether they would *believe* that GP can enhance their quality decisions. This is an empirical question, and can only be solved with a lab based on computational equivalence. A full understanding of its technical details may be neither a necessary nor a sufficient condition for the formation of this belief.

Just as in the case of Objection (2), Objection (3) proposes another possible reason why people may not use GP. This criticism is commonly shared in relation to other CI tools characterized by complex and nonlinear behavior. Our response to Objection (3) is similar to that to Objection (2). Whether or not a comprehensive understanding is crucial for humans to accept a state-of-the-art technology can only be answered empirically. It is quite common in behavioral economics for human choices to not necessarily be rational or scientific. Various biases have been well established empirically in behavioral economics.

In summary, the relevance of computational intelligence to human adaptive behavior cannot be appropriately studied without a CE laboratory (a lab that satisfies the computational equivalence condition).

3   Complex Systems Comprising Human and Software Agents

The CE lab described above not only serves as a starting point toward a foundation of agent engineering but also function as a platform to study the behavior of *electronic markets*. In this type of markets, all decisions are either made by humans aided by software or are automated completely. The former is exactly the architecture depicted in Figure 4, whereas the latter is equivalent to a CE lab where all human agents are replaced by software agents as shown in the same figure.

There are already many economic and financial applications of these two architecture. For example, in Internet auctions, software agents, such as *esnipe* and *auctionblitz*, support human bidders with routine task to improve performance precision ([23, 25]). Another example is in financial markets where programmed trades on the computerized trading platform can be used to help day traders in determining their bid and ask decisions ([32]). Our CE lab can be viewed as a simple model of these complex adaptive systems, and, via agent-based simulation, can be used to enrich our understanding of this type of systems.

However, our CE Lab is not designed only for specific applications, such as electronic markets. Its framework is very general so that we can use it to address a very fundamental question: *What will happen for a complex adaptive system when the participated human agents are equipped with CI tools?* We try to answer this question using a picture. Figure 4 gives four different types of

Fig. 4. Complex Systems Composed of Human and/or Software Agents

agent-based models. On the left of the top row, we have an agent-based model that is completely composed of human agents. On the right of the top row, we have a model that is purely composed of software agents. Two models on the bottom are agent-based models that are composed of both human and software agents. The difference between the two is that human agents on the left model are aware of the existence of software agent while the human agents on the right model are not.

Most experimental economic models only consider human agents, whereas most agent-based computational models only have software agents. While the original motivation of agent-based models has been to understand the equivalent systems composed of human agents, human participation and interface with the system and with the artificial agents have been excluded. In other words, human agents have been completely replaced by artificial agents.[3] Recently, the literature has started to look at the issue of interaction between software agents and human agents in complex adaptive systems, such as auction games ([11, 17, 16, 28, 33]), oligopoly games ([22]) and the stock market ([19]). Nonetheless, in

---

[3] Having said that, we would like to point out that the modern definition of artificial intelligence has already given upon the dream of replicating human behavior. Now, a more realistic and also interesting definition is based on the *team work* cooperatively performed by artificial agents and human agents ([20]).

these setups, human agents are only exposed to limited computational resources, and are not equipped with high-performance computing; therefore, the potential feedback relation between human agents and the system, including the artificial agents, has not been greatly exploited. We believe that the CE lab is the first step toward a formal study of the fundamental question posed above.

Our CE lab enables us to conduct experiments based on the four different types of agent-based models and hence makes it possible for us to perform a comparative study on the complex dynamics of the four agent-based models. Moreover, in addition to the comparative study, the CE lab also allows us to examine the possible *structural changes* or *regime changes* when a society that is solely composed of human agents is gradually or suddenly transforming itself into a society with a mixed population of software agents and human agents. The main points of interest are as follows:

- First, in general, how do humans react to the nonlinear complex dynamics? Would they tend to behave in a more complex manner when situated in such a complex environment?
- Second, if they do behave in a more complex manner[4], what are the consequences of such behavior? Will the aggregate dynamics become more (or less) complex and nonlinear?
- Third, what are the additional impacts of the inclusion of artificial agents (human agents) on an already-existing society composed of only human agents (artificial agents)? Do artificial agents on markets influence human behavior? ([16])

Regarding question (1), an interesting hypothesis is that humans may not necessarily respond to a complex environment with complex behavior. On the contrary, they may just follow a *rule of thumb*. This *simplicity hypothesis* is partially supported by some theoretical and empirical work.[5] For example, the winning strategy in trading tournament involving many agents is simple ([26, 27]). In trading, the simple trading strategy *buy-and-hold* was found to exhibit superior performance to many other sophisticated strategies. In making predictions, the simple predictor *random walk* was also shown to predict more accurately than other sophisticated predictors. Nonetheless, these findings are not strong enough to discourage people to devote a great deal of effort to develop sophisticated nonlinear predictors as well as trading strategies. Therefore, what determines people's search intensity for a "best" perception (representation) of complex nonlinear phenomena remains an interesting issue.

Through these experimental designs and the associated agent-based simulations of the CE lab, we can watch and study how human agents react to a complex nonlinear environment. In particular, it helps us to understand under what circumstances human agents tend to behave in ways that are more

---

[4] For example, they incorporate some of the CI tools into their decisions.

[5] This hypothesis can be loosely connected to the famous *Occam's razor* or the *parsimony principle*.

complex than simple.[6] More generally, can we find an effective characterization or implicit constraint of agents' choices of adaptive schemes? For example, we need to ask whether they tend to prefer qualitative schemes over quantitative schemes, linguistic schemes over crisp schemes, and simple (comprehensible) but sub-optimal schemes over complex (incomprehensible) but accurate schemes,...., etc. Needless to say, these are important questions that need to be addressed before we can lay a solid foundation for agent engineering.

One important recent development in agent-based social simulation has occurred in the use of *natural language* ([17, 31]). People frequently and routinely use natural language or linguistic values, such as high, low, and so on, to describe their perception, demands, expectations, and decisions. Some psychologists have argued that our ability to process information efficiently is the outcome of applying *fuzzy logic* as part of our thought process. Evidence on human reasoning and human thought processes supports the hypothesis that at least some categories of human thought are definitely fuzzy. Yet, early agent-based economic models have assumed that agents' adaptive behavior is *crisp*. [31] made progress in this direction by using the *genetic-fuzzy classifier system* (GFCS) to model traders' adaptive behavior in an artificial stock market. [31] provided a good illustration of the *non-equivalence* between the acknowledgement of the *cognitive constraint* and the assumption of *simple agents*. It is well-known that the human mind is notoriously bad at intuitively comprehending exponential growth. However, there is no evidence that traders on Wall Street are simple-minded. [31] recognized the difference, and appropriately applied the GFCS to *lessen* the agents' reasoning load via the use of natural language.

The thing that concerns the second issue is the casual relation between the complexity of macro dynamics and the complexity of micro- dynamics, or simply the *emergent phenomena*. While a series of studies regarding the emergent phenomena were conducted in the past in the ACE context ([14, 9, 6]), there is also no empirical evidence in relation to experimental economics.

A particularly interesting thing is that the micro behavior can sometimes be quite different from the macro behavior. Both the work done by [14] on the cobweb model and by [9] on the asset pricing model has shown that the time series of the market price (an aggregate variable) follows a simple stochastic process. However, there is no simple description of the population dynamics of individual behavior. The simple stochastic price behavior was, in effect, generated by a great diversity of agents whose behavior was constantly changing. [9] proposed a measure for the *complexity* of an agent's behavior and a measure of the *diversity* of an agent's complexity, and it was found that both measures can vary quite widely, regardless of the simple aggregate price behavior.

In addition, using micro-structure data, [6] initiated an approach to study the *emergent property*. By that definition, they found that a series of aggregate properties, such as the efficient market hypothesis, the rational expectations hy-

---

[6] While [8] simulates the evolving complexity of software agents in the artificial stock markets, the empirical counterpart of human behavior is not available in the literature due to the lack of an appropriate lab, such as the CE Lab.

pothesis, the price-volume relation and the sunspot effect, which were proved by rigorous econometrics tests, were generated by a majority of agents who did not believe in these properties. Once again, our understanding of the micro behavior does not lead to a consistent prediction of the macro behavior. The latter is simply not just the linear scaling-up of the former. Conventional economics tends to defend the policy issues concerned with the individual's welfare, e.g., the national annuity program, based on the macroeconometrics tests, e.g., the permanent income hypothesis. Agent-based macro-economics may invalidate this approach due to emergent properties.

By using the CE lab, one can vary the computational resources under different experiments. For example, in one experiment, human agents are exposed only to simple adaptive schemes, whereas in the other they can gain access to sophisticated adaptive schemes. In this way, we can examine whether a society of naive agents will tend to result in less complex aggregate dynamics than a society of sophisticated agents.

The third issue in a sense concerns the effects of the appearance of software agents on human agents. When human agents are explicitly informed of the presence of anonymous software agents in the system, would they behave differently as compared to the case where such a presence is uncertain ([16])? Furthermore, when human agents are provided with more detailed information regarding how software agents behave, such as their adaptive schemes, would that affect their own choice of adaptive schemes? This question is particularly relevant for electronic trading systems, such as *ebay*. In a sense, this question can be viewed in terms of the *socio-psychological impact* on human behavior in the presence of interacting machine intelligence. An equally important issue is concerned with the associated market dynamics and efficiency ([7]).

4   Concluding Remarks

This paper has two aims. The first is to build a laboratory with human subjects, which satisfies the *computational equivalence* condition. The second is so that the lab, referred to as the *CE lab*, can then serve as a platform to integrate the current research in experimental economics, behavioral economics (finance) and agent-based computational economics. These three fields share a common research goal with regard to the relevance and significance of adaptive behavior to economic dynamics. While, from the agent-based computational economics, it is now quite clear that aggregate dynamics can crucially depend on the learning dynamics, the issue as to the choice or the design of the learning dynamics (the so-called *agent engineering*) has not been effectively resolved. In particular, it cannot be resolved solely on the basis of experimental economics in the way Robert Lucas suggested. This is because most labs in which experiments involving human subjects are conducted do not provide subjects with high-performance computing facilities. Consequently, many adaptive schemes studied in agent-based computational economics are virtually impossible for human agents to compute, and the empirical relevance of adaptive schemes such as fuzzy logic, neural networks, and genetic algorithms is beyond the current research capacity of experimental economics.

Computational equivalence is about *replictability*. It basically requires that the lab have the same computational power as ACE generally has. To achieve this goal, software agents are introduced to and work with human agents in the lab, as suggested by the MIT approach (to artificial intelligence). By means of computational equivalence, what is done by the software agents (autonomous agents) in ACE may in principle be replicated by human agents in this lab. Only when replictability is guaranteed, can one ground the foundation of agent engineering in experiments involving human agents.

Leaving aside ACE, the failure to incorporate these computational intelligence techniques into the current experimental economics naturally limits the computational complexity of human decision rules. This limitation can be a real concern when the human behavior which experimental economics tries to study is largely inspired by a computationally-rich environment. Specifically, in an era of electronic commerce, when more and more automated trading techniques are being made available to human agents, questions regarding the dynamics and the efficiency of different auction designs may no longer be properly answered by the experiments conducted in the conventional lab. However, the use of the CE lab would help. Furthermore, more intriguing questions may arise when human agents do not only interact (play, compete) with human agents, but also with the possible presence of software agents, as is often seen in the case of e-bay or Nasdaq. What are the impacts of software agents on human agents? What is the effect on market dynamics and efficiency when autonomous agents are introduced to the markets? More generally, how do human agents adapt to their digital surroundings and what are the consequential dynamics? The CE lab, by effectively integrating ACE and experimental economics, provides us with a starting place to explore the richness of the nonlinear complex digital economy.

Acknowledgements

The authors are grateful to Dr. Tina Yu for her deliberate suggestions made to improve the writing of the paper, and Prof. Chiu-Che Tseng's for his comments in network architecture.

References

[1] Arifovic, J. (1994), "Genetic Algorithm Learning and the Cobweb Model," *Journal of Economic Dynamics and Control* **18(1)**, pp. 3–28. 19

[2] Arifovic, J. (1995), "Genetic Algorithms and Inflationary Economies," *Journal of Monetary Economics* **36(1)**, pp. 219–243. 19

[3] Arifovic, J., and M. Maschek (2003), "Expectations and Currency Crisis–An Experimental Approach," paper presented at the *9th International Conference on Computing in Economics and Finance*, University of Washington, Seattle, July 11–13. 19

[4] Axelrod, R. (1997), "Advancing the Art of Simulation in the Social Sciences," in R. Conte, R. Hegselmann, and P. Terna (Eds.), *Simulating Social Phenomena*, Lecture Notes in Economic and Mathematical Systems, pp. 21–40. 18

[5] Chen, S.-H., and C.-H. Yeh (1996), "Genetic Programming Learning and the Cobweb Model," in P. Angeline (Ed.), *Advances in Genetic Programming*, Vol. 2, Chap. 22. MIT Press, Cambridge, MA, 443–466. 19

[6] Chen, S.-H. and C.-C. Liao (2004), "Agent-Based Computational Modeling of the Stock Price-Volume Relation," forthcoming in *Information Sciences*. 28

[7] Chen, S.-H. and C.-C. Tai (2003), "Trading Restrictions, Price Dynamics and Allocative Efficiency in Double Auction Markets: Analysis Based on Agent-Based Modeling and Simulations," forthcoming in *Advances in Complex Systems*. 20, 22, 29

[8] Chen, S.-H., and C.-H. Yeh (2001), "Evolving Traders and the Business School with Genetic Programming: A New Architecture of the Agent-Based Artificial Stock Market," *Journal of Economic Dynamics and Control* **25**, pp. 363–393. 28

[9] Chen, S.-H., and C.-H. Yeh (2002), "On the Emergent Properties of Artificial Stock Markets," in *Journal of Economic Behavior and Organization*, Vol. 49, pp. 217–129. 28

[10] Cliff, D. (1997), "Minimal-Intelligence Agents for Bargaining Behaviors in Market-Based Environments," *HP Technical Report*, HPL-97-91, 1997. 20

[11] Das, R., J. Hanson, J. Kephart, and G. Tesauro (2001), "Agent-Human Interactions in the Continuous Double Auction," *Proceedings of the International Joint Conference on Artificial Intelligence*. 26

[12] Dawid, H (1999), "On the Convergence of Genetic Learning in a Double Auction Market," *Journal of Economic Dynamics and Control*, 23, pp. 1545–1567. 20, 22

[13] Feltovich, N. (2000), "Reinforcement-based vs. Belief-based Learning Models in Experimental Asymmetric-Information Games," *Econometrica*, Vol. 68, pp. 605–641. 19

[14] Franke, R. (1998), "Coevolution and Stable Adjustments in the Cobweb Model," *Journal of Evolutionary Economics* **8(4)**, pp. 383–406. 28

[15] Gode, D. K., and S. Sunders (1993), "Allocative Efficiency of Market with Zero-Intelligence Trader: Market as a Partial Substitute for Individual Rationality," *Journal of Political Economy*, Vol. 101, No. 1, pp. 119–137. 20

[16] Grossklags, J. and C. Schmidt (2003), "Interaction of Human Traders and Artificial Agents on Double Auction Markets: Simulations and Laboratory Experiments," in K. Chen, et al. (Eds.), *Proceedings of 7th Information Sciences*, pp. 1269–1272. 26, 27, 29

[17] He, M., H.-F. Leung, and N. Jennings (2002), "A Fuzzy Logic-Based Bidding Strategy for Autonomous Agents in Continuous Double Auctions," *IEEE Transactions on Knowledge and Data Engineering*. 26, 28

[18] Kirman, A. P., and N. Vriend (2001), "Evolving Market Structure: An ACE Model of Price Dispersion and Loyalty," *Journal of Economic Dynamics and Control* **25(3-4)**, pp. 459–502. 24

[19] Kurumatani, K., T. Yamamoto, H. Kawamura, and A. Ohuchi (2004), "Market Micro-Structure Analysis by Multi-Agent Simulation in an X-EconomyíX Comparison among Technical Indices," *Information Sciences*, forthcoming. 26

[20] Lieberman, H. (1996), "Software Agents: The MIT Approach," Invited speech delivered at the *7th European Workshop on Modelling Autonomous Agents in a Multi-Agent World* (MAAMAW'96), Eindhoven, The Netherlands, Jan 22–25, 1996. 26

[21] Lucas, R. E., Jr. (1986), "Adaptive Behavior and Economic Theory," *Journal of Business* **59**, pp. 401–426. 19

[22] Midgley, D., R. Marks, and L. Cooper (1997), "Breeding Competitive Strategies," *Management Science* **43 (3)**, pp. 257–275. 26

[23] Ockenfels, A. and A. Roth (2002), "The Timing of Bids in Internet Auctions: Market Design, Bidder Behavior, and Artificial Agents," *Artificial Intelligence Magazine*, Fall, pp. 79–87. 25

[24] Ringhut, E. and S. Kooths (2003), "Modeling Expectations with GENEFER - An Artificial Intelligence Approach," *Computational Economics*, Vol. **21**, pp. 173–294. 23

[25] Roth, A., and A. Ockenfels (2002), "Last Minute Bidding and the Rules of Ending Second Price Auctions: Evidence from eBay and Amazon Auctions on the Internet," *American Economic Review* **92(4)**, pp. 1093–1103. 25

[26] Rust, J., J. Miller and R. Palmer (1993): "Behavior of Trading Automata in a Computerized Double Auction Market," in D. Friedman and J. Rust (Eds.), *The Double Auction Market: Institutions, Theories, and Evidence*, Addison Wesley. Chap. 6, pp.155–198. 20, 27

[27] Rust, J., J. Miller, and R. Palmer (1994), "Characterizing Effective Trading Strategies: Insights from a Computerized Double Auction Market," *Journal of Economic Dynamics and Control*, Vol. 18, pp. 61–96. 20, 27

[28] Shachat, J. and J. Swarthout (2002), "Procurement Auctions for Differentiated Goods," IBM Watson Research Center Working Paper. 26

[29] Smith, V. L. (1991), *Papers in Experimental Economics*, Cambridge: Cambridge University Press. 20

[30] Smith V. L., G. L. Suchanek, and A. W. (1988), "Bubbles, Crashes, and Endogenous Expectations in Experimental Spot Asset Markets," *Econometrica* **56(6)**, pp. 1119–1152. 22

[31] Tay, N., and S. Linn (2001), "Fuzzy Inductive Reasoning, Expectation Formation and the Behavior of Security Prices," *Journal of Economic Dynamics and Control* **25**, pp. 321–361. 28

[32] Varian, H. R. (1988), "Effect of the Internet on Financial Markets," School of Information Management and Systems, University of California, Berkeley. 25

[33] Wellman, M., A. Greenwald, P. Stone, and P. Wurman (2002), "The 2001 Trading Agent Experiment," in *Proceedings of Fourteenth Innovative Applications of Artificial Intelligence Conference*, pp. 935–941. 26

Market-Based Resource Allocation for Information-Collection Scenarios

Shih-Fen Cheng[1], Michael P. Wellman[1], and Dennis G. Perry[2]

University of Michigan, Ann Arbor, MI 48109, USA
{chengsf,wellman}@umich.edu
dgperry@acm.org

Abstract. Dynamic decentralized resource allocation for information-collection can play a critical role in emergency scenarios. We explore two simplified scenarios for information-collection, and define market games for allocating resources to interdependent tasks. Experiments with a market game for disaster-response illustrate our general methodology for analyzing strategic interactions in such an environment.

1 Introduction

1.1 Market-Based Resource Allocation

In a *task allocation problem*, the object is to determine which of a set of tasks to accomplish and how, in an environment of limited resources. In a central optimization approach, the allocation is controlled by a central planner, who collects all the problem-related information and formulates a model that can then be optimized to determine the commanded allocation. In a decentralized environment, such a planner is not available, for either or both of two reasons:

Decentralized Control. Authority may be by construction decentralized, such that individual decision makers, or *agents*, have control over respective elements of the overall problem. For example, agents may have discretion over which tasks they perform, or rights over portions of the resources.

Decentralized Information. Information bearing on possible or preferred allocations may be distributed among the agents. For example, each agent may have its own preferences over task accomplishments, and knowledge of its own capabilities and resources. Such information is generally incomplete, asymmetric, and privately held, so that no central source could presume to obtain it through simple communication protocols.

Arguably [1], markets comprise the best-understood class of mechanisms for decentralized resource allocation. In *market-based resource allocation*, or *market-based control* [2], agents representing end users (those requiring task accomplishments), resource owners, and service providers issue bids representing exchanges or deals they are willing to execute, and the market mediators allocate resources

K. Kurumatani et al. (Eds.): MAMUS 2003, LNAI 3012, pp. 33–47, 2004.

and tasks as a function of these bids. In a well-functioning market, the price system effectively aggregates information about values and capabilities, and directs resources toward their most valued uses as indicated by these prices. As Ygge and Akkermans put it:

$$local\ data\ +\ market\ communication\ =\ global\ control. \qquad [3]$$

Although markets do not in general guarantee optimal control, the conditions under which they perform successfully are well known, and can be characterized in precise technical terms. Moreover, the conditions under which they tend to fail (e.g., asymmetric information, nonconvexities in preference and production) generally present difficulties for any approach to decentralization, typically requiring some degree of centralization of information and authority to remedy regardless of the form of underlying allocation mechanism.

One further advantage of adopting this perspective is that it is readily implementable. Automation of market interfaces in the guise of electronic commerce increasingly (albeit at a slower pace than a few years ago) provides computational support for market-based interactions across networks, and promises to support more dynamic and flexible forms of deal-making among software agents than hitherto possible.

1.2 Advanced ISR Management

One important problem resistive of centralized control techniques is managing the allocation of intelligence, surveillance and reconnaissance (ISR) assets. Such assets are generally distributed geographically, may be owned by different organizations (private and public), and may be subject to interoperability constraints. Historically, this has led to great inefficiencies in the deployment of ISR assets, and use levels well below their potential aggregate capacity. More recent improvements in Command, Control, Communications, Computers, and Intelligence (C4I) infrastructure have enabled the connection of once-isolated ISR assets, thus opening the possibility of achieving an actual capacity closer to the potential. Bridging this gap, however, requires a suitable global planning methodology for the task allocation problem.

The United States Defense Advanced Research Project Agency's Advanced ISR Management (AIM) program was initiated to explore possible approaches to global planning in this environment. The ultimate goal of AIM is to allocate the ISR resources efficiently in order to provide the command and control (C2) decision maker with timely and sufficient information. AIM scenarios can occur in either military or civilian settings where coordination among friendly units and consistent environment understanding are essential. The information required may come from various sources including all sorts of military and civilian sensors, databases, and geographical information systems. Besides the effort in retrieving the information, considerable amounts of information processing and integration are also required to turn raw information into usable form.

The allocation of ISR assests as well as processing capacities pose a formidable task for AIM planners. The difficulties arise not only from the complexity of the decision problem, but also the distributed nature of the tasks involved. Although AIM problems are generally not completely decentralized (e.g., reconnaissance platforms may be operated by units within the same military service), we address a fully decentralized version in order to stress this aspect of the problem environment.

Applin et al. [ ] describe a market-oriented approach to ISR management, in which they calculate prices by solving a linear program modeling the domain. This amounts to centralized analysis of a distributed system, providing insights into the relative values of alternative resources and costs of alternative tasks. The approach we pursue here is complementary, deriving prices themselves in a distributed manner, through market interactions of self-interested agents. The remainder of this paper describes our investigation of such market-based approaches to decentralized resource allocation in simplified AIM scenarios.

2 Playing Market Games

Modeling a resource-allocation scenario and associated market mechanisms is tantamount to defining a *market game*. In a market game, a collection of agents— each with private information, objectives, capabilities, and resource rights— exchange resources among themselves through a given configuration of market mechanisms.

There is a great variety of resource allocation issues arising in the ISR domain, and many other domains of interest in our research on decentralized resource allocation. To support investigation of a broad range of market games, we have developed flexible infrastructure for specifying and running market games, employed in this study and elsewhere. The core of our *generic market gaming system* is a configurable auction engine, the Michigan Internet AuctionBot [ ]. The AuctionBot supports a wide range of market mechanisms, specified in terms of parameters characterizing the space of bidding, information revelation, and allocation policies [ ].

In addition to the market rules, specifying a market-game scenario entails description of the agents, initial allocations, and other features of the problem environment. Components of our generic market gaming system include the following.

1. Preference generator. Constructs and disseminates agent-specific information, including preferences, allocations, capabilities, and any other characteristics that are private to the agent and vary from game to game.
2. Scorer. Evaluates the performance of each agent on completion of the game. Scoring typically entails assembly of transactions to determine final holdings, and for each agent, an allocation of resources to activities maximizing its own objective function.

3. Agent interface. The game system implements a communication interface
through which bids, queries, and any other game interactions are transmit-
ted.

Our current game system is a generalization of the infrastructure we developed to operate an open research event called the "Trading Agent Competition" (TAC) [7]. Held annually since 2000, the TAC market game is based on
a challenging scenario in the domain of travel shopping [8]. The TAC series has
produced several interesting ideas about the design of trading agents [9, 10], and
has served as a useful testbed for studying market-based resource allocation.

Our generic game system is a modular re-specification of the TAC market
infrastructure. By configuring the preference generator, scorer, and other modules through parameter files and scripts, we can run the TAC game (both 2000
and 2001 variants), as well as the AIM scenarios described here, and some others
currently under development.

3   AIM Scenarios

We have defined two AIM resource allocation scenarios, and implemented them
as market games through our generic game server. The first scenario emphasizes
the dependence of tasks in a chain of information collection and exploitation activities. The second focuses on a broader allocation of resources to tasks, without
explicit chains of activity. The second game has been analyzed in greater depth,
and is the subject of the study described in subsequent sections.

3.1   Scenario 1: Allocation of Collection and Exploitation Assets

Our first scenario was designed to model the allocation of ISR assets to alternative reconnaissance tasks, with variable value. As illustrated by Fig. 1, this
scenario posits two regions of hostile territory ("North" and "South"), and two
time periods ("days") of interest. The goal of each agent is to produce reconnaissance reports, where such a report covers a given region on a given day. The
value of reports for particular (region,day) pairs varies across agents, as specified by the private information generated for each agent at the beginning of the
game.

To produce a report, an agent must arrange for both collection (imaging)
and exploitation of reconnaissance information. ISR collection assets (e.g., spy
planes, satellites) provide capabilities for gathering information in the form of
images, and exploitation assets (e.g., human analyst teams) serve to process the
raw images into complete intelligence reports. Assets are owned by the various
agents, who trade usage rights through the markets in order to achieve their
own tasks. For example, an agent owning aircraft platforms might sell some of
their use on day 1 to another agent collecting information on the North region. It
might simultaneously buy analysis services on day 2 for the South region in order
to accomplish its own task of interest. The assets possess distinct capabilities,

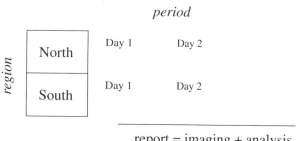

Fig. 1. AIM Scenario 1: Collection and exploitation. Agents strive to produce reports for particular regions on particular days, based on their preferences and resource availabilities

for example, certain platforms might be based in a given region, whereas others can cover both regions. Their exchange is mediated by various kinds of market mechanisms, such as continuous double auctions (CDAs) [11] or multi-unit English auctions [12].

Although the two-region/two-period model is exceedingly simple, it captures an important form of *task dependence*, which we view as a critical issue for decentralized resource allocation. In prior work, we have studied market-based allocation with task dependencies in the context of supply-chain formation [13]. For our AIM project, we employed this scenario primarily as a prototype exercise testing the capacity of our generic gaming system, devoting more investigative effort to a second scenario in this domain.

3.2   Scenario 2: Task Allocation for Disaster Response

Our second scenario was designed to model the ISR component of crisis management after a major earthquake hits the San Francisco Bay area. It was imagined that the San Jose valley falls below sea level, with openings at the north and south sides causing the whole valley to be filled with incoming sea water, thus creating a new "San Francisco Bay Island". In this disaster scenario, regional crisis management teams are faced with the immediate task of assessing damage to major facilities in the city, and to identify the subsequent actions that should follow. Investigations are to be organized by each crisis management team in its governing area, through utilizing undamaged ISR resources owned by it or other crisis management units.

Figure 2 presents a block diagram of this scenario. Five agents represent regional crisis management teams, who interact with each other through markets for the various ISR assets. There are four types of asset: for reconnaissance by air, sea, and land, the last available in two modes (land1 and land2).

The scenario operates over a two-day planning horizon, with each day divided into three time slots. Each agent is presented with five tasks, each specifying a priority (in units of value), deadline, and required resource. For example,

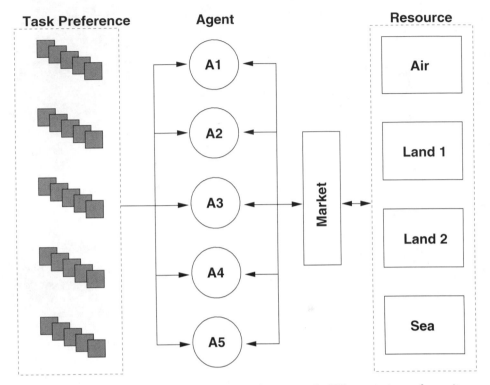

Fig. 2. AIM Scenario 2: Disaster response. Agents trade ISR assets to perform situation assessment tasks

Agent 1 might have a task to perform an air survey of its region by time slot 4 (the first third of the second day), at priority 250. Tasks take one time slot, and may be performed any time at or before the given deadline. To accomplish the task, the agent must assemble the associated resources (in the example above, just the air platform) for the time slot they will be employed.

The basic tradeable resource is the right to employ an asset in a particular time slot. The agents' *endowments* define their initial allocation of such resources. In our simulations, we assign endowments randomly, giving each agent one unit of each asset-slot combination with probability 0.4.

The agents' tasks are also generated randomly, with the following characteristics:

- Priority: distributed uniformly between 100 and 1000.
- Deadline: distributed uniformly between 1 and 6.
- Resource requirements: Each type required with probability 0.5.

Given its tasks, the agent's objective is to maximize the value of task completion (accruing priority value for each task achieved by its deadline), net of market transactions. In other words, the agent's utility function is the sum of task achievement value plus net proceeds (which may be positive or negative) from trading ISR assets in the market.

Asset rights are traded in 24 CDAs, one for each combination of resource type (air, sea, land1, land2) and slot index (1..6). Bids submitted to the CDAs offer to buy or sell units of the slot-indexed resource at a specified price. If a new bid matches another currently standing in the auction, the transaction clears at the standing-bid price, and the two bids are removed from the auction. On each new bid, the auction releases a revised *price quote*, revealing the greatest current offer to buy (the *bid*), and the least current offer to sell (the *ask*).

To simulate a game instance, we assign the agents' endowments and tasks, and open up the auctions for trading. The game proceeds for five minutes, upon which the markets close, and the game system determines the final holdings as the sum of initial holdings and any transactions during the game. The score for each agent is its net cash plus the value of its optimal task performance given its resource holdings.

4   Agent Strategies for the Disaster-Response Game

Although the disaster-response game is relatively simple compared to a real AIM scenario, determining an equilibrium strategy profile, or even the best response to other plausible strategies, is far from analytically tractable. Thus, our analysis proceeds by exploring some simple strategies, and evaluating their quality and plausibility. We have experimented with three agent strategies, of increasing sophistication.

4.1   Strategy A: Baseline

Before implementing the more sophisticated strategies, we first construct a myopic, greedy strategy that can serve as a comparison baseline. In strategy A, the agent tries to fulfill its tasks in order, starting from the task with highest value. If the resources required for the current task are not possessed by the agent but are available on the market, the agent will try to buy them at task's value. Otherwise, the agent will give up this task. At the end of each iteration, the agent will sell all redundant resources on hand, at a random price.

A step-by-step description of strategy A follows:

Step 0: Retrieve task preferences and resource endowments. Sort tasks by priority value in descending order. Set the current task to the first. Set available resources to the endowment.

Step 1: Update available resources to reflect transaction information, and retrieve price quotes for each good.

Step 2: Determine the slot (at or before deadline) that minimizes the cost of assembling the required resources for the current task, at the current prices. Resources with positive availability (i.e., in current holdings but not committed to higher-priority tasks) are considered free. If any resource is not

available in the market currently, its cost will be taken as infinite. Break ties
in favor of later slots.

Step 3: For the slot selected, decrement the availability count for each resource
required, and make a note of the task associated with this resource.

Step 4: If the current task is the lowest priority, proceed to **Step 5**. Otherwise,
set the next-priority task as current, and go to **Step 2**.

Step 5: For each resource, place buy bids corresponding to negative availability
values, and sell bids for positive availability values. Set the price of buy bids
to the value of associated tasks, and set random prices for sell bids. Go to
Step 1.

4.2   Strategy B: Optimal Task Allocation

Strategy A assigns resources to tasks in a greedy manner, with no direct consideration of overall optimality. We thus introduce strategy B, which allocates
resources optimally using an integer linear programming (ILP) model. Given
current price quotes, strategy B calculates the best choice of resources for each
of its tasks, then acts accordingly to acquire those resources in the market.

Steps 0 and 1 of strategy B are the same as for A. The remaining steps are
as follows:

Step 2: Calculate an optimal resource allocation using the ILP model,
parametrized by given task preferences and resource availabilities. Our model
assumes that at most one unit of each good may be purchased at the current
price quote.

Step 3: For each resource, place buy or sell bids corresponding to the comparison of optimal allocation and current availabilities. Set the price of buy bids
to a constant value exceeding the last price quote, and set random prices for
sell bids. Go to **Step 1**.

4.3   Strategy C: Marginal Value Bidding

A disadvantage of strategies A and B is that both sell only when the resource
is of zero value to the agent. However, this neglects the possibility of selling a
resource that may generate higher value in another agent's possession. Thus, the
main improvement in strategy C is to calculate the actual value of any single
unit of resource. If adding an additional unit of resource can bring in some value
to the agent, the agent will be willing to pay at most this value to buy that
resource. If removing any unit of resource will cause the agent to lose any value,
the agent will have to receive at least this value to sell that resource. In Strategy
C, therefore, the agent submits bids to buy and sell every resource type, at its
determined valuation.

The agent assess goods at their *marginal value*, that is, the difference between the agent's optimal allocation with and without the good in question. In
calculating marginal values, the agent assumes it can buy at most one unit of
other goods at their going prices.

Steps 0 and 1 of strategy C are the same as for A and B. The remaining steps are as follows:

Step 2: Calculate marginal values for each good using the ILP model, parametrized by given task preferences and resource availabilities. The model assumes that at most one unit of any other good may be purchased at its current price quote.

Step 3: For each resource, place buy and sell bids corresponding to the calculated marginal values. Go to **Step 1**.

5   Searching for Equilibrium

In previous work, we have described a general methodology employing evolutionary search for exploring bidding strategies in trading games [ ]. The basic idea is to construct the game's payoff matrix, and search for equilibrium, using the *replicator dynamics* formalism [,]. In replicator dynamics, relatively successful strategies are rewarded by an increase in their proportion of the population, with less successful strategies penalized accordingly. The replication function defines an evolutionary game, effectively serving as an iterative algorithm to search for an equilibrium in the underlying stage game. When this algorithm terminates (reaches a stationary state), the resultant population is a candidate mixed-strategy Nash equilibrium of the system.[1]

The first step of the approach is to transform the market game into standard *strategic form* [ ]. Note that every instance of our market game starts with a set of agents endowed with randomly generated preferences, and the result of the game is determined by the subsequent bidding activities from all agents. From this we can define the strategy as a mapping from the product of market prices and client preferences to the bidding actions. Since market prices are determined by the interaction of strategies, the actions chosen are ultimately a function of preferences and other agents' strategies. However, rather than consider all possible strategies in the natural extensive-form description of the game, we fix the space of strategies to a finite set, and define payoffs directly as a function of strategy choices and preference assignments. Given that preferences are assigned probabilistically, this induces an *expected payoff* as a function of strategy profiles.

We construct an *expected payoff matrix* by sampling from market simulations. In general, this matrix is of size S^N, for a game with N agents and S available strategies. In our scenario, we have five agents and three strategies (A, B, C), leading to $3^5 = 243$ cells. By symmetry, however, the order of strategies in a profile is irrelevant. For example, given the profile $(4, 1, 0)$—four A agents and one B agent—it does not matter *which* agent plays strategy B. This reduces the size of the matrix to 21 cells.[2]

---

[1] Friedman [ ] establishes that replicator dynamics is guaranteed to converge to symmetric Nash equilibrium under a variety of assumptions, for two-player games.

[2] The general formula for the number of distinct profiles is $\binom{N+S-1}{N}$.

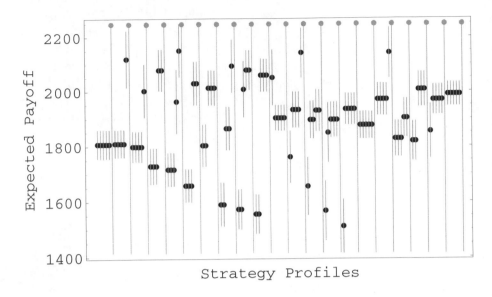

Fig. 3. Payoff matrix for all possible strategy profiles. Each column represents a strategy profile, in lexicographic order left-to-right, from $(5,0,0)$ to $(0,0,5)$. The five dots of a profile represent the mean utility values for the respective agents, with vertical lines specifying 95% confidence intervals

To obtain this payoff matrix as required, we ran 200 simulated games for each strategy profile. To uniquely represent each profile, we use a three-element tuple (N_1, N_2, N_3), in which N_i denotes the number of agents playing strategy i in this profile, $\sum N_i = N$. Figure 3 shows the results of the simulations.

5.1   Experimental Results

The payoff matrix apparently validates our expectation that strategy C is superior to A and B. However, the conclusion is not entirely immediate, as C is not a *dominant strategy*. For strategy dominance to hold, it would have to be that C is better than A and B given any other fixed profile of other strategies. We can test this by inspection of the payoff matrix. The first three columns displayed in Fig. 3 correspond to strategy profiles (5,0,0), (4,1,0), and (4,0,1) respectively. Given four agents playing A, the profiles represent the three available options for the fifth agent. We can see that this agent does best in the second column, where it plays strategy B. Thus, C is not a dominant strategy.

It turns out that C does represent a pure-strategy Nash equilibrium for this game. That is, given four agents playing C, C is a unique best response for the fifth agent. This too can be verified by inspection of the payoff matrix.

This equilibrium is also the one found through replicator dynamics. Starting from a uniform population $(\frac{1}{3}, \frac{1}{3}, \frac{1}{3})$, the proportions evolve as shown in Fig. 4.

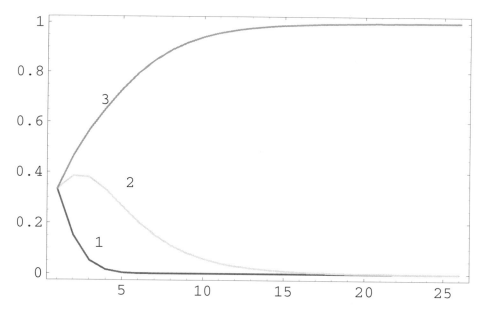

Fig. 4. Evolutionary dynamics for initial population $(\frac{1}{3}, \frac{1}{3}, \frac{1}{3})$

Although the replicator dynamics never quite reach $(0, 0, 1)$ (by construction they require nonzero fractions of each component), they exhibit clear convergence toward the pure strategy.

Although we have not found significant sensitivity to initial conditions in previous studies [14], in principle the end result may depend on the starting population. Therefore, we also explored the extreme cases where we start with nearly pure strategies of of A or B. Figure 5 depicts these respective cases. Note that for the case where we start with a predominantly A profile, B initially increases faster than C. This result is in accord with our observation above that B is a better response than C to four A players. However, once the population contains a substantial mix of Bs, then C quickly comes to the fore and predominates.

One further issue to consider is sampling error. Our depiction of the payoff matrix in Fig. 3 presents confidence intervals for each value in the strategy profile. Naturally, a simulation in terms of mean values may not reflect the reality of an expected payoff matrix generated by a simulation of sample size 200. Therefore, we also implemented a version of the replicator dynamics that samples from value distributions, instead of using mean values. These produced results consistent with those shown.

Finally, for a problem of this size we can also verify the result using available algorithms for solving games analytically. In this case, Gambit[3] [19] is able to

---

[3] http://www.hss.caltech.edu/gambit/

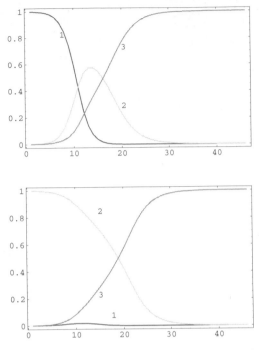

Fig. 5. Evolutionary dynamics for initial populations $(1 - 2\epsilon, \epsilon, \epsilon)$ and $(\epsilon, 1 - 2\epsilon, \epsilon)$. ($\epsilon$ is a small positive constant.)

verify that the pure strategy $(0, 0, 5)$ is the unique symmetric Nash equilibrium for this payoff matrix. There also exist several asymmetric equilibria.

5.2   Market Efficiency

The preceding analysis identifies an equilibrium given the restricted strategy-space identified for our disaster-response scenario. This result can be viewed as a provisionally suggested policy for playing the market game. A logical next question is how well does this strategy profile perform, in comparison with alternative profiles as well as other possible benchmarks. The primary benchmark of interest is the global optimum, that is, the allocation of resources that would be chosen by a central planner, given all information and the objective of maximizing the aggregate value of tasks accomplished.

For each strategy profile, we calculated the sum of utility achieved by agents in the market (column "Agent Sum"), and the globally optimal allocation for the given preferences and endowments. The results are presented in Table 1. We can see that the equilibrium strategy $(0,0,5)$ does not achieve the greatest total utility, even among this restricted strategy set. Instead, the mixed profile $(0,4,1)$ performs best. Inspection of Fig. 3 indicates that this too is a Nash equilibrium, although not the one selected by replicator dynamics. Note that on a percentage

Table 1. Efficiency of market compared to global optimum

Profile	Agent Sum	Global Opt	Efficiency (%)
(0,0,5)	9944	11510	86.40
(0,1,4)	9732	11042	88.13
(0,2,3)	9659	11026	87.61
(0,3,2)	9287	10754	86.36
(0,4,1)	10024	11497	87.19
(0,5,0)	9383	10843	86.53
(1,0,4)	9251	10792	85.71
(1,1,3)	9161	10737	85.32
(1,2,2)	9305	10932	85.12
(1,3,1)	9700	11366	85.34
(1,4,0)	9661	11336	85.23
(2,0,3)	9289	11074	83.88
(2,1,2)	9311	11138	83.60
(2,2,1)	9003	10794	83.41
(2,3,0)	9648	11353	84.99
(3,0,2)	9037	10922	82.73
(3,1,1)	9266	11253	82.34
(3,2,0)	9347	11130	83.98
(4,0,1)	9201	11133	82.65
(4,1,0)	9364	11100	84.36
(5,0,0)	8949	11010	81.28

basis, (0,1,4) generates the highest efficiency rating, over 88%. The variation in the "Global Opt" column suggests that additional samples may be required to characterize the set of Nash equilibria with satisfactory confidence. In general, however, the best performance is clearly obtained from settings where strategies B and C (the ones performing task optimization) predominate; introducing As tends to degrade efficiency.

6   Conclusion

We have presented two simple ISR allocation scenarios, and market games implementing decentralized solutions. In-depth analysis of one of the games, albeit with a highly restricted strategy space, reveals that determining equilibrium is feasible, and that the market itself can achieve almost 90% of the available utility. Since agents in the market optimize local decisions with respect to prices (not expressly considering each other's strategies), the allocation method scales quite well in principle with the number of agents.

Ongoing work is extending this methodology in several ways:

– Defining more, larger, and varied market games, and deploying them on our generic game server.

- Comparing results of the market to alternative allocation mechanisms.
- Scaling up the size of strategy spaces amenable to evolutionary search.
- Bootstrapping improved trading strategies, through interleaved equilibrium analysis, and online learning within the strategy space itself.

Acknowledgements

Daniel Reeves implemented the evolutionary search algorithm and provided assistance with that component of the analysis. Dave Applin provided essential guidance in modeling the ISR domain. We also thank the anonymous reviewers for raising questions of clarification. This research was supported in part by the DARPA/IXO AIM program, under subcontract to SAIC.

References

[1] Wellman, M.P., Wurman, P.R.: Market-aware agents for a multiagent world. Robotics and Autonomous Systems **24** (1998) 115–125 33

[2] Clearwater, S., ed.: Market-Based Control: A Paradigm for Distributed Resource Allocation. World Scientific (1995) 33

[3] Ygge, F., Akkermans, H.: Decentralized markets versus central control: A comparative study. Journal of Artificial Intelligence Research **11** (1999) 301–333 34

[4] Applin, D., Coleman, P., McCoy, P., Rouff, C.: An agent-based and market-oriented approach to distributed isr resource allocation. In: IEEE Aerospace Conference, Big Sky, MT (2002) 35

[5] Wurman, P.R., Wellman, M.P., , Walsh, W.E.: The michigan internet auctionbot: A configurable auction server for human and software agents. In: Second International Conference on Autonomous Agents, Minneapolis (1998) 301–308 35

[6] Wurman, P.R., Wellman, M.P., , Walsh, W.E.: A parametrization of the auction design space. Games and Economic Behavior **35** (2001) 304–338 35

[7] Wellman, M.P., Wurman, P.R., OMalley, K., Bangera, R., de Lin, S., Reeves, D., , Walsh, W.E.: Designing the market game for a trading agent competition. IEEE Internet Computing **5** (2001) 43–51 36

[8] Wellman, M.P., Greenwald, A., Stone, P., , Wurman, P.R.: The 2001 trading agent competition. Electronic Markets **13** (2003) 4–12 36

[9] Greenwald, A.: The 2002 trading agent competition: An overview of agent strategies. AI Magazine **24** (2003) 83–91 36

[10] Stone, P., Littman, M.L., Singh, S., Kearns, M.: Attac-2000: An adaptive autonomous bidding agent. Journal of Artificial Intelligence Research **15** (2001) 189–206 36

[11] Friedman, D., Rust, J., eds.: The Double Auction Market. Addison-Wesley (1993) 37

[12] Cramton, P.: Ascending auctions. European Economic Review **42** (1998) 745–756 37

[13] Walsh, W.E., Wellman, M.P.: Decentralized supply chain formation: A market protocol and competitive equilibrium analysis. Journal of Artificial Intelligence Research (2003) 37

[14] Wellman, M.P., MacKie-Mason, J.K., Reeves, D.M., , Swaminathan, S.: Exploring bidding strategies for market-based scheduling. In: Fourth ACM Conference on Electronic Commerce, San Diego (2003) 41, 43

[15] Taylor, P., Jonker, L.: Evolutionary stable strategies and game dynamics. Mathematical Biosciences **40** (1978) 145–156 41

[16] Schuster, P., Sigmund, K.: Replicator dynamics. Journal of Theoretical Biology **100** (1983) 533–538 41

[17] Friedman, D.: Evolutionary games in economics. Econometrica **59** (1991) 637–666 41

[18] Fudenberg, D., Tirole, J.: Game Theory. MIT Press (1991) 41

[19] McKelvey, D., McLennan, A.: Computation of equilibria in finite games. In: Handbook of Computational Economics. Volume 1. Elsevier (1996) 43

Modeling of Theme Park Problem with Multiagent for Mass User Support

Hidenori Kawamura[1], Koichi Kurumatani[2], and Azuma Ohuchi[1]

[1] Graduate School of Engineering, Hokkaido University
N13W8, Kita-ku, Sapporo, Japan
[2] National Institute of Advanced Industrial Science and Technology
Aomi 2-41-6, Koto-ku, Tokyo, Japan

Abstract. We propose the Theme Park Problem as one example of test bed for mass user support. The objective of the problem's solution is to coordinate many visiting agents' behavior in a way that increases social welfare without reducing individual satisfaction. For the computer simulation, we design four types of basic coordination algorithms, and the simulation's results are used to discuss the basic characteristics of the problem.

1 Introduction

Recent technological progress in ad-hoc network environments related to Personal Digital Assistant (PDA), cellular phone, and wireless LAN use has indicated the increasing importance of ubiquitous environments [WE1, WE2]. In a ubiquitous environment, various independent communication devices, sensors, and processors are distributed in the user environment for supporting his daily activities. Moreover, the information technology for supporting such personal activity on the Internet might include technology for airline, bus, and railway scheduling and reservations, car navigation, or hotel and services reservation.

The information technology for supporting the user's daily activities needs a new type of artificial intelligence based on the linkage between the digital information space and the real world, and certain infrastructures of information processing based on agent architecture and sensing technology have been studied as base of such an artificial intelligence [SA1, SA2]. In particular, new type artificial intelligence called mass user support has been studied [KU1, KU2]. Its goal is not only to optimize individual life utility but also to support a social system made up of a group of individuals. Mass user support research aims to develop a social coordination mechanism that increases social welfare without reducing individual utility.

How to increase social welfare and individual utility is theoretically studied in terms of Game Theory [NE], and it is basically a difficult problem because of its multiple-objective. On the other hand, recent multiagent researches have studied the relationship between individual bounded rationality and emergent sociality by embedding the practical complexity as agents [EP]. Here, the purpose of our

K. Kurumatani et al. (Eds.): MAMUS 2003, LNAI 3012, pp. 48–69, 2004.

study is not to construct a detailed theory of social coordination but to pursue mass user support by investigating a more practical problem.

In this paper, we propose the "Theme Park Problem," denoted as TPP, as one example of mass user support research. The TPP consists of two kinds of element, a spatial segment and a software agent. The spatial segment is one component of the theme park, and it may be one of several types, i.e., attraction, road, plaza, entrance, and exit. The software agent represents a visitor to the theme park, and it has individual preferences regarding each attraction. The objective of TPP is to develop an algorithm that dynamically coordinates agents' visiting behavior in order to reduce congestion and increase the individual visitor's satisfaction. In other words, TPP is a dynamic coordination problem which needs to coordinate many individual behavior and to optimize individual and social satisfaction by using distributed information. We focus on the theme park as the research target for the following reasons.

- The problem is closed; namely, only information related to the theme park has to be considered, and it is possible to model the individual agent's visiting activity and preferences for the attractions.
- It is possible to measure the effectiveness of coordination based on congestion degree, wait time for admission to the attractions, throughput, and so on.
- The size of the agents' activities reflects on the order of $10^2 \sim 10^5$ agents, and should be large enough for the initial study of mass user support.
- It is possible to compare the problem's solutions with real theme park data.
- The algorithm should be implementable in a real theme park with a kind of PDA or cellular phone.

The same type problem is proposed by J. E. Prado et al. [PR], and they constructed a coordination algorithm based on bottom-up market-type reservation system. The algorithm was applied for a simple setting, and effectiveness of it was evaluated by comparing with other typical algorithms. In this paper, to clarify the characteristics under this kind of problem, we investigate more variety environments with some simulation settings by usage of simple coordination algorithms.

This paper is organized as follows. Section 2 explains the basic definition of TPP, and Section 3 is related to some kinds of coordination algorithms. Section 4 describes the experimental computer simulations. Section 5 discusses these results, and Section 6 concludes the paper.

2   Definition

2.1   Theme Park Problem

The theme park of TPP is constructed from N spatial segments that provide a particular kind of service for the visitor agents. The segment i has one of five types defined as attraction, road, plaza, entrance, and exit. It also has two static attributes, c_i and st_i, and each type of segment is characterized by these

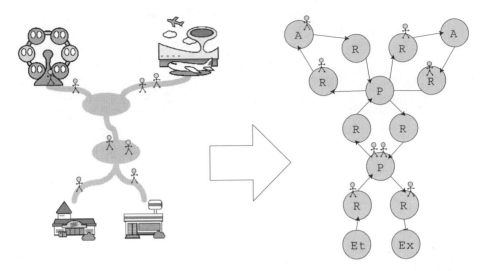

Fig. 1. The example of small theme park. The left figure shows the image of theme park, and the right shows the directed graph representation of it. In the right graph representation, the notations, A, R, P, En, and Ex represent an attraction, road, plaza, entrance and exit segment, respectively

parameters. The parameter c_i represents the service capacity of the segment i, which means the maximum number of visitors that can be served in the segment i at once. st_i is the service time for a visitor agent. The agent requires st_i times to receive its service in the segment i; e.g., the agent requires st_i times to move through an road segment. The theme park is defined as a directed graph in which the segments are represented as nodes and each segment is connected by directed edges. Figure 1 shows an example of a small theme park, which consists of two attractions, two plazas, one entrance and exit. The visitor agents transit these segments according to the directed edges.

In the theme park, n agents visit attraction segments through road and plaza segments. The visitor agent j has a preference value p_{ji} which represents the agent j's preference degree for the segment i. Each p_{ji} is a real value between 0 and 1 that has been determined in advance. For example, a higher value of p_{ji} indicates the agent j strongly hopes to visit the segment i. The preference values for segments other than type attraction are set to 0.

The dynamical definition of the model is as follows. Let t be the time step of the simulation. The simulation is iterated until t reaches the termination time t_{max}. The agent j has five dynamical attributes, $cs_j, pt_j, vt_{ji}, wt_j$ and mt_j. cs_j represents the current segment where the agent j is on at time t. The agent j belongs to only one segment at any time, and starts from the entrance segment at the beginnings of the simulation. The past time pt_j represents how long the agent j spends in the segment i. This variable is increased by one when the time step of the simulation proceeds. The visiting time vt_{ji} is the number of times

Table 1. The variables for the agent

Variable	Explanation
p_{ji}	The preference degree of the agent j for the segment i
cs_j	The current segment where the agent j is on
pt_j	The past time for that agent j spends in the segment i
vt_j	The number of times the agent j visits the segment i
wt_j	The total wait time of the agent j
mt_j	The total moving time of the agent j

the agent j has visited node i. wt_j and mt_j represent the total wait time and total moving time of the agent j, respectively.

As dynamical attributes, the segment i has the set of agents a_i and the queue q_i. a_i consists of agents visiting the segment i at time t. The queue consists of agents which desire to visit the segment i when the service capacity of the segment i is full. The priority order of queue is based on First-In First-Out buffers, and an earlier agent has prior admittance over that of a later one. When the agent j goes inside the segment i, the agent j is erased from the queue q_i.

The procedure of simulation proceeds as follows. At time t, the agent j acts in turn according to the agent number. For simplification, let i be the current segment of the agent j, namely, corresponding to cs_j. The agent can choose the next segment to transit to if the following condition is satisfied.

$$st_i \leq pt_j \tag{1}$$

The condition indicates that the service of current segment i has finished. Otherwise, the agent j spends more time in the current segment until the service has finished.

Next, suppose that the agent j satisfies the above condition and chooses the segment k as the next one. In the simulation, the next segment is indicated by a coordination algorithm explained later. If the following condition is also satisfied, the agent j can transit from the current segment i to the next segment k.

$$|a_k| + 1 \leq c_k \text{ and } |q_k| = 0, \tag{2}$$

or,

$$|a_k| + 1 \leq c_k, |q_k| \neq 0 \text{ and}$$
$$\text{the priority of the agent } j \text{ is the first in } q_k. \tag{3}$$

The notation $|\cdot|$ means the cardinality of elements.

When the agent j moves to the next segment after satisfies of the condition 2 or 3, the total wait time of the agent j is updated as

$$wt_j \leftarrow wt_j + (pt_j - st_i). \tag{4}$$

```
1  procedure Theme_Park_Problem()
2    initialize();
3    while (t < t_max) do
4      agent_activity();
5      t ← t + 1;
6    end while
7    output evaluation();
8  end procedure

9  procedure agent_activity()
10   for each agent j do
11     pt_j ← pt_j + 1;
12     i ← cs_j;
13     if (st_i ≤ pt_j)
14       k ← next_segment_navigation();
15       if the condition 2 or 3 is satisfied
16         wt_j ← wt_j + pt_j − st_i;
17         if the segment i is a road or plaza
18           mt_j ← mt_j + st_i;
19         endif
20         cs_j ← k;
21         vt_k ← vt_k + 1;
22         pt_j ← 0;
23         delete the agent j from a_i;
24         delete the agent j from q_k;
25         add the agent j to a_k;
26       else if j is not registered in q_k
27         add the agent j to q_k;
28       end if
29     end if
30   end for
31 end procedure
```

Fig. 2. The pseudo-code for simulating TPP

Moreover, if the segment i is an road or plaza segment, the total moving time is updated as

$$mt_j ← mt_j + st_i. \tag{5}$$

After updating, the agent j moves to the segment k by changing the current segment cs_j to k, and pt_j is reset to zero. If the agent does not satisfy condition 2 or 3, the agent j is added to the queue q_k and waits until the segment k is available for the agent j.

The pseudo-code for simulating TPP is shown in Figure 2.

2.2   Evaluation

The main purpose for the TPP is to optimize the social welfare based on the set of
agents' individual utilities. However, it is not so easy to optimize such multiple-
objectives because the possibility of visiting and the wait time is complexly
related to mutual agents' behavior. The one of most important concept for multi-
objective optimization is Pareto optimality. We define the social welfare based
on the concept of Pareto optimality as follows.

If t reaches termination time t_{max}, the simulation is stopped, and the evaluation of the agent j is calculated as follows.

$$u_j = p_j^* + \epsilon \cdot p_j^*/(wt_j + mt_j) \tag{6}$$

$$p_j^* = \sum_i f(p_{ji}, vt_{ji}) \tag{7}$$

$$f(p_{ji}, vt_{ji}) = p_{ji} \cdot min[1, vt_{ji}] \tag{8}$$

$f(p_{ji}, vt_{ji})$ represents the utility function for visiting the attraction i according
to the preference p_{ji} and the visiting time vt_{ji}. Prado et al. proposed three kinds
of utility function, (a) utility that is constant, (b) utility that decreases linearly
with the number of visits, and (c) utility that is constant to some threshold
number of visits, and zero thereafter [ ]. We adopt the same manner of (c)
with the threshold of visiting time 1. ϵ is the weight parameter.

The social welfare of the TPP is calculated as follows.

$$U = \sum_j w_j \cdot u_j, \tag{9}$$

where,

$$w_j > 0, \sum_j w_j = 1. \tag{10}$$

Here, it is known that the set of optimal solutions of the equation 9 for various
weight sets is a partial set of Pareto optimal solutions for the multiple-objectives.
We can compare with some coordination algorithms based on the above social
welfare. In addition, we simply define all weights as $w_j = 1/n$.

3   Coordination Algorithm

For mass user support, a coordination algorithm provides the agents with theme
park information and tries to control a sequence of agents' action for optimizing
individual utility and social welfare. To coordinate the behavior of agents, there
are two basic ways, i.e., reactive coordination and deliberative coordination. The
reactive coordination is based on only current situation, and does not utilize the
sophisticated projection of future situation. Namely, it does not require exact
future assurance of agent's behavior, and reactively coordinates. The deliberative

coordination unfolds projection of whole behavior to the future situation based on a kind of reservation system, and closely coordinates the whole behavior.

If the situation is not changeable and treated reservation is not so huge and stable, the deliberative coordination would work better, but the changeable situation, e.g., operation of attractions is not strict and unstable along time table, attitudes of visitors are not cooperative for reservation, and visitors easily modify their plans, would make the deliberative coordination failure. The reactive coordination potentially has adaptiveness for such situation, but it is a rough heuristic mechanism and has no guarantee of optimality. On the other hand, if a fully-connected information system can be constructed, the deliberative coordination works better, otherwise the reactive coordination might work better.

Then, it is important to classify basic characteristics of the TPPs and effectiveness of coordination algorithms for various settings. But, pure classification based on only problem setting is difficult because dynamic characteristics of the problems can not be separated from the property of applied coordination algorithms. As first step of investigation, we construct simple reactive coordination algorithms with no specific prediction and reservation system.

Here, a coordination algorithm informs each agent of the next segment after the service on current segment has finished. We simply suppose that the function $next\_segment\_navigation()$ shown in Figure 2 corresponds to the algorithm. The algorithm can utilize the information about $c_i, st_i, p_{ji}, q_i, cs_j$, and vt_{ji}. We assume the situation that the algorithm obtains the information p_{ji}, cs_j and vt_{ji} from visitors' PDAs or cellular phones, and measures q_i by observing each attraction's condition. c_i and st_i are given by the theme park setting.

For the TPP, we prepare four kinds of coordination algorithms. Each agent always follows the information provided by these algorithms.

Greedy Algorithm (G)

1. If the destination of the agent j is not determined or the agent j reaches the destination, this algorithm chooses the unvisited attraction whose preference is highest value among the unvisited attraction segments. If no unvisited attraction exists, the exit segment is set to the destination. The shortest path from the current segment to the destination is found by Dijkstra's algorithm.
2. Inform the agent of the next segment that are on the shortest path.

This algorithm merely makes the agent select the most preferred attraction segment. Namely, each agent independently visits with unconscious of the others and theme park information aggregated from whole agents' behavior. This algorithm might represent no-coordination case.

Congestion-Avoidance Algorithm (CA) This algorithm utilizes an alternative way to choose the destination segment for it of algorithm G. This algorithm chooses the unvisited attraction whose expected wait time w_i is lowest value among the unvisited attraction segments. The value of w_i is calculated with the simple equation $w_i = |q_i| \times st_i/c_i$ based on the current time data. Other procedure is same as algorithm G. This algorithm uses a part of information aggregated by whole agents' behavior, and this type of assist for a real theme park is easy to realize because it merely broadcasts congestion information or expected wait time. For more intelligent service, it may be effect to show the expected wait time including moving time to the destination and dealing with the prediction of situation change by moving time lag.

Stochastic Congestion-Avoidance Algorithm (SCA) This algorithm decides the destination by stochastically selected way either of algorithm G or CA. Here, γ is the probability parameter for selection, and the destination is decided by algorithm G with the probability γ; otherwise, it is by algorithm CA. Other procedure is also same as algorithm G. Agents following algorithm SCA does not know which of way to choose the destination is used, and simply follow the navigation. The parameter γ is simply set to 0.5 here.

Preference-Congestion Coordination Algorithm (PCC) To determine the destination, this algorithm calculates the following value v_{ji} for each unvisited attraction, and selects the segment which has the highest value of all unvisited attraction.

$$v_{ji} = \begin{cases} 0 & \text{if } vt_{ji} \geq 1 \\ (p_{ji}/\hat{p}_j)^\alpha \cdot (1 + w_i/\hat{w})^\beta & \text{otherwise} \end{cases} \qquad (11)$$

$\hat{p}_j$ and $\hat{w}$ are the average values of p_{ji} and w_i of the unvisited attraction segments. The parameters α and β indicate the balance of preference and wait time. Usually, α is set to a positive value, and β is set to a negative value. This algorithm coordinates the destination based on the balance of preference and congestion. Here, we chose $\alpha = 1, \beta = -0.3$ based on preliminary experiments. Other procedure is also same as algorithm G.

4   Computer Simulation

4.1   Problem Settings

The setting consists of nine attraction segments, three plaza segments, one entrance and exit segments, and twenty six road segments, i.e., $N = 40$ segments. These segments are connected with directed edges like in Figure 3. The notations, A, R, P, En, and Ex represent an attraction, road, plaza, entrance and exit segment, respectively.

The settings of each segment are shown in Tables 2 and 3. In particular, the attraction segments have the five settings shown in Table 3 because the service time setting of the attraction segments may directly affect the characteristics of the problem, and the unevenness of attractions' service time may cause stagnation of agent flow. The preference p_{ji} of each agent the agent j is randomly arranged from the set of $\{1.0, 0.9, 0.8, \ldots, 0.2\}$ with no duplication. The popularity of attraction segments does not exist in this case.

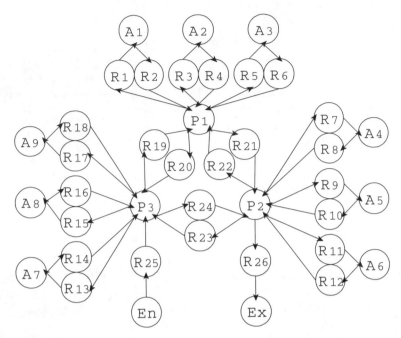

Fig. 3. The graph representation of the theme park for computer simulations

4.2   Experiment 1

The computer simulation was executed with several settings that were combinations of {st103050, st153045, st203040, st253035, st303030} and {n = 200, 400, 600}. The total number of settings was 15. We carried out 100 trials for each setting, and all results are shown as averages of 100 trials. In addition, the preference values p_{ji} of the agent j were randomly set in each trial.

Figures 4 (a), 4 (b) and 4 (c) show the averaged total wait time, wt_j. The X axes indicate the standard deviation of attractions' service time in the experimental settings, and the Y axes represent the value of wt_j. The indexes G, CA, SCA and PCC correspond to the algorithms. In Figure 4 (a), the total wait time of each algorithm gradually increases according to the increase of standard deviation of service time. For n = 200, most agents could visit all attraction segments, and the higher values of st103050, which corresponds to the case that standard debiation is 20, are due to the wait times of A_3, A_6, and A_9, which had the longest service time. In contrast, A_1, A_4 and A_7 had no wait time. For n = 400 and 600, there were some agents which could not visit all attraction segments, and the tendencies of the algorithms were different. In the st103050 case, which corresponds to the case that standard deviation is 20, algorithm CA and PCC could effectively reduce the wait time by using the mechanism to avoid jammed attraction segments, and succeeded in temporally distributing the congestion. It is difficult for these algorithms to coordinate in a flat load case like st303030 corresponding to the case that standard deviation is 0 because in such

Table 2. The setting of road, plaza, entrance, exit segments

Segment	st_i	c_i	Segment	st_i	c_i
$R_{1\sim18}$	5	∞	$P_{1\sim3}$	0	∞
$R_{19\sim24}$	30	∞	En	0	∞
$R_{25\sim26}$	5	∞	Ex	0	∞

Table 3. The values of st_i in each experimental settings and the standard deviation of the values of st_i. The service capacity c_i of each segment is set to 1

	st303030	st253035	st203040	st153045	st103050
$A_{1,4,7}$	30	25	20	15	10
$A_{2,5,8}$	30	30	30	30	30
$A_{3,6,9}$	30	35	40	45	50
Std. Dev.	0	5	10	15	20

case the preference of each agent is uniformly distributed and concentration of agents scarcely occurs.

Figures 5 (a), 5 (b) and 5 (c) show the averaged total moving time, mt_j. The X axes indicate the standard deviation of attractions' service time in the experimental settings, and the Y axes represent the value of mt_j. In the $n = 400$ and 600 cases shown in Figures 5 (b) and 5 (c), mt_j shows the opposite tendency compared with wt_j. The reason is simply that the time of each agent is mostly used for waiting and moving. Thus, reduction of wait time leads to increase in moving time for visiting more attractions. In the $n = 200$ case shown in Figure 5 (a), the result is slightly different from the other cases. The time of each agent is almost enough to visit all attraction segments due to the smaller number of agents in the theme park, and most agents finished visiting attraction segments with in the simulation time and went out of the theme park. The difference between algorithms might be caused by the topology of theme park. In the experimental setting, each longest service time attraction locates in one of vertices of the triangle topology, and agents often visit from current vertex to another vertex for reducing the wait time according to coordination of the algorithms. The tendency to avoid the congestion leads such difference.

Figures 6 (a), 6 (b) and 6 (c) show the averaged preference value summation of the visited attraction, p^*. The X axes indicate the standard deviation of attractions' service time in the experimental settings, and the Y axes represent the value of p^*. Comparing with the results of algorithm G and CA, algorithm G is superior in the st303030 case, which corresponds to the case that standard debiation is 0, and algorithm CA is superior in the st103050 case, which corresponds to the case that standard deviation is 20. Algorithm G based on preference works well in the flat load case, and effective load balancing is automatically achieved by the characteristics of algorithm G. This enables agents to visit attraction segments without reducing preference value. On the other hand, if the service time of attraction segments is unequal, algorithm CA enables agents to visit more attraction segments because it effectively distributes the load of attraction segments having a longer service time and agents can visit more attraction segments than the could while using algorithm G. The results of algorithm SCA are interesting in that algorithm SCA performs better than algorithm G and CA in the cases st153045 and st203040, which correspond to the cases that standard deviation is 15 and 10, respectively, although algorithm SCA merely randomly selects algorithm G or CA. Algorithm PCC stably gives higher values in all problems. This is evidence that algorithm PCC could achieve effective coordination with load distribution. The important characteristic of the preference summation is that visiting more segments and selecting more prefer segments are related as a trade-off. If an algorithm pursues more preferred segments, congestion occur locally at long-service attraction segments. Thus, a good algorithm should have an effective balance between the preference and distribution.

Figures 7 (a), 7 (b) and 7 (c) show the evaluation value of social welfare, U. The X axes indicate the standard deviation of attractions' service time in the experimental settings, and the Y axes represent the value of U. The tendency of each graph is similar to the graph of p^* because the total time $(wt_j + mt_j)$ of each result is almost constant, and the evaluation is strongly affected by p^*. In most cases, algorithm PCC performed the best, and the other algorithms' performance changed according to the problem settings. This indicates that the performance of the algorithm depends on the problem environment, and it is difficult to easily coordinate in various situations. Although the experiment shows the good performance of algorithm PCC, it is still necessary to investigate a larger varieties of problems and constraints.

4.3   Experiment 2

In the experiment 2, to investigate the scale effectiveness of visiting agents, the number of agents was set for $n = 200$ to $n = 1200$ at intervals of 200. The applied settings were st103050 and st303030. We tried 100 trials for each setting, and all results are shown as averages of 100 trials. Other settings were same as the experiment 1.

Figures 8 (a) and 8 (b) represents the averaged wait time in the case st103050 and st303030, and Figures 9 (a) and 9 (b) represents the averaged moving time in each case. The X Axes indicates the number of agents, n. According to Figures 8 (a) and 9 (b), the results of moving time and wait time are different with each algorithm in the case st303030. This result indicates that coordination for reducing the wait time might be effective for the setting like that the bias of service time exists even if the number of agents is large. In fact, although the average visiting time of each agent in the case st103050 was less than 2, the waiting and moving time are improved by the effectiveness of algorithms. On the other hand, the waiting and moving time of each algorithm are almost same values in the case 303030 shown by Figures 8 (a) and 9 (b). This result suggests it is difficult to improve the waiting and moving time in the case like st303030. In a case

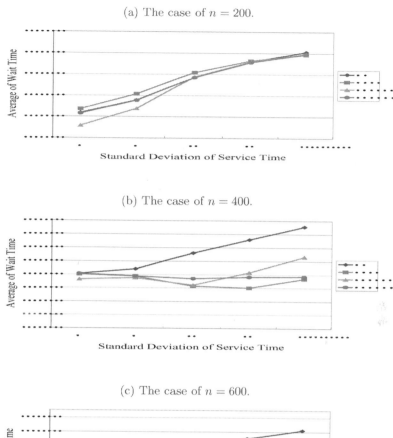

(a) The case of $n = 200$.

(b) The case of $n = 400$.

(c) The case of $n = 600$.

Fig. 4. The results of average of wait time wt_j. In each figure, the X axis indicates the standard deviation of attraction's service time in each experimental setting. The Y axis indicates the average value of wait time wt_j. The notations of "G," "CA," "SCA" and "PCC" correspond to the algorithm Greedy, Congestion-Avoidance, Stochastic Congestion-Avoidance and Preference-Congestion Coordination, respectively

with flat load, the congestion of visiting agents is automatically distributed by the characteristic of service time setting, and the improvement is difficult for the

(a) The case of $n = 200$.

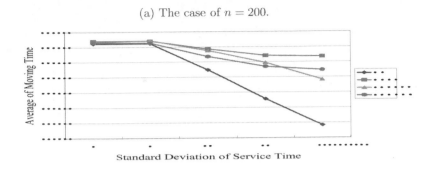

(b) The case of $n = 400$.

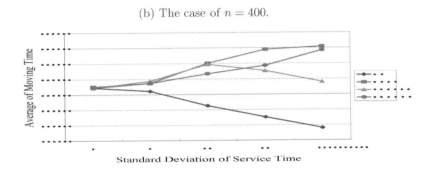

(c) The case of $n = 600$.

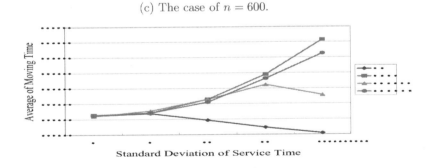

Fig. 5. The results of average of moving time mt_j. In each figure, the X axis indicates the standard deviation of attraction's service time in each experimental setting. The Y axis indicates the average value of moving time mt_j. The notations of "G," "CA," "SCA" and "PCC" correspond to the algorithm Greedy, Congestion-Avoidance, Stochastic Congestion-Avoidance and Preference-Congestion Coordination, respectively

(a) The case of $n = 200$.

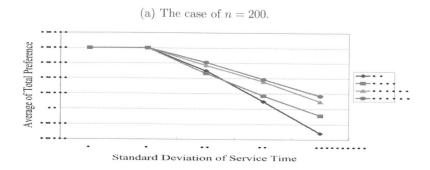

(b) The case of $n = 400$.

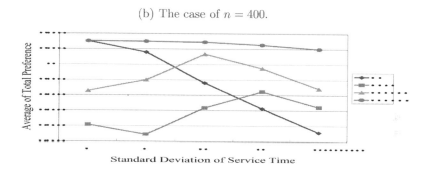

(c) The of case $n = 600$.

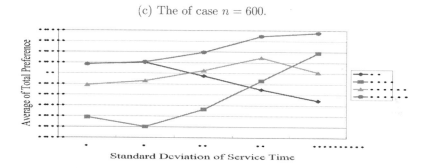

Fig. 6. The results of average of preference value p_j^*. In each figure, the X axis indicates the standard deviation of attraction's service time in each experimental setting. The Y axis indicates the average value of preference value p_j^*. The notations of "G," "CA," "SCA" and "PCC" correspond to the algorithm Greedy, Congestion-Avoidance, Stochastic Congestion-Avoidance and Preference-Congestion Coordination, respectively

(a) The case of $n = 200$.

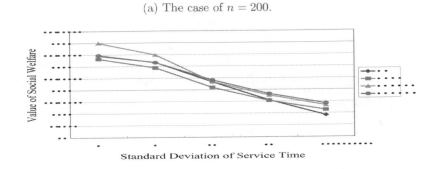

(b) The case of $n = 400$.

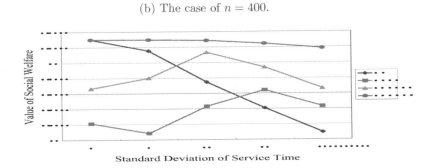

(c) The case of $n = 600$.

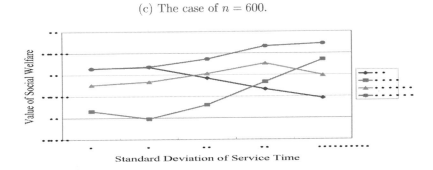

Fig. 7. The results of value of social welfare U. In each figure, the X axis indicates the standard deviation of attraction's service time in each experimental setting. The Y axis indicates the average value of social welfare U. The notations of "G," "CA," "SCA" and "PCC" correspond to the algorithm Greedy, Congestion-Avoidance, Stochastic Congestion-Avoidance and Preference-Congestion Coordination, respectively

coordination algorithms. In the case that the preference of agents is set to biased values, e.g., the popular attraction exists, the result of st303030 might show like the case st103050.

Figures 10 (a) and 10 (b) shows the averaged preference summation values in the case st103050 and st303030. In each case, the effectiveness of algorithms is different with each other. This result shows it might be possible for a coordination algorithm to improve individual utility in the situation that the theme park is crowded and agents can visit only two or three attractions. The evaluation of social welfare U represents same feature as shown in Figure 11 (a) and 11 (b).

5   Discussion

For developing mass user suport, we adopted the multiagent system to model the theme park environment. The flexibility of the multiagent system enables us to introduce practical and complicated situations into the model, but theoretical analysis of the model is difficult, and we have to carefully research this type of agent-based simulation. In particular, the coordination algorithm for the TPP needs the following new characteristics compared with classical industry scheduling problems.

- **Quality**
  - how to make satisfying coordination socially and personally.
- **Scalability**
  - how to process many agents' requirements reasonably.
- **Robustness**
  - how to coordinate more agents that may follow the instructions or not.

These characteristics needs a new type algorithm which attaches importance to adaptability.

According to the results of the computer simulation, TPP has the characteristic that it is dynamically changed by the problem settings and that it is strongly affected by the applied algorithm because the behavior of visiting agents are directly affected by the algorithms. The TPP setting here is simple in that the number of visiting agents is fixed in advance to 10^2 order and has no fluctuation, all agents must follow the guidance offered by the algorithm, the preference of agents is evenly distributed, service time and capacity of each segment are fixed and have no temporal events with changing parameters, and the size of the theme park is not large. However, the behavior of the simulation is complex enough with its interaction between agents, coordination algorithm and theme park situation. In addition, the basic experimental problem has no specific constraint, e.g., precedence of visiting. We can only gain an understanding of the TPP characteristics from computer simulations because TPP is considered to be complex systems.

To extend the simulation to include practical problems, we have to introduce following elements.

(a) The case of setting $st103050$.

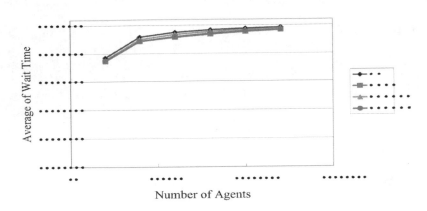

(b) The case of setting $st303030$.

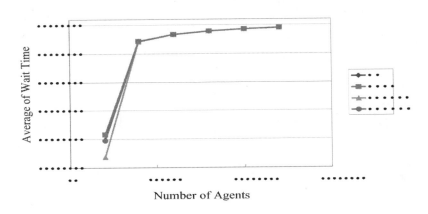

Fig. 8. The results of average of wait time wt_j. The figures (a) and (b) show the result of the setting $st103050$ and $st303030$, respectively. The X axis indicates the total number of visiting agents. The Y axis indicates the average value of wait time wt_j. The notations of "G," "CA," "SCA" and "PCC" correspond to the algorithm Greedy, Congestion-Avoidance, Stochastic Congestion-Avoidance and Preference-Congestion Coordination, respectively

- Enlargement of theme park size
- Complication of the structure of spatial segments
- Fluctuation of visiting agent number
- Bias of preference

(a) The case of setting $st103050$.

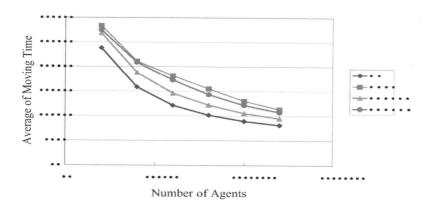

(b) The case of setting $st303030$.

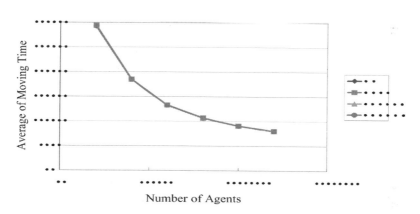

Fig. 9. The results of average of moving time mt_j. The figures (a) and (b) show the result of the setting $st103050$ and $st303030$, respectively. The X axis indicates the total number of visiting agents. The Y axis indicates the average value of moving time mt_j. The notations of "G," "CA," "SCA" and "PCC" correspond to the algorithm Greedy, Congestion-Avoidance, Stochastic Congestion-Avoidance and Preference-Congestion Coordination, respectively

To clarify the basic aspect of coordination algorithm for mass user suport, it is necessary to investigate various situations with computer simulations and perform many experiments with various problem settings.

(a) The case of setting *st*103050.

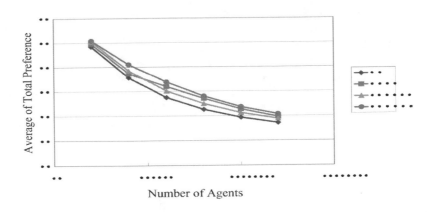

(b) The case of setting *st*303030.

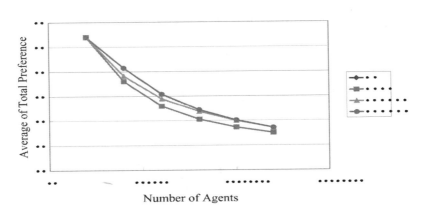

Fig. 10. The results of average of preference value p_j^*. The figures (a) and (b) show the result of the setting *st*103050 and *st*303030, respectively. The X axis indicates the total number of visiting agents. The Y axis indicates the average value of preference value p_j^*. The notations of "G," "CA," "SCA" and "PCC" correspond to the algorithm Greedy, Congestion-Avoidance, Stochastic Congestion-Avoidance and Preference-Congestion Coordination, respectively

It is also important to design an effective TPP algorithm. The algorithm must reactively coordinate many agents' activities by using distributed information because it is difficult to ascertain all the conditions of all the theme

(a) The case of setting *st*103050.

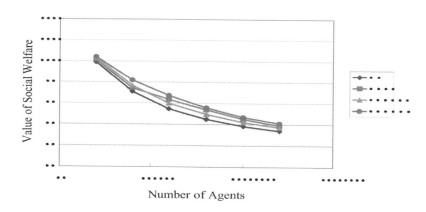

(b) The case of setting *st*303030.

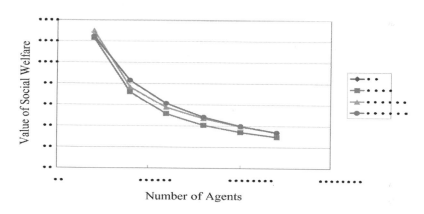

Fig. 11. The results of value of social welfare U. The figures (a) and (b) show the result of the setting *st*103050 and *st*303030, respectively. The X axis indicates the total number of visiting agents. The Y axis indicates the average value of social welfare U. The notations of "G," "CA," "SCA" and "PCC" correspond to the algorithm Greedy, Congestion-Avoidance, Stochastic Congestion-Avoidance and Preference-Congestion Coordination, respectively

park elements. Algorithm G is based on only local information, the preference of agent. Algorithm CA uses real-time global information, the queue numbers and service time of attraction segments. Algorithms SCA and PCC use both local and global information. The utilization of information is not based on another agent's information and it is reasonable to develop distributed coordination for this type of problem. As a similar mechanism to coordinate many local behaviors, the market mechanism is remarkable because the market mechanism can reach an efficient equilibrium point balancing many individual behaviors with only global information [PR, KU3, WL]. On the other hand, an algorithm which locally uses and coordinates other agents' intentions [MI, LI], or the biological-inspired approach based on stigmergy of multiagents [DO] might be effective.

6   Conclusions

We proposed the theme park problem as one example of a test bed for social coordination and mass user suport. The problem has various aspects according to setting, and the performance of the applied algorithms is dynamically changed by them. The problem is complex, and it is necessary to construct an adaptive coordination algorithm to deal with the various dynamic situations. We have studied on this problem and have developed coordination algorithms from a practical standpoint.

Acknowledgements

We wish to thank Dr. Masahito Yamamoto, Hokkaido University, Dr. Joshua M. Epstein and Dr. Robert Axtell, The Brookings Institution, Dr. Katia P. Sycara, Carnegie Mellon University, Dr. Kazuo Miyashita, Dr. Itsuki Noda, Dr. Kiyoshi Izumi, Dr. Noriaki Izumi, Mr. Akio Sashima and Dr. Tomohisa Yamashita, National Institute of Advanced Industrial Science and Technology, and the annonymous reviewers for their considerable cooperation and valuable advices.

References

[DO]   M. Dorigo and G. D. Caro. Ant Algorithms for Discrete Optimization. Journal of Artificial Life, 5 (2): 137–172, MIT Press, 1999. 68

[EP]   J. M. Epstein and R. Axtell. Growing Artificial Societies Social Science from the Bottom Up. The Brookings Institution Press, 1996. 48

[KU1]   K. Kurumatani. Coordination with Architecture for Ubiquitous Agents: CONSORTS. Proceedings of the International Conference on Intelligent Agents IAWTIC2003, in printing, 2003. 48

[KU2]   K. Kurumatani: Mass User Support by Social Coordination among Users, Working Note of The IJCAI-03 Workshop on Multiagent for Mass User Support, pp. 58-59 (2003). 48

[KU3]   K. Kurumatani. User Intention Market for Multi-Agent Navigation - An Artificial Intelligent Problem in Engineering and Economic Context. Proceedings of the AAAI-02 Workshop on Multi-Agent Modeling and Simulation of Economic Systems, MAMSES2002 (Edmonton), Technical Report WS-02-10, AAAI Press, 1–4, 2002. 68

[LI]   J. S. Liu and K. P. Sycara. Multiagent Coordination in Tightly Coupled Task Scheduling. Proceedings of the International Conference on Multi-Agent Systems 96, 181–188, 1996. 68

[MI]   K. Miyashita. CAMPS: A Constraint-Based Archtecture for Multiagent-Planning and Scheduling. Journal of Intelligent Manufacturing, 9: 147–154, 1998. 68

[NE]   J. von Neumann and O. Morgenstern Theory of Games and Economic Behavior. Prinston University Press, 1944. 48

[PR]   J. E. Prado and P. R. Wurman Non-cooperative Planning in Multi-Agent, Resource-Constrained Environments with Markets for Reservations Papers from the AAAI Workshop, Planning with and for Multiagent Systems, Technical Report WS-02-12, 60–66, 2002. 49, 53, 68

[SA1]   A. Sashima and K. Kurumatani. Seamless Context-Aware Information Assists Based on Multiagent Cooperation. Proceedings of the Second International on Agent-based Approaches in Economic and Social Complex Systems, AESCS'02, 39–46, 2002. 48

[SA2]   A. Sashima, K. Kurumatani and N. Izumi. Physically-Grounding Agents in Ubiquitous Computing. Proceedings of the Joint Agent Workshop JAWS2002 (Hakodate), 196–203, 2002. 48

[WE1]   M. Weiser Hot Topic: Ubiquitous Computing. IEEE Computer, 71–72, 2003. 48

[WE2]   M. Weiser Some Computer Science Problems in Ubiquitous Computing. Communications of the ACM, 2003. (reprinted as Ubiquitous Computing. Nikkei Electronics, December 6, 137–143, 1993.) 48

[WL]   M. P. Wellman and W. E. Walsh. Auction Protocols for Decentralized Scheduling. Games and Economic Behavior, 35: 271–303, 2001. 68

Story-Based Planning in Theme Park

Yutaka Matsuo[1,2], Shigeyoshi Hiratsuka[1,2], Tomohisa Yamashita[1],
Akira Takagi[1], Naoaki Okazaki[3], Takuji Tokiwa[1], and Koichi Kurumatani[1,2]

[1] National Institute of Advanced Industrial Science and Technology (AIST)
Aomi 2-41-6, Tokyo 135-0064, Japan
y.matsuo@aist.go.jp
http://www.carc.aist.go.jp/~y.matsuo/
[2] Japan Science and Technology Agency (JST)
[3] The University of Tokyo

Abstract. This study develops a planning system to make a tour plan
both in a theme park and a town with multi-agent architecture. The
main part of the system comprises two kinds of agents: a Story Writer
agent and a Story Miner agent. A Story Writer agent makes a schedule for a user based on the user's preferences, goals, and interests with
a consistent plot such as "ride all the coasters in the park" or "go to see
a trendy movie." It contributes to a user's satisfaction by generating an
interpretable plan that matches the plot. On the other hand, the Story
Miner agent discovers some characteristic from the generated plan and
produces an explanation for why the plan is good. It contributes to user
satisfaction by explicitly providing the reason for the plan being good.
We describe two scenarios: a theme park scenario and a date support
scenario. Especially, we detail algorithms for both types of agents for
theme park scenario.

1 Introduction

Personalization benefits both users and providers of personalized services. For
personalized information support, it is important to consider a user's preferences
and intentions. Various studies of user modeling have been done already, but it
remains difficult to model a user's preferences and intentions which are widely
useful in many domains [9, 8].

From the view point of mass user support and social coordination [11, 10],
the method of approximating a user's utility according to that user's preferences
and intentions is of utmost importance. A user's utility is fundamental material
to make a model of multiple users and thereby achieve a socially appropriate
solution. For example, navigation in a city and in a theme park is considered as
a model problem for social coordination. If users are motivated to take directed
paths to their destination, the transportation system will function better overall.
However in a recent stage, a crude approximation is made as to a user's utility:
for example, a user's utility is measured as the time to reach a destination.

More attention to a user's utility may indicate several important facts that
are usually ignored in the problem modeling process:

K. Kurumatani et al. (Eds.): MAMUS 2003, LNAI 3012, pp. 70–85, 2004.

- A user can never assign a true utility value for an action before acting. The utility value is only an estimation based on some attributes of the action. The utility value is constantly updated after one action is made and evaluation of the utility is obtained.
- A user can never determine that a plan is actually superior to others unless the user repeats visits many times. An experience such as visiting a theme park and going to a trendy movie sometimes occurs only once, so a user never fully evaluate a plan without actually choosing and experiencing the plan. A user can take only one plan at a time. For that reason, comparison between multiple plans has no meaning after a user selects one plan. (Of course, a user can tell ex-post that the plan might be better in the scope of understanding the situation. For example, another attraction may seem very nice, but we may have been unable to visit it.)
- Explanation is very important for a user's satisfaction. Consider a travel plan. A travel plan sometimes has a title, for example "Visit old towns and ruins in Turkey." It also contains a fragment of the story: for example, "This hotel was originally built for a King's summer palace," "We will also visit the King's hunting ground," and so on. These explanations are important to induce a user to accept, interpret and assign meaning to the plan. A user can tell a friend that "I will visit old towns and ruins in Turkey" or "The hotel I stayed at was once the King's summer palace. That was very good!" The interpretability of the plan is important for a user's satisfaction.

This study proposes a new direction to approximate and improve a user's satisfaction, especially for making a good tour plan for a user. The study objective requires that we focus on a *story*. A story is meant in this paper as a consistent explanation with high interpretability. By story-based planning, we intend planning which has a consistent explanation that can be easily accepted and interpreted by a user.

Interpretability is an essential aspect of a story. In this paper, it is realized by two forms: a *plot* and a *side story*. A plot is a planning strategy to make a plan interpretable. A side story is a short story that is included in a plan. We propose two kinds of agents to build an interpretable plan. One is the *Story Writer* agent, which generates a plan based on a plot. Another is the *Story Miner* agent, which discovers a sidestory of a given plan. Those two agents contribute to a satisfiable plan for a user.

In this paper, we will overview our overall concept. The rest of the paper is organized as follows: The next section details the concept of story-based planning. Section 3 describes two scenarios, a theme park scenario and a date support scenario, which can be attained by story-based planning. Section 4 explains a concrete algorithm in the case of the theme park scenario, followed by discussions in Section 5. Related works are presented in Section 6. We conclude the paper with Section 7.

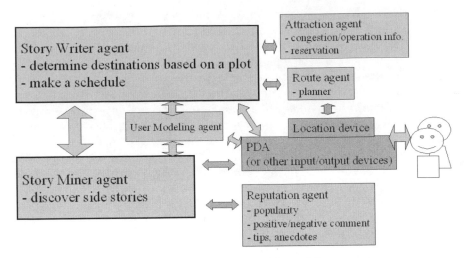

Fig. 1. Story Writer agent and Story Miner agent

2   Story-Based Planning

To improve a user's satisfaction, a tour plan is preferably generated with a story, that is, with a consistent explanation with high interpretability. By constructing a plan with a story, we can improve a user's satisfaction. This paper refers to a planning based on a story as *Story-based planning*.

Story-based planning is realized by two types of agents.

— Story Writer agent: it makes a plan based on a *plot*.
— Story Miner agent: it discovers a *side story* from the given plan.

Multiple agents manage resources and information such as attractions, a user model, a route and popular topics. Such agents are called *Resource* agents in this paper. The overall architecture of Story Writer agent, Story Miner agents, and Resource agents are shown in Fig. 1. The Story Writer agent generates a plan consulting with the User Modeling agent, Route planner, and Attraction agent. The Story Miner agent discovers side stories by consulting with the Reputation agent and the User Modeling agent (and sometimes with the Attraction agent). We assume that a user's direction and location are obtained through a PDA (Personal Degital Assistant) and some location devices.

We don't go into details in this paper about the Resource agents, PDAs and location devices, because our focus is on how to improve user's satisfaction by a story. Below, we describe two agents, the Story Writer agent and the Story Miner agent in detail.

2.1   Story Writer Agent

Story Writer agent is an agent that generates a plan according to a plot to form an interpretable story. For example, assume a Story Writer agent covers a plot

"Go to a trendy movie," and generates a plan that includes a trendy movie as a destination and a restaurant and shopping before and after the movie.

Story Writer agent calls other Resource agents to generate a plan if necessary. In this example, it calls a Movie agent (a Resource agents) with emphasis on the "trendy" attribute. The Story Writer agent also calls a Restaurant agent, Cafe agent, and Shopping agent categorized as Resource agents with emphasis on the "trendy" attribute to fix the schedule before and after the movie. Finally, the Story Writer agent checks whether the obtained plan is consistent with the plot or not. Thereby, we can get a plan to go to a trendy movie with a trendy cafe and so on.

A *plot* is a planning strategy to generate a plan and make it interpretable. For example, a plot is labeled as "Go to a trendy movie," "Go and stay at a theme park," and so on. It corresponds to a title of a travel package tour or a title of a model course in a theme park.

A plot consists mainly of

- a strategy to choose destinations,
- a strategy to choose subsidiary destinations before and after the destination.

We describe an inner design of Story Writer agent in detail in the next section.

2.2   Story Miner Agent

Story Miner agent finds side stories from a given plan. A *side story* is an explanation to improve the interpretability of the plan. It includes an explanation for why a given plan is good or information addressing the multiple destinations. For example, "This plan includes all the coasters in the park," "You can view the catsle from different angle from attraction A and attraction B," or "The restaurant you went is a top-ranked restaurant in the ranking of New Casual Italian Restaurants 2002."

The Story Miner agent functions to improve a user's satisfaction by explicitly presenting explanations as to why it is a good plan. This function can be used when generating a plan, but it can also be used during or after the practice. For example, the system may say that "This restaurant is very good, it is featured on TV." If you failed to visit that restaurant because of congestion, it may suggest that "Though that restaurant is popular, the meal quality is absolutely better in this restaurant!" or "That restaurant has no view for the bridge. We can see the beautiful bridge from the best angle in this restaurant." What the system says is all true. However, such a statement depends upon the points the system focuses. In other words, we seek an explanation to justify the quality of a given plan.

This is mainly done in several approaches:

- Attribute-based approach: find a criterion and the range to make the given plan the best and explain it. For example, "This plan includes all the coasters in the park."

– Keyword-based approach: collect the descriptions of attractions. Then, find common keywords or relevance between two descriptions. For example, "Attraction A shows you Mickey and Minnie's dance. Attraction C provides some pictures of Mickey."
– Rule-based approach: apply pre-defined rules and generate an explanation. For example, if a given plan includes attraction A and B, then output "You can view the castle from a different angle from attraction A and attraction B."

2.3   Resource Agent

Resource agents are agents that manage resources and information. In the theme park case, there are several types of Resource agents.

An Attraction agent, which is one of the Resource agents, provides information on opening times, fees, menus, merchandises, and so on for each attraction, show, restaurant, or shop. Congestion information and reservations are sometimes available through the agent.

The Route agent seeks a path from point to point. Sometimes it must also collect congestion or availability information of routes. The User Modeling agent collects information regarding a user. It includes user's attributes such as pre-defined demographic attributes or interests, predicted user's interests and objectives, features derived from user's interaction history, user's location history, and so on.

A Reputation agent provides popularity of each attraction, positive and negative comments on each attraction, some tips, and anecdotes related to those attractions.

3   Two Scenarios

This section describes two scenarios that we intend to realize through story-based planning. One is a *theme park scenario* and another is a *date support scenario*. The former is easier to realize than the latter in that the problem can be defined clearly. All attractions, operation times, and average congestion are known beforehand; futhermore, attractions are characterized by some attributes like those shown in Fig. 2.

3.1   Theme Park Scenario

Theme parks such as DisneyLand and Universal Studios have many attractions, restaurants and shops. Sometimes, all the attractions cannot be visited in a day because of the many attractions and vast area of a park.

Therefore, some guidebooks suggest a variety of model courses for visiting the park efficiently. A model course is a sequence of several attractions, shows, restaurants, and so on that allows a user to enjoy the entire day. For example, several books show courses such as for typical types of user groups.

Big coaster	
TIME	
waiting time to ride (weekday)	30 min. on average
waiting time to ride (holiday)	90 min. on average
duration	3 min.
open	9:00 a.m. to 9:45 p.m.
EVALUATION	
for children	2
for adults	4
Disney degree	5
exciting	5
trendy	4
romantic	1
EXPLANATION	
constructed year	1999
character	Mickey and Pluto
description	This coaster is one of the most popular atttraction in this park. It runs about 130 km/h for 2044 m. Very hard attraction. The view of Fujiyama is very beautiful.

Fig. 2. Example of attributes for an attraction

- Family courses
- Couples' courses
- Group courses

Family courses often include attractions and restaurants that can also be enjoyed by children. They may include merry-go-rounds, small coasters, and short-time comedy shows, but they would not include exciting coaster-type attractions or expensive French meals. On the other hand, Couples' courses would include coaster-type attractions, serious shows, and romantic French meals for a couple to enjoy a wonderful time.

There can be more advanced distinctions among users, especially for repeat visitors. For example, some visitors want to see mainly shows and performances. Other visitors want to visit attractions with a favorite character (e.g., Mickey Mouse). Some repeat guests want to visit new attractions first. Therefore, there are many model courses based on user preferences, such as

- Show-intensive course,
- Coaster-intensive course,
- Character-intensive course,
- New attraction-intensive course,

and so on.

Therefore, in a theme park scenario, we assume that users' needs are typically classified by a type of a user group for first visitors, and by users' preferences for repeaters.

Story Writer Agent The Story Writer agent generates a course, i.e., a full-day or half-day schedule, in a theme park as a model course suggested by some guidebooks. A model course in a guidebook is static: it has no flexibility concerning congestion, unavailability of some attractions, and user preferences. In contrast, Story Writer agent can generate a plan dynamically based on the current user and the environmental situation.

The parameters for Story Writer agent differ according to the target type of user group and user preferences. For example, a Story Writer agent for a family course emphasizes attributes of "for children" for each attraction. A Story Writer agent for a couple course emphasizes attributes such as "exciting," "romantic," and "for adults." A Story Writer agent for a coaster-intensive course will give special priority to coasters.

In the theme park scenario, we can define attributes for all attractions in a consistent way. Therefore the role of Story Writer agent is mainly to transform the attributes into utility using some criteria. Then, it will choose some attractions as destinations.

In addition, we must consider lunch time, dinner time, and time to buy souvenirs. For a couple, it is good to boost the mood by scheduling good shows and a good restaurant in the latter half of the plan. However, for a family it is good to place main destinations in a plan as early as possible because children quickly become bored or sleepy. Therefore, the generated plan must have a structure to improve user satisfaction, just as a story has a structure. A strategy to choose destinations is described in Section 4.

Story Miner Agent The Story Miner agent will detect a side story based on the descriptions and reputations of attractions.

For example, if a given plan includes all the attractions that are newly built in this year, it generates an explanation "Your plan includes all the newest attractions" by focusing on "constructed year" attributes. If a plan includes an attraction with a good view of a harbor and a restaurant with a good view of the harbor in the different direction, it generates "You can see the harbor from different angles from two points; they are both very good views" from the descriptions of attractions and a rule to describe this.

3.2   Date Support Scenario

Another scenario that we intend to realize through story-based planning is date support scenario. When a couple have a date, one of them is expected to make a date plan. Sometimes that person checks a good restaurant and make a reservation. The person might make a more elaborate plan: check a trendy date spot, check a good restaurant around it and make a reservation, and check transportation. If one plans a date for a half a day, for a full day, or for a couple of days, one must make a plan for a combination of date spots (movie, museum, park, shopping, and so on), restaurant, transportations, and so on.

This scenario subsumes that users are a couple and can go to many sites in a city. For a date, there can be numerous candidates of a date course. Many books and magazines suggest good date spots, restaurant, and so on. Some books also suggest some model date courses for a couple. The problems are

- Conditions differ among users. For example, time (afternoon, evening, or night), location (residential location and possible locations to visit), budget and preference are different according to the case. Therefore, we want to have a tailored plan for each couple depending on their situation.
- There are many sources of information on date spots. We want to gather information for deciding destinations such as date spots to visit, good restaurants to visit and, so on. Especially, we want an interpretable explanation of a plan to enhance satisfiability of a couple.

The date support scenario has the characteristic that the order of destinations is important. For example, a plan to visit "Shopping, Movie, Restaurant, Bar" is better than "Bar, Restaurant, Movie, Shopping," because, when we do shopping, we can go to a movie when it starts. And if one sees a movie, one might want to have time to talk about it in a good restaurant. On the other hand, having meals in a restaurant engenders less time flexibility, so one might be late for the movie unless allowance for that eventuality is made beforehand. In this sense, the order of destinations is very important for the date support scenario, just as the plot of a story is important.

Story Writer Agent There can be many types of Story Writer agents that generate date plans for "Going to a trendy movie," "Going to a hot spot," "Going to Yokohama," and so on. In contrast to the theme park scenario, there is no one Story Writer agent, but many Story Writer agents.

For example, a Story Writer agent for "Going to a trendy movie" will first determine a movie to go to see considering users' preferences and objectives. Information on movies are obtained via the Web sites [1]. These sites have sometimes a retrieval system. The Story Writer agent can put a query to a retrieval system by emphasizing more on the "trendy" attribute. Some sites can also retrieve movies by specifying options "for date."

Then it generate a schedule before or after the movie, such as cafe or restaurant near the movie site. In this case, if a dinner is scheduled before the movie, it is desirable to make a reservation that allows sufficient time for going to the movie. If a dinner is to be scheduled after the movie, a restaurant with a good mood or a good night view is nice. Such information on restaurants, cafes, and date spots can be all collected through Web sites. Retrieval and reservation will be also possible via Web services in the future.

There are many types of such Story Writers. They offer different strategies to select destinations and make date plans, because different story writers will write different types of plans.

---

[1] Such as The Internet Movie Database (http://www.imdb.com/), Hollywood.com (http://www.hollywood.com) and so on.

Story Miner Agent In the date support scenario, attributes of each destination are inconsistent and unavailable. Therefore, there are a couple of ways to generate a side story:

- Utilize a search engine and retrieve commments or descriptions that are relevant to one or more destinations.
- Find a ranking where the destination is evaluated as the best.

This is a rather challenging research theme, but there are already some studies that address reputation searches from the Web [15, 6].

3.3   Differences between Two Scenarios

The main differences between the above two scenarios are these two. First, a theme park is, so to speak, a closed world. All attractions, restaurants, and shops can be assigned attribute values in a consistent manner. On the other hand, in a date support scenario, consistency is not expected. Although there are sources of information to evaluate restaurants, movies, and hot spots within the same category in a consistent manner, the consistent attributes over different categories are hard to obtain. Therefore, the Story Writer agent is the only one for theme park scenario, while there are a number of different Story Writer agents for date support scenario.

Second, in the theme park scenario, information can be obtained beforehand. All attractions are operated in a predetermined way. Congestion information or operation information (e.g., in a case where an attraction is not operational during rain) are the few exceptions that are realtime information: otherwise, information is static. On the other hand, in a date support scenario, one can not acquire all information beforehand. For example, it is very demanding to prefetch all movie operation information in Tokyo beforehand. Information is constantly updated. For that reason, we must gather information online, or with frequent updates.

Therefore, a theme park scenario is more tractable to handle than date support scenario, but in both scenarios a story plays an important role to make good interpretable plans for users. In the next section, we describes more concrete algorithms for the theme park scenario.

4   Algorithm of Agents for Theme Park Scenario

In this section, we describe an algorithm of Story Writer agent and Story Miner agent for the theme park scenario.

4.1   Story Writer Agent

The main functions of Story Writer agent are:

- to calculate a user's utility based on attraction attributes considering a user's preferences,
- to choose destinations, and produce a schedule.

We first describe how to calculate a user's utility based on attraction attributes, and then describe the strategy to choose destinations.

Calculating Utilities Attributes for each attraction are shown in Fig. 2. These attributes are considered as a vector. For example, "EVALUATION" (for children, for adults, Disney, exciting, trendy, romantic) attributes are shown as

$$A_{BigCoaster} = (2, 4, 5, 5, 4, 1).$$

"Magical coaster" is represented as

$$A_{MagicalCoaster} = (5, 2, 4, 2, 3, 2).$$

If target users are a family, the transformation vector f is defined as

$$f_{Family} = (0.6, 0, 0.2, 0.1, 0.1, 0)^T.$$

Then the utilities of Big coaster and Magical coaster are calculated as

$$A_{BigCoaster} \cdot f_{Family} = 1.2 + 1.0 + 0.5 + 0.4 = 3.1$$

$$A_{MagicalCoaster} \cdot f_{Family} = 3.0 + 0.8 + 0.2 + 0.3 = 4.3.$$

MagicalCoaster has a higher utility than BigCoaster for a family type. We can also define the coaster-intensive type as $(0, 0.3, 0, 0.7, 0, 0)$ and get different utilities. This is a very straightforward approach, but in the case of the theme park scenario, this works well.

Of course, there are other factors to calculate utilities: for example, if an attraction is popular, we increase the utility. If the user expresses a desire to visit an attraction, we increase the utility greatly.

Choice of Destination Scheduling a full day in a theme park is a very difficult problem. There are many variables such as which attractions, restaurants, shops to visit, and when. A schedule is not represented by a combination of destinations, nor a sequence of destinations. It is represented by a list of a destination-time pair as shown in Fig. 3 because there are three types of destinations.

- Attraction type: one can go anytime, wait, and ride.
- Show type: one must wait until scheduled times to see a show.
- Shop type: we can go anytime and leave anytime.

A restaurant for which reservation is necessary is considered as show type with regard to time constraint. Some theme park employs a reservation system for popular attractions, sometimes called "fast pass." In this case, the reserved attraction is also considered as show type. Other restaurants are considered as attraction type. Exceptionally, a restaurant like a food court is considered as shop type, because you can have an option to eat or not, and also to leave and to stay.

To address such time constraints, we must manage a time stamp with destinations. Unlike popular scheduling problems such as job shop scheduling or scheduling for micro-processors that address a sequence of actions but do not use a time stamp, our problem is more difficult to solve.

9:00   Gate
9:15   Storm Riding (wait and ride)
10:25 Aquarina (wait and ride)
11:00 Shopping at Harbour Sweets
11:30 Big Coaster (reservation)
13:00 Lunch at Casba Food Court (no reservation)
14:00 Magic Musical Show
. . .   . . .

Fig. 3. Example of schedule

Therefore, we employ a procedural method to determine a schedule, rather than describing as an optimization problem and apply general search methods.

First we define three kinds of destinations:

– Prime destination,
– Secondary destination, and
– Binding destination.

A *prime destination* is an indispensable destination for a target story. For example, if the target story is the coaster-intensive type, then the plan must have visits to coaters. A failure to go to the prime destination constitutes a failure to attain the story, more or less.

A *secondary destination* is a destination that contributes to enhance the plan. It includes destinations for lunch, dinner, rest, souvenirs, and other attractions if time is available.

A *binding destination* is a destination that improves the feasibility of the plan. It includes shopping with the aim of waiting for the next reservation; destination that is in the path to the next destination. It prevents boredom, allows rest and toilet breaks and so on.

Algorithm The algorithm to generate a schedule for a given story type is described as follows:

1. **Obtain Utility Value**: Calculate a utility value for each attraction (including restaurant and shop) by multiplying attributes of each attraction and a user type vector.
2. **Choose Prime Destinations**: Choose several destinations with top utility values. (Sometimes these destinations are predefined.)
3. **Choose Secondary Destinations**: Choose several destinations of lunch, dinner, rest, and so on.
4. **Place Destinations**: Place destinations on a schedule with time stamps. Show type destinations are settled first, then attraction type destinations are placed.
5. **Improve the Schedule**: Change the order of destinations, and put binding destinations.

6. **Select a Schedule**: Go to 2 and repeat generation of a schedule for a given number. Different schedules are generated with randomness. After a given number of iterations, one of them is selected as a solution considering each plan's utility and feasibility.

The improvement phase is very complicated. We should consider the path and exchange the order of two destinations so that the whole path gets shorter. The order is also evaluated from the perspective of appropriateness for each story type.

4.2   Story Miner Agent

The following steps are executed for the Story Miner agent for the theme park scenario.

- **Find Side Story for Single Destination**:
  - 1. If the plan includes a destination with good descriptions or good comments, output the description. For example, "Big coaster was the No. 1 coaster in the World until 1999."
  - 2. If a destination in the plan is the best in some ranking, show that ranking. For example, "Haunted House is the most preferred attraction by couples."
- **Find Side Story for Multiple Destinations**:
  - 3. Find a set of common attributes that are not identical with a user type vector. If there is such attributes, generate an explanation. For example, "this plan includes many new attractions."
  - 4. Apply rules to generate an explanation. For example, the rule is described as: If a plan includes Magellan restaurant and the Water show, then explain it as "From the Magellan restaurant, you can see some boats that will be used in Water shows."

Item 1 is realized using the description of each destination. We input descriptions or comments into data base with scores of credibility and quality. Item 2 is realized using many ranking lists. Such rankings are easily available in some guidebooks because ranking is a common way to convey overall images of a theme park to a reader.

Items 3 and 4 require more complex processing. To realize item 3, we must seek common attributes and generate an explanation, mainly by template matching. Item 4 is a more straightforward approach whereby comments are transformed and stored in the form of rules.

5   Discussion

This paper has outlined story-based planning that is intended to improve a user's satisfaction through constructing a plan based on a plot and finding side stories. The concept proposed herein is new in the field of navigation and user modeling.

When we build an information support system for a user, we model a user's interests and objectives in some ways. Ultimately we are likely to summarize user's utility as a value. Of course, this is effective in many domains such as finding interesting news article or recommendation of popular tourist spots. A user may want to read an article of personal interest, and desire to visit a tourist spot to serve that interest to broaden and deepen their own knowledge.

However, when visiting a theme park or having a date, the situation is different. In most cases, there is no concrete objective for users when visiting a theme park or having a date. The abstract goal of users is to enjoy the experience or induce enjoyment in a partner. In this sense, the user's utility for the goal is highly subjective. There is no clear distinction of whether a user will enjoy an attraction or not. A user may enjoy an attraction in some cases, but not in other cases, depending on mood, physical condition, and many other factors.

In this situation, it is very difficult to pursue the objectivity of utility value for a user. Instead, this paper addresses provision of a "story" so that a user can interpret the action sequence and justify what the user actually enjoys. People who visit a theme park or have a date want to enjoy the experience, and seek explanations for that. For example, one prefers to hear "This restaurant is the best French restaurant in this town" rather than "This is the 207th best restaurant in the US," assuming that these two are true statements. In an objective and scientific sense, these two statements are equal, but for a user's satisfaction it is different. The former is easier for the user to interpret as "I went to a good restaurant."

In the current stage, we are developing a proto-type of the system for both the theme park scenario and the date support scenario. We are goint to use the system experimentally after finishing the development and make evaluations comparing our system with other scheduling strategies from a view point of user's satisfaction.

6   Related Work

There has been much research on planning, such as STRIPS style [18]. We introduce several other planning methods that may be relevant to our work.

Hierarchical task network (HTN) [4] is a task network representing a set of tasks to be done. Each task is decomposed until all the tasks will become primitive, that is executable. In our work, for example "go to a movie" might be decomposed into "find a movie to see," "find a route to travel," and "get a ticket" in a date support scenario. Therefore, it can be used for date support scenario. However, in the theme park scenario, there are no prominent hierarchical tasks, so we employ procedural scheduling.

Dufree and Lesser developed Partial Global Planning (PGP) [3], in which each agent maintains a partial global plan, that stores its own partial picture of the plans of all members of the group. PGP focuses on distributed execution and run-time planning: it uses a specialized plan representation, where a single agent's plan includes a set of objectives, a long-term strategy for achieving those objectives, a set of short-term details, and a number of predictions and ratings. Surveys on distributed planning are detailed in [2]. PGP might be useful in the inner architecuture of the Story Writer agent.

On the other hand, scheduling techniques are useful when operations or jobs to be scheduled are determined. Tom my knowledge, none of the scheduling techniques are applicable directly to our problem, because our problem includes a subproblem to determine where to visit. For example, job shop scheduling [7] is one of the most popular models in scheduling theory. It is formalized by a finite set of jobs to be processed on a finite set of machines. Each job must be processed on every machine and consists a chain or complex of operations which have to be scheduled in a predetermined given order. However, our problem has several kinds of time constraints, such as attraction type, show type, and shop type constraints, which is over the scope of job shop scheduling.

Scheduling problems can be found in several different application areas, such as the scheduling of production operations in manufacturing industry, computer processes in operation systems, aircraft crews, and so on. Sauer et. al proposes multi-site scheduling [10] for transportation which is two-layered scheduling and relevant to our system. However, to apply to our problem, some modifications are necessary.

Recently many studies have addressed tour guides in a city or museum:

- The GUIDE system is an intelligent and context-aware tourist guide. The system has been deployed in the city of Lancaster using handheld GUIDE units [1]. Personal context including the user's location and profile and the environmental context are used to tailor the presentation of information to the user. For example, if a visitor makes a return visit to an attraction, then the information presented should reflect this fact, e.g., by welcoming the visitor back.
- Deep Map is a project that aims at building an intelligent next-generation spatial information system. It realizes the vision of a future tourist guidance system that functions as a mobile guide and as a web-based planning tool [13]. Fink and Kobsa develops user modeling for a personalized city tour in the Deep Map project [5]. The WebGuide sub-project aims at the provision of personalized tour recommendations for the city of Heidelberg that cater to an individual user's interests and preferences. WebGuides identifies geographical points of interest and computes a tour that connects these points via, presumably, interesting routes.
- Hippie is a "nomadic" guide that can be used all along the process of a visit in a museum, i.e., for preparation, the visit itself, and its evaluation [14]. An information system is said to be nomadic when the user has access to personal information space from all places independent from specific devices. The electronic guide provides information access at home via the museum information access provided via wireless technologies. The user can access information by moving in physical space and navigating in the information space concurrently. A Web-based client-server approach allows for adaptive selection and presentation of information based on a user model.

- The CRUMPET project aims at "Creation of User-friendly Mobile Services Personalised for Tourism" [17]. The design concepts of the project are: personalized and location-aware support of mobile users, and adaptive, ontology-based user model, scalability with respect to clients and providers, and multi-agent architecture with middle-agents performing brokerage.
- Hyperaudio is a system able to organize the presentation of museum content taking into account the visitor's needs and the layout of the physical space [12]. It can provide the visitor with information tailored on his own interests and interaction history; it can also support the visitor in his own exploration of the physical space, helping him to find information and suggesting new interesting physical locations.

Though a good amount of research on tour guide or museum guide based on user's interests and locations exists, the navigation employed is rather on the spot: in typical usage, the system displays the point of interests based on a user model, the user selects one of them, and the system guides a user there. There is no long-term strategy to improve a user's satisfaction. For example, if the system can predict that a user will be thirsty after a couple of hours' walk, the system should plan a visit to a nice cafe beforehand. Such a long-term plan, what we call a plot, is necessary for more advanced navigation.

7   Conclusion

All the world's a stage,
And all the men and women merely Players;

— W. Shakespeare, *As You Like It*

Our project for developing a support system based on story-based planning is called *SHAKESPEAR* (Sympathetic Handholding Assistant by Knowledge intensivE Story-based Planning for Entertainment AREa). As a play by Shakespeare is thoughtfully created and touches our heart, we aim at making a thoughtful plan and want to create a wonderful time for users.

This paper introduces story-based planning especially for a theme park scenario and a date support scenario. In such situations, the user's utility is highly subjective, so providing interpretable stories to improve user satisfaction seems a promising approach. Story-based planning is realized by two agents: Story Writer agents and Story Miner agents, both of which play different roles to improve user satisfaction. We are currently developing a system to function in a real environment. Evaluation and strengthening methodologies for story-based planning are our future objectives.

Our work will contribute to mass user support because story-based planning enables us to have several alternative plans for each user that increase user satisfaction. Therefore, we have more degrees of freedom to enhance social coordination, which will further increase both a user's utility and overall system performance.

References

[1] K. Cheverst, N. Davies, K. Mitchell, and P. Smith. Providing tailored (context-aware) information to city visitors. In *Proc. International Conference on Adaptive Hypermedia and Adaptive Web-Based Systems (AH'2000)*, pages 73–85, 2000. 83

[2] M. desJardins, E. Durfee, C. Ortiz, Jr., and M. Wolverton. A survey of research in distributed, continual planning. *The AI Magazine*, 20(4):13–22, 1999. 83

[3] E. Durfee and V. Lesser. Partial global planning: A coordination framework for distributed hypothesis formation. *IEEE Transactions on Systems, Man, and Cybernetics*, 21(5):1167–1183, 1991. 82

[4] K. Erol, D. Nau, and J. Hendler. HTN planning: Complexity and expressivity. In *Proc. AAAI-94*, 1994. 82

[5] J. Fink and A. Kobsa. User modeling for personalized city tours. *Artificial Intelligence Review*, 18:33–74, 2002. 83

[6] S. Fujimura, N. Matsumura, N. Okazaki, and M. Ishizuka. Decision support based on reputation from bulletin board. In *Proc. 17th Annual Conf. of the Japanese Society for Artificial Intelligence*, pages 2B1–05, 2003. in Japanese. 78

[7] A. S. Jain and S. Meeran. A state-of-the-art review of job-shop scheduling techniques. Technical report, Department of Applied Physics, Electronics and Mechanical Engineering, University of Dundee, 1998. 83

[8] A. Kobsa. Generic user modeling systems. *User Modeling and User-Adaptied Interaction*, 11:49–63, 2001. 70

[9] A. Kobsa. *User Modeling and User-Adapted Interaction*. Kluwer Academic Publisher, 2001. 70

[10] K. Kurumatani. Mass user support by social coordination among users. In *Working Note of the IJCAI-03 Workshop on Multiagent for Mass User Support*, pages 58–59, 2003. 70

[11] K. Kurumatani. Social coordination with architecture for ubiquitous agents - CONSORTS. In *Proc. IAWTIC '03*, 2003. 70

[12] C. Strapparava M. Sarini. Building a user model for a museum exploration and information-providing adaptive system. In *Proc. the 2nd Workshop on Adaptive Hypertext and Hypermedia, HYPERTEXT'98*, 1999. 84

[13] R. Malak and A. Zipf. *Deep Map – Challenging IT Research in the Framework of a Tourist Information System*, pages 15–27. Springer-Verlag, 2000. 83

[14] R. Oppermann and M. Specht. A nomadic information system for adaptive exhibition guidance. In *Proc. ICHIM*, pages 103–109, 1999. 83

[15] D. Rafiei and A. Mendelzon. What is this page known for? computing web page reputations. In *Proc. 9th WWW Conf.*, 2000. 78

[16] J. Sauer, T. Freese, and T. Teschke. Towards agent-based multi-site scheduling. In *Proc. the ECAI 2000 Workshop on New Results in Planning*, pages 123–130, 2000. 83

[17] B. Schmidt-Belz, P. Stefan, A. Nick, and A. Zipf. Personalized and location-based mobile tourism services. In *Workshop on Mobile Tourism Support Systems*, pages 18–20, 2002. 84

[18] D. Weld. Recent advances in AI planning. *AI Magazine*, 20(2):93–123, 1999. 82

Effect of Using Route Information Sharing to Reduce Traffic Congestion

Tomohisa Yamashita, Kiyoshi Izumi, and Koichi Kurumatani

Cyber Assist Research Center (CARC)
National Institute of Advanced Industrial Science and Technology (AIST)
Aomi 2-41-6, Koto-ku, Tokyo 135-0064, Japan
tomohisa@carc.aist.go.jp
kiyoshi@ni.aist.go.jp
k.kurumatani@aist.go.jp

Abstract. In this research, our aim is to increase the utility of road transportation systems by reducing traffic congestion for the benefit of both individuals and society as a whole. To attain our purpose, we propose a simple route guidance mechanism based on mass user support. Through multiagent simulation, we examine the ability of our proposed mechanism for improving traffic efficiency of both individual drivers and whole systems. Our simulation results that i) our proposed mechanism improves efficiency for the drivers who use it and the entire transportation system, and ii) the social dilemmas in route choice behaviors occur in a radial and ring network.

1 Introduction

Recently, cellular phone and personal digital assistants (PDA) have been developed, and network environments for short-range communication, i.e., wireless LAN have also been improved. Due to such technological progress, ubiquitous computing environments with various kinds of devices, sensors, and processors installed in social infrastructure have become more and more important. In ubiquitous computing environments, acquiring current states and position of users and the intentions and preferences in real time while protecting users' privacy is possible. Therefore, based on information about users collected by such devices and sensors, new information services can be provided. For example, home automation with intelligent home appliances, virtual communities based on the always-connected high-speed Internet, and on-line distributed meetings and electric ordering systems in companies are anticipated.

Especially, ubiquitous computing environments in road transportation systems have developed rapidly; car navigation systems have spread widely, and the accuracy of GPS (Global Positioning System) is constantly advancing. A vehicle information and communication system (VICS) was started and then the range over which the VICS can provide congestion information was extended [14].

K. Kurumatani et al. (Eds.): MAMUS 2003, LNAI 3012, pp. 86–104, 2004.

These advances were med possible by the development of in-vehicle communication devices, sensors, and processors. [1]

One of most important information services in road transportation systems is navigation from an origin to a destination. Based on such developments, many researchers have been trying to develop navigation systems, and to examine what kind of traffic information is variable [1, 9]. Generally, the purpose of navigation systems is to maximize the efficiency of individual users by providing routes that satisfy their intensions, e.g., reducing travel distance or travel time. However, previous research has revealed that optimizing performance by merely providing information about congestion in road transportation systems is difficult [7, 11, 13]. Usually, navigation systems recommend routes for decreasing travel time based on the current state of traffic congestion. To decrease travel time, a driver using a navigation system chooses a recommended route. However, if other drivers simultaneously choose the same recommended route, traffic is concentrated on that route. As a result, traffic congestion is caused on the selected route. Therefore, traveling the recommended route takes longer even though navigation systems recommended it for decreasing travel time.

To make matters worse, traffic congestion increases even more rapidly as more drivers choose the recommended route. As car navigation systems have been spreading rapidly, this is a serious problem. Furthermore, because this kind of phenomena is observed not only in road transportation systems but also at large scale theme parks [3] and event halls [10], general solutions for reducing congestion are strongly demanded.

In our work, we introduce the concept of mass user support [5, 6] in order to avoid the unintentional traffic congestion caused by use of navigation systems. Mass user support provides information services to users, or groups, or mass that go beyond conventional personal services. Although conventional services only considers utility for individual users, mass user support considers not only the sum of personal services provided to individual users but also interactions among users. The purpose of mass user support is to increase utility for individuals and for society as whole, and without increasing the benefit to society by sacrificing benefits to individuals. That is to say, mass user support requires some kind of social coordination that leads to mutual concessions among users [5].

In road transportation systems, the best solution that maximizes the performance of the system is not necessarily required. The reason is that, if the performance of road transportation systems can be improved slightly by mass user support, the profit to society is immeasurable because of the large-scale of road transportation systems. Even if a reduction traffic congestion is marginal, we can derive the following benefits: i) direct reduction of economic loss, ii) a decrease in the harmful effects from pollutants in exhaust gas, and iii) a more

---

[1] The VICS Center [11] collects, processes and edits information about traffic congestion, road control, and other traffic information in real time, and then provides road traffic information in words and graphics through communications and broadcast media (FM multiplex broadcasting and beacons). Drivers can receive traffic information via navigation devices installed in vehicles.

comfortable driving environment for drivers. Moreover, a service based on mass user support is required to provide not only an increase of utility but also fairness among users, stability of the service, transparency of the mechanism, and robustness against disturbance because mass user support deals with many users at the same time,

In our research, we aim to increase individual's utility and social benefits of road transportation systems by decreasing traffic congestion. For this purpose we propose a simple route guidance mechanism based on mass user support that promotes a mutual concessions among users autonomously. Using multiagent simulation, we examine the effect of our proposed mechanism from the following two points of view. i) as the drivers using our proposed mechanism increases, the efficiency, e.g., travel time from their origins to their destinations, should increase monotonously, ii) the efficiency of drivers using our proposed mechanism should always be better than that of the drivers using other mechanisms.

Traffic flow is represented so that each link (each road between intersections) is divided into several blocks and a velocity-density relationship is applied to each block. We apply multiagent simulation on our traffic flow model to confirm the cause of traffic congestion caused by the route choice based on personal user support, and to examine the effect of our proposed route choice mechanism.

2   Multiagent Modeling

2.1   Traffic Model

In our work, we constructed a traffic flow model as simply as possible in order to examine interdependency between traffic congestion and route choice behaviors in road transportation systems. Therefore, we did not consider the following factors: traffic signals (i.e., stopping at a red lights), waiting for oncoming cars when making turns at intersections, turn lanes, multi-lanes, overtaking, blind allies, U-turn in lanes not at intersections.

In our traffic flow model, a road between intersections is called a link, and is divided into several blocks. The length of a block is equal to the distance that a vehicle runs at free flow speed V_f of the link during one simulation step. After division of a link, an order is assigned to each block from downstream to upstream. Concerning the block assigned to be the i-th, we define K_i as the density of block i, L_i as the length of block i, N_i as the number of the vehicles in block i, and V_i as the feasible speed of vehicles in block i. Here, K_i is the division of N_i by L_i. In block i, V_i is revised based on Greenshield's V-K relationship, described as

$$V_i = V_f(1 - \frac{K_i}{K_{jam}}), \qquad (1)$$

where K_{jam} is jam density, which means the minimum density prevents vehicles in a traffic jam from moving. In this simulation, we set these coefficients as $V_f = 13.89$ and $K_{jam} = 0.14$.

The process of the flow calculation between the two neighboring blocks i and $i + 1$ is as follows. At every step, the speed of vehicles in each block is revised

order of revision of block state

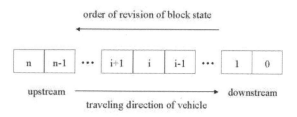

Fig. 1. Direction of vehicle's movement of and revision of blocks

according to the V-K relationship, and then vehicles move forward based on this speed. The vehicle's movement is processed from downstream to upstream as shown in Fig. 1. Based on V_i, vehicle j can move forward. When vehicle j moves into block i from block $i+1$, its speed changes to V_i from V_{i+1}. If K_i is exceeds jam density K_{jam}, no vehicles can move into block i from block $i+1$. After the movement of vehicle j_1 in front of vehicle j_2, if vehicle j_1 is within a distance that allows vehicle j_2 to move forward at the speed of vehicles V_i, vehicle j_2 approaches vehicle j_1 to the minimum distance between two cars. Although vehicle j_2 has enough speed to move further, it must stay behind vehicle j_1. At the next step in block i, when V_i is revised based on K_i, vehicles can accelerate or slowdown to V_i immediately regardless of the speed in the previous last step.

In terms of applying the Q-K or V-K relationship to each block, the method of flow calculation in our model to is similar to that of the Hybrid Block Density Method [2, 12]. Although the Hybrid Block Density Method treats traffic flow as a continuum, i.e., with a continuous approximation of vehicles, our method treats each individual vehicle discretely, i.e., a multiagent approach. In terms of treating each individual vehicle discretely, our model is similar to the Nagel-Schrekenberg model [8]. However, using that model to deal with large-scale road transportation systems is difficult. The number of blocks increases as the scale of systems becomes larger because the length of a block is fixed to one vehicle. Accordingly, computational cost for calculating state of all blocks increases significantly. By contrast, in our model, computational cost can be controlled by extending the length of a block because the length of one block can be variable. Therefore, our model is suitable for dealing with phenomena caused by route choice behaviors in large-scale traffic transportation systems.

2.2   Route Choice Behavior

We prepared three types of drivers in examining route choice behavior. The first and second types are well-known and easy-to-understand because they simply attempt to minimize travel distance or travel time. The third type is our proposed mechanism based on the concept of mass user support. This mechanism is assumed to be used in an ubiquitous computing environment because it is necessary to communicate for route information sharing.

Shortest Distance Route The drivers using the shortest distance route (SD) decide a route based on their knowledge of a map without information about traffic congestion. The drivers using the SD simply choose the route that provides the shortest distance from their origin to their destination. They only consider the distance of a link and search for the shortest route for that distance.

Shortest Time Route The drivers using the shortest time route (ST) decide a route based on their knowledge of a map and information about current traffic congestion. The drivers using the ST represent the dynamic route choice based not only on map information but also on current congestion information about the entire network at anytime as obtained from a traffic information center (e.g., VICS Center) via vehicle equipment. They search fro the route that has the shortest travel time from their origins to their destinations, and revise their routes whenever they approach an intersection.

A driver using the ST is assumed to receive information about the current traffic density of all blocks from a traffic information center via vehicle equipment. They consider the expected travel time of a link as calculated based on the current density of each block as follows. First, the speed on block i is calculated based on the V-K relationship with density K_i. Next, the passage time of block i is calculated based on length L_i of block i and speed V_i on block i. Finally, the passage time of a link is calculated by summing the passage time of all blocks on the link. We define expected travel time ETT_l as the summation of the passage times of all blocks on link l. Drivers using the ST search for the shortest route based on the expected travel time from their current position to their destination at every intersection.

Shortest Time Route with Route Information Sharing The drivers using the shortest time route with route information sharing (RIS) choose a route based on their knowledge of a map, information of current traffic congestion, and accumulative information about the routes of other drivers using RIS. The drivers using RIS also search for their routes and revise them whenever they approach an intersections. The difference between RIS and ST is that the drivers using RIS share their route information from origins to destinations. This sharing can be achieved easily by communication with a route information server via devices, e.g., cellular phone. The route information server needs to be the same as that of traffic information center.

First, drivers using RIS searches the shortest route from their origins to their destinations in the expected travel time. Then, the drivers notify the route information server of their routes. The route information server collects the routes of all drivers using RIS, and assigns passage assurance of a driver to a link based on their routes, current positions, and destinations as follows. Passage assurance means the degree of assurance that a driver will pass through a link in the future. We define passage assurance $PA_{l,j}$ of driver j to link l as follows. If a route passes through p links from driver's current position to a destination, the route information server assigns a order to each link from the destination to driver's

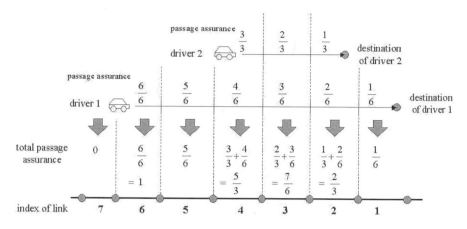

Fig. 2. Example of total passage assurance calculation for each link

current position on the route. Next, the route information server divides the order by p and regards it as the weight of a link. For example, $1/p$ is assigned a link including a destination, 1 ($=p/p$) is assigned to a link including a current position. [2]

Furthermore, we define total passage assurance TPA_l as the sum of the passage assurances of all drivers to link l. The route information server calculates TPA_l as,

$$TPA_l = \sum_{k \in RIS}^{k} PA_{l,k}, \tag{2}$$

where RIS is the set of the drivers using the RIS.

Fig. 2 shows an example of calculating total passage assurance of all links. Driver 1 has the route through six links 6, 5, 4, 3, 2, 1 from a current position on link 6 to a destination on link 1. Based on the current position, destination, and route of driver 1, passage assurances for link 1 to 7 of driver 1 are calculated as

$$PA_{1,1} = 1/6, PA_{1,2} = 2/6, PA_{1,3} = 3/6,$$
$$PA_{1,4} = 4/6, PA_{1,5} = 5/6, PA_{1,6} = 6/6, \tag{3}$$
$$PA_{1,7} = 0.$$

Driver 2 has the route through three links 4, 3, 2 from current position on link 4 to a destination on link 2. Similarly, passage assurances of link 1 to 7 of driver 2 are calculated as

$$PA_{2,2} = 1/3, PA_{2,3} = 2/3, PA_{2,4} = 3/3,$$
$$PA_{2,1} = PA_{2,5} = PA_{2,6} = PA_{2,7} = 0. \tag{4}$$

---

[2] In this model, we assume that there are driver origins and destinations on links.

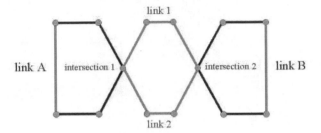

Fig. 3. Simple road network with two routes

According to the passage assurances for links 1 to 7 of drivers 1 and 2, total passage assurances of link 1 to 7 are calculated as

$$TPA_1 = 1/6, TPA_2 = 2/3, TPA_3 = 7/6,$$
$$TPA_4 = 5/3, TPA_5 = 5/6, TPA_6 = 1, \qquad (5)$$
$$TPA_7 = 0.$$

The route information server provides the total passage assurance of all links for the drivers using RIS. Finally, we define the prospective traffic volume PTV_l of link l as the product of ETT_l and $(TPA_l + 1.0)$. Drivers using RIS search the shortest route in the prospective traffic volume from their current positions to their destinations.

In this mechanism, route information server needs to know the route from a current position to a destination for each driver. However, the route information server does not need to know which drivers pass through the route. Accordingly, this mechanism has the advantages of anonymity and simplicity.

3   Computer Simulation

3.1   Simulation Settings

At first, in order to evaluate the effectiveness of our proposed route guidance mechanism in various conditions, we performed simulation in some combinations of the ratio of three route choice types. Specifically, we prepared three kinds of combinations of three route choice types. In Cases 1 and 2, we treated simple situation to examine how the drivers using ST and RIS would perform only with the drivers using SD. In Case 1, we omitted the drivers using RIS, and altered the ratio of the drivers using SD and ST. On the other hand, in Case 2, we omitted the drivers using ST, and altered the ratio of the drivers using SD and RIS. In Case 3, we fixed the number of the drivers using SD to 20%, and altered the ratio of the drivers using ST and RIS. This last setting is based on an estimation of the future use of traffic information systems as traffic information will be easier for many drivers to access because of the wide spreading of navigation systems.

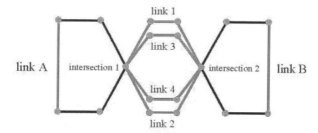

Fig. 4. Simple road network with four routes

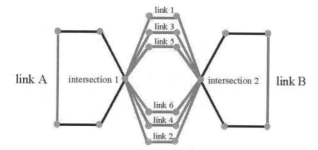

Fig. 5. Simple road network with six routes

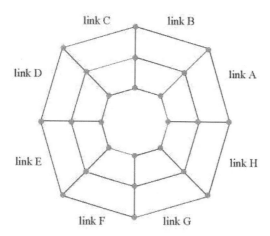

Fig. 6. Radial and ring network

Next, in order to evaluate the effectiveness of our proposed mechanism in different configurations of road networks, we used two kinds of road networks. One network was a simple one in that all drivers could choose one route from two, four, or six routes to reach a destination. These configurations are shown in Figs. 3, 4, 5, and described in Table 1. In the case of the simple road networks

Table 1. Conditions of the simple network and the radial and ring network

	simple network			radial and ring network
	2	4	6	
Number of links	16	22	28	40
Number of nodes	14	18	20	24
Number of vehicles	1200	1530	1860	1650
Total length (km)	125.9	162.9	200.0	173.1

with four routes, links 1 and 3 have the same length, and links 2 and 4 also have the same length. In the case of the simple road networks with six routes, links 1, 3, and 5 have the same length, and links 2, 4, and 6 also have the same length. The length of links 1, 3, and 5 is slightly longer than that of links 2, 4, and 6. The route origin of a driver was assigned randomly to any block on link A or B in Figs. 3, 4, and 5. If the origin of a driver is on link A, the destination was assigned to any block on link B. On intersections 1 and 2, a driver chooses from two, four, or six routes. Most links had a standard capacity except links 1 and 2 in Fig. 3, links 1 to 4 in Fig. 4, and links 1 to 6 in Fig. 5. The capacity of links 1 and 2 was 1/2 of that of standard links. The capacity of links 1 to 4 was 1/4 of the standard capacity. The capacity of links 1 to 6 is 1/6 of the standard capacity. That is to say, although the number of routes between intersection 1 and 2 was increased, the total capacity of routes from intersection 1 to 2, and 2 to 1 was not increased.

The other network is the radial and ring network described in Fig. 6 and Table 1. In this road network, all links had the same capacity. The origin of drivers' route were assigned randomly to any block on link A to H in Fig. 6. And then, their destination were assigned to any block on a symmetric link. For example, if the origin was assigned to link B, the destination was assigned to link F.

In order to make the vehicle density in all networks the same value, we arrange the number of vehicles based on each total route length. At every simulation step, twenty vehicles were generated randomly on links A or B in the simple road networks, or on links A to H in the radial and ring network. After reaching their destinations, drivers returned to their points of origin. And then, the drivers returned to their destinations again. All drivers repeated these round-trips throughout the simulation.

To compare our simulation results for the different road networks, we defined the ideal travel distance, the ideal travel time, and the travel time efficiency. The ideal travel distance of a driver was defined as the distance from an origin to a destination when a driver passes through the shortest route for the distance. The ideal travel time was defined as the time required from an origin to a destination when a driver passes through the shortest route for the distance at free flow speed. The travel time efficiency was defined as the ratio of the actual time taken to travel from an origin to a destination and the ideal travel time.

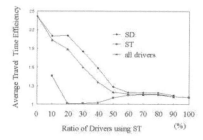 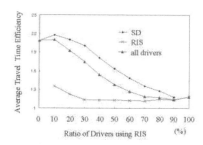

Fig. 7. Average travel time efficiency for Case 1 in simple road network with two routes

Fig. 8. Average travel time efficiency for Case 2 in simple road network with two routes

3.2 Simulation Results

In estimating the results of simulations conducted under the conditions of various ratios of drivers types and the configurations of road networks, we especially focused on a comparison of the average travel time efficiency of the drivers using SD, ST, and RIS, and that of all drivers. The results of our simulation based on the average of 10 trials are shown in Figures 7 to 18. In these graphs, the horizontal axis is the ratio of the drivers using ST or RIS, and the vertical axis is the average travel time efficiency.

Figures 7, 8, and 9 show the results in the simple network with two routes. Figure 7 shows the average travel time efficiency in Case 1, i.e., averages of the drivers using SD, ST, and all drivers. The efficiency of drivers using ST in almost was equal to 1.0 when the ratio of the drivers using ST was 20, 30, and 40%. After 50%, as the ratio of the drivers using ST increased, the efficiency of the drivers using ST increased to 1.12 gradually. On the other hand, as the ratio of the drivers using ST increased, the efficiency of the drivers using SD and all drivers decreased steadily until 60% and then remained constant. Figure 8 shows the average travel time efficiency in Case 2, i.e., averages of the drivers using SD, RIS, and that of all drivers. Until the ratio of the drivers using RIS was 70%, the efficiency of the drivers using RIS declined relatively. After that, that of the drivers using RIS rose slightly. As the ratio of the drivers using RIS increased similarly to Case 1, the efficiency of the drivers using SD and all drivers decreased monotonously. Figure 9 shows the average travel time efficiency in Case 3, i.e., the efficiency of the drivers using SD, ST, RIS, and that of all drivers. Until the ratio of the drivers using RIS was 60%, there were no significantly changes in the efficiency of the drivers using SD, ST, RIS, and that of all drivers, and their values were similar. After 60%, although the efficiency of the drivers using SD increased and that of the drivers using ST decreased, no significant changes occurred in that of the drivers using RIS and that of all drivers.

Figures 10, 11, and 12 show the results for the simple network with four routes. Figure 10 shows the average travel time efficiency in Case 1. The efficiency

96   Tomohisa Yamashita et al.

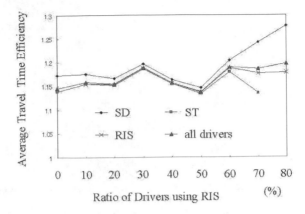

Fig. 9. Average travel time efficiency for Case 3 in simple road network with four routes

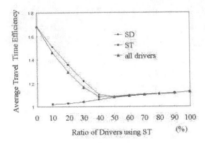

Fig. 10. Average travel time efficiency for Case 1 in simple road network with four routes

Fig. 11. Average travel time efficiency for Case 2 in simple road network with four routes

of the drivers using ST continued rising monotonously from beginning to end. Until the ratio of the drivers using ST was 50%, the efficiency of the drivers using SD and that of all drivers fell steadily, and then increased slightly. After 50%, all of them were almost the same. Figure 11 shows the average travel time efficiency in Case 2. Until the ratio of the drivers using RIS was 30%, the efficiency of the drivers using RIS rose slightly. After that, the efficiency of the drivers using RIS went down slightly. Until 50%, the efficiency of the drivers using SD and that of all drivers dropped steadily from beginning to end. Figure 12 shows the average travel time efficiency in Case 3. Until the ratio of the drivers using RIS was 60%, the efficiency of all decreased steadily. After 60%, however the efficiency of the drivers using SD went up slightly, the rest remained almost constant. Furthermore, the efficiency of the drivers using RIS was worse than all others before a 60%. After that, that of the drivers using RIS was better than that of the others. Throughout the simulation, all of them were very close.

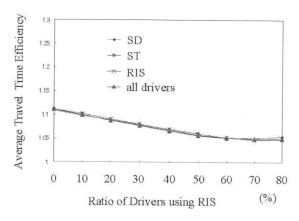

Fig. 12. Average travel time efficiency for Case 3 in simple road network with four routes

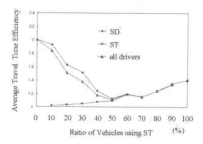

Fig. 13. Average travel time efficiency for Case 1 in simple road network with four routes

Fig. 14. Average travel time efficiency for Case 2 in simple road network with four routes

Figures 13, 14, and 15 show the results for the simple network with six routes. Figure 13 shows the average travel time efficiency in Case 1. Similarly to the simple network with four routes, the efficiency of the drivers using ST kept rising monotonously from start to finish. Until the ratio of the drivers using ST was 50%, the efficiency of the drivers using SD and that of all drivers reversed from decreasing to increasing. After 50%, the efficiency of all were very close. Figure 14 shows the average travel time efficiency in Case 2. Until the ratio of the drivers using RIS was 30%, the efficiency of the drivers using RIS rose marginally. After that, the efficiency of the drivers using RIS declined slightly except for a steep jump at 80%. Throughout, the efficiency of the drivers using SD and that of all drivers fell steadily. However, alike the efficiency of the drivers using RIS, that of the drivers using SD and that of all drivers jumped at 80%. Figure 15 shows the average travel time efficiency in Case 3. Except for jumps when the ratio of the drivers using RIS was 10 and 40%, the efficiency of all

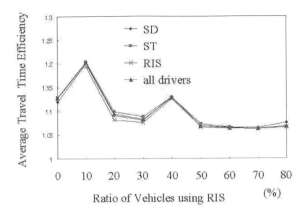

Fig. 15. Average travel time efficiency for Case 3 in simple road network with six routes

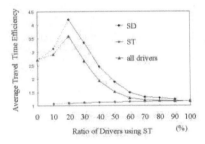

Fig. 16. Average travel time efficiency for Case 1 in the radial and ring network

Fig. 17. Average travel time efficiency for Case 2 in the radial and ring network

declined gradually. Although the efficiency of the drivers using RIS was a little better in 20 and 30%, almost all were equal.

Figure 16, 17 and 18 show the result in the radial and ring network. In the graphs in Fig. 16 and 17, there are partially dashed lines. This means that values for the travel time efficiency of these parts was not valid. In the conditions that 0 to 10% drivers use the ST and the rest use the SD, 80% of all vehicles were caught in deadlock. In our traffic simulation, deadlock was defined as meaning that vehicles in the top of a link cannot move into the next links because these are filled completely with other vehicles. Furthermore, the vehicles in the top of those next links also could not move into the following links for the same reason. Under conditions of deadlock, no drivers reached thier destinations even once, so the travel time efficiency could not be calculated accurately.

Figure 16 shows the average travel time efficiency in Case 1. After 20%, the efficiency of the drivers using ST increased slightly and steadily. At first, the efficiency of the drivers using SD and that of all drivers dropped dramatically.

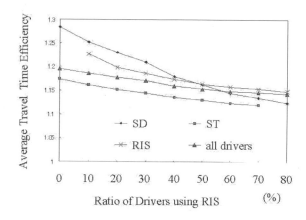

Fig. 18. Average travel time efficiency for Case 3 in the radial and ring network

After the ratio of the drivers using ST was 80%, that of all of them declined marginally. Figure 17 shows the average travel time efficiency in Case 2. Although the shapes of lines for the efficiency of the drivers using SD and that of all drivers were similar to these in Fig. 16, that of the drivers using RIS decreased slightly and steadily. Fig. 18 shows the average travel time efficiency in Case 3. From beginning to end, all of the efficiencys continued to decrease steadily. Until the ratio of the drivers using RIS was 50%, the efficiency of all were ranked in ascending order as the drivers using ST, all drivers, the drivers using RIS, and the drivers using SD. After that, the rank was changed to the drivers using ST, the drivers using SD, all drivers, and the drivers using RIS.

4   Discussion

In this section, we discuss the effect of our proposed mechanism on the efficiency of the drivers using it and on all systems.

At first, concerning the results in the simple network with two routes, results suggest that no reduction of traffic congestion was obtained by the increased of the drivers using RIS because the travel time efficiency of the drivers using RIS and all drivers given in Fig. 8 was not always better than that of the drivers using ST in Fig. 7. Furthermore, Fig. 9 did not show a change for the drivers using RIS and all drivers. However, the reason no improvement was obtained by using the RIS was not a failure of the RIS. In our simulation, we used the assumption that drivers repeatedly went to their destinations and return to their origins throughout the simulation. The introduction of the RIS prevents the cause of traffic congestion by drivers simultaneously concentrating on one route where no traffic congestion exists currently. Our assumption of the drivers' round-trips between origins and destinations resulted in a deviation of caused traffic congestion.

In the simple network with two routes, there are two sides. One side includes link A and intersection 1, and the other includes link B and intersection 2. During generation of vehicles from the beginning of the simulation, if the inflow from one side (e.g., side A) is more than that from the opposite side (e.g., side B), the vehicles moving from side B to A increases some steps later. As vehicles are generated, if traffic congestion is caused in the routes from side B, feasible outflow from side B to A decreases, i.e., the vehicles moving from side B to A will decrease some steps later. At that time, feasible outflow from side A to B is kept high because the number of vehicles in side A decreases. And then, the vehicles in side B increase because to return from side A to B takes a short time, while to return from side B to A because of traffic congestion takes a long time. As a result, traffic congestion is caused in both of the two routes from side B to A. Therefore, in Case 3, the increase of the number of the drivers using RIS didn't improve the travel time efficiency of the drivers using SD, ST, RIS, and that of all drivers although traffic congestion caused by drivers simultaneously concentrating on one route out of two could be avoided.

Secondly, concerning the results for the simple networks with four and six routes, traffic congestion was reduced with the increased use of the driver using RIS. In Figs. 10 and 13, as the number of the drivers using ST increased, the travel time efficiency of the drivers using SD and all drivers was improved until the ratio of the drivers using ST was 50%, the efficiency of all drivers became worse. The reason is that the drivers using the ST often concentrated simultaneously on one route that the traffic information system told them that had less traffic congestion than other routes. In contrast, in Fig. 11 and 13, as the number of the drivers using RIS increased, the travel time efficiency of the drivers using RIS and SD became better except before the ratio of the drivers using RIS was 30%. The drivers using RIS can improve their efficiency, the drivers using SD and all drivers more than that the drivers using ST in relatively high low ratio of the drivers using RIS. Without the drivers using ST, our proposed mechanism achieved a mutual concession among the drivers using the SD and RIS. In Fig. 12 and 15, the efficiency of the drivers using SD, ST, RIS and all drivers was improved as the ratio of the drivers using RIS rose. Although the efficiency of the drivers using RIS was not always better than those of the drivers using SD and ST, differences between the efficiency of the drivers using RIS and the other types were slight. The drivers using RIS were able to avoid concentrating simultaneously on one specific route with the minimum expected travel time. Even with the interaction between the drivers using ST and RIS, our proposed mechanism also achieve a mutual concession among the drivers using SD, ST and RIS. The efficiency of the drivers using RIS roughly satisfied with the two features that we require. Therefore, we can say that our proposed mechanism works efficiently for both each individual utility and the whole system in the simple networks with four and six routes.

Next, concerning the results in the radial and ring network, traffic congestion was improved as the ratio of the drivers using RIS increased. In Fig. 16, as the ST increases, the travel time efficiency of the drivers using ST becomes worse.

On the other hand, in Fig. 17, as the ratio of the drivers using RIS increased, the efficiency of the drivers using RIS became better. Without the drivers using ST, our proposed mechanism achieved a mutual concession among the drivers using SD and RIS.

As shown in Fig. 18, as the ratio of the drivers using RIS rose, the travel time efficiency of all was improved monotonously. Similar to the results in the simple networks, the drivers using RIS were able to avoid concentrating simultaneously on one specific route. The difference is that the travel time efficiency of the drivers using ST was always better than that of the drivers using RIS and SD was better than that of the RIS after the ratio of the drivers using RIS was 50%. Therefore, with the interaction between the drivers using ST and RIS, making a concession to the drivers using the ST did not improve the efficiency. The reason is that in the radial and ring network a driver using RIS had to take the longer route when that driver gave up to move on the short route.

Here, we take up these relationships between the drivers using ST and RIS in the travel time efficiency, i.e., i) as the number of the drivers using RIS increased, the travel time efficiency of the drivers using ST and RIS was improved monotonously, and ii) the travel time efficiency of the drivers using ST was always better than that of the drivers using RIS. These relationships satisfy the conditions of the social dilemmas [1]. According to Dawes, the social dilemmas are required to satisfy the following conditions. Suppose that each of N players has a choice between two strategies, contributing (Cooperate: C) or not contributing (Defect: D) to a group. Let $D(m)$ be the payoff of a player choosing D when m players choose C, and let $C(m)$ be the payoff of a player choosing C when m players choose C. The D choice is dominant strategy for each player, i.e., each player obtains a better payoff by choosing D than C regardless of the number of the players choosing C.

$$D(m) > C(m+1). \tag{6}$$

If all players choose their dominated C strategies, the outcome is more profit than the outcome when every player chooses D.

$$C(N) > D(0). \tag{7}$$

The payoffs of a player choosing both D and C are monotone increasing functions of m, i.e., whichever the player chooses; the more the player chooses C, the more the payoff obtained.

$$D(m+1) > D(m) \quad and \quad C(m+1) > C(m). \tag{8}$$

In the radial and ring network, if cooperative behavior is regarded as being the use of RIS and defective behavior as the use of ST (and SD), the transition of the travel time efficiency of the ST and RIS satisfies the conditions of a social dilemma. The reason is that the travel time efficiency of all drivers increases as the drivers using RIS increases, and the drivers using ST always obtain greater efficiency. Actually in the radial and ring network a mutual concession among the drivers using RIS, i.e., avoiding the congested route and each taking the longer route, reduced traffic congestion on the whole system. However, the drivers using ST can pass through the shorter distance without heavy traffic congestion and can only improve it own the travel time efficiency at the expense of a mutual concession among the drivers using RIS, i.e., mutual avoidance of the shorter route in both distance and time. Although the drivers using RIS improves their travel time efficiency and that of all drivers, the other drivers' time efficiency are better than the drivers using RIS because the drivers using ST and SD free-ride contribution of the drivers using RIS. Therefore, we can say that our proposed mechanism works efficiently for the whole system but not efficiently for the individual utility of the drivers using it in the radial and ring networks.

To construct an effective mechanism based on route information sharing, we must improve our proposed mechanism. Currently, it is very simple because the route information server receives route information from individual drivers, calculates the prospective traffic volume, and returns macro information to them. Our proposed mechanism has many variables in determining the passage assurance, the total passage assurance, and the prospective traffic volume. Moreover, it doesn't regard current traffic congestion and the intention and status of drivers. Therefore, if our mechanism is designed more precisely, it will be able to improve the efficiency of drivers using it and that of all other drivers.

However, in the radial and ring network, we observed that the route choice behaviors created the problem of the social dilemmas. The drivers using SD and ST free-ride the mechanism based on mass user support making a mutual concession. To develop the mechanisms that can continue improving the travel time efficiency monotonously as their number increases will not be difficult. However, to develop the mechanisms that can achieve the better travel time efficiency of the divers using RIS over that of the others will be significantly difficult. In order to solve the social dilemmas presented by route choice behaviors, we need to construct new types of route navigation mechanisms. Because the social dilemmas have been taken up in various research fields, we can apply that knowledge to our mechanism, and then we will be able to acquire new solutions suited to the features of traffic flow.

5   Conclusion

In this paper, we proposed a route guidance mechanism with route information sharing. The aim of our proposal is to improve the traffic efficiency of both individual drivers and whole systems. With multiagent modeling, we constructed a simple traffic flow model based on the V-K relationships. Three types of route choice behavior were prepared: the Shortest Distance (SD), the Shortest Time (ST), and the Shortest Time with Route Information Sharing (RIS), are prepared. To examine the effect of this mechanism in various conditions, we used three cases of the ratio of the drivers using SD, ST, and RIS, and two kinds of road networks. One kind of network was the simple one with two, four, and six routes from origin to destinations. The others were radial and ring networks.

From simulation results, we found that i) in the simple networks with four and six routes, the RIS works efficiently, ii) in the radial and ring network, the RIS can promote a mutual concessions, and can improve the efficiency of the drivers using RIS and all drivers. However, a social dilemma situation was caused, and then the drivers using ST and SD free-rode the drivers using RIS. Therefore, for the drivers using RIS to achieve the best travel time efficiency was difficult. Based on these results, we discovered the necessity of modifying our proposed mechanism and constructing new types of mechanisms to conquer the social dilemmas in route choice behaviors.

References

[1] Dawes, R., M.: Social Dilemmas. Annual Review of Psychology 31 (1981) 169-193 101

[2] Horiguchi, R., Kuwahara, M., Nishikawa, I.: The Model Validation of Traffic Simulation System for Urban Road Networks: 'AVENUE'. In Proceedings of the Second World Congress on Intelligent Transport Systems'95 (IV) (1995) 1977-1982 89

[3] Kawamura, H., Kurumatani, K., Ohuchi, A.: Modeling of Theme Park Problem with Multiagent for Mass User Support, In Working Note of The International Joint Conference of Artificial Intelligence 2003, Workshop on Multiagent for Mass User Support (2003) 1-7 87

[4] Klugl, F., Bazzan, A. L. C., Wahle, J.: Selection of information types based on personal utility: a testbed for traffic information markets. In Proceedings of the second International Joint Conference on Autonomous Agents and Multiagent systems (2003) 377-384 87

[5] Kurumatani, K.: Mass User Support by Social Coordination among Users. In Proceedings of the International Joint Conference of Artificial Intelligence 2003, Workshop on Multiagent for Mass User Support MAMUS-03 (2003) 58-59 87

[6] Kurumatani, K.: Social Coordination with Architecture for Ubiquitous Agents: CONSORTS. In Proceedings of International Conference on Intelligent Agents, Web Technologies and Internet Commerce 2003 (CD-ROM) (2003) 87

[7] Mahmassani, H. S., Jayakrishnan, R.: System Performance and User Response under Real-Time Information in a Congested Traffic Corridor. Transportation Research 25A(5) (1991) 293-307 87

[8] Nagel, K., Schreckenberg, M. A.: A cellular automaton model for freeway traffic. Journal de Physique I (2) (1992) 2221-2229 89

[9] Shiose, T., Onitsuka, T., Taura, T.: Effective Information Provision for Relieving Traffic Congestion. In Proceedings of 4th International Conference on Intelligence and Multimedia Applications (2001) 138-142 87

[10] Suzuki, R., Arita T.: Effects of Information Sharing on Collective Behaviors in Competitive Populations. In Proceedings of the Eight International Symposium on Artificial Life and Robotics (2003) 36-39 87

[11] Tanahashi, I., Kitaoka, H., Baba, M., H. Mori, H., Terada, S., Teramoto, E.: NETSTREAM, a Traffic Simulator for Large-scale Road Networks, R & D Review of Toyota CRDL, 37(2) (2002) 47-53 (in Japanese) 87

[12] TeramotoüCE., Baba, M., Mori, H., Asano, Y., Morita,H.: NETSTREAM: Traffic Simulator for Evaluating Traffic Information Systems. In Proceedings of IEEE International Conference on Intelligent Transportation Systems '97 (CD-ROM) (1997) 89

[13] Yoshii, T., Akahane, H., Kuwahara, M.: Impacts of the Accuracy of Traffic Information in Dynamic Route Guidance Systems. In Proceedings of The 3rd Annual World Congress on Intelligent Transport Systems (CD-ROM) (1996) 87

[14] http://www.vics.or.jp 86, 87

Is Dial-a-Ride Bus Reasonable in Large Scale Towns? Evaluation of Usability of Dial-a-Ride Systems by Simulation

Kousuke Shinoda[1,2], Itsuki Noda[1,2,3], Masayuki Ohta[1], Yoichiro Kumada[1,2], and Hideyuki Nakashima[1,2]

[1] Cyber Assist Research Center, AIST
135-0064 Aomi, Koto-ku Tokyo, Japan
[2] Japan Advanced Institute of Science and Technology
923-1292 asahidai, Tatunokuti Nomi Ishikawa, Japan
[3] PRESTO, Japan Science and Technology Corporation

Abstract. Dial-a-ride systems are attracting attention as a new style of transportation systems for urban areas. While it has been reported that such systems improve the usability of bus systems when applied in a small town or area, it is not obvious how and under what conditions the systems are effective in comparison to traditional fixed-route bus systems. We conducted two computer simulations of dial-a-ride and fixed-route systems in order to compare the usability and profitability of both systems. Simulation results indicated that: (1) The usability of the dial-a-ride system with a fixed number of buses drops very quickly when the number of requests(demands) increases. (2) When we increase the number of buses proportionally to the number of demand, the usability of the dial-a-ride system is improved more significantly than that of the fixed-route system. (3) When frequency of demands is sufficiently, the dial-a-ride system is a reasonable solution from the both usability and profitability perspectives.

1 Introduction

Dial-a-ride is a door-to-door public transport service for individuals who, because of a disability, are prevented from using transports, the city's fixed-route bus service. It is a system in which a passenger calls a control center of buses and tells his/her destination; and the center re-plans route of an appropriate bus to service the request.

The dial-a-ride system is also attracting attention as a new public transportation system that provides convenient transportation for disabled persons while solving traffic-jams in urban areas. It is, however, applied to limited and small-scale cases for the following several reasons:

- It is difficult to handle a huge number of passengers with many buses. Generally, the problem of finding an optimal assignment of a passenger's request to a bus is a NP-hard problem.

K. Kurumatani et al. (Eds.): MAMUS 2003, LNAI 3012, pp. 105–119, 2004.
© Springer-Verlag Berlin Heidelberg 2004

- Traditional fixed-route systems cannot obviously be replaced by the dial-a-ride system. Especially, it is not well-studied how the usability of the dial-a-ride system changes when the number of passenger increases compared with the fixed-route systems.

Many researchers have already attacked the first issue. Assignment of passengers' requests and planning bus routes is considered a variation of the *traveling-salesman problem*[1, 2] and the *vehicle routing problem*[3, 4, 5, 6, 7]. Various optimization techniques are used to solve the problem. [8] and [9] makes use of local search and tab search, respectively. Simulated annealing and GA has also been applied in [10, 11]. Complexity of calculation has been investigated by [12].

In addition to these studies, various studies have addressed the dial-a-ride problem from the following various perspectives:

- comparison of performance under various constraints on buses:
  Many studies [13, 3, 14, 15, 16] have investigated changes of performance when the dial-a-ride system is run with various numbers of buses.
- on-line and off-line algorithms:
  Various operation research techniques have been applied to solve assignment and re-routing problems under on-line and off-line conditions[17, 18, 13, 19, 20].
- relation to other traffic constraints:
  [21] investigated how the dial-a-ride system interacts with other long-distance transportation systems such as trains. [22] addressed the relation between efficiency of buses and town size. [18, 23] took traffic conditions into account to evaluate the performance of dial-a-ride systems.

On the other hand, however, few studies have examined the problem from the viewpoint of the second issue stated above. Currently, dial-a-ride systems serve mainly disabled persons. It is difficult for the system to garner sufficient revenue from passengers' fees because the number of disabled persons is limited. We should conceptualize a way for traditional fixed-route system users to use the dial-a-ride system to increase the number of passengers. For that purpose, a comparison of usabilities of fixed-route and dial-a-ride systems is necessary in order to determine the conditions in which the dial-a-ride system will provide a better solution for whole social systems. This article, shows the results of a comparison of the usability of both of fixed-route and dial-a-ride systems by simulations of transportation in a virtual town. In the rest of the article, we formalize the problem of dial-a-ride systems in Section 2 and in Section 3 describe a detailed setup of simulations. Finally, simulation results are shown and analyzed in Section 4.

2 Formalization

2.1 Dial-a-Ride System

There are several frameworks of dial-a-ride systems according to styles of accepting *demands*[1] and policies of bus routing. Two major style variations are:

- **Reservation Style**:
  A passenger calls and makes a request to the bus control center a certain period ahead of the requested departure time. For example, a passenger must make a reservation one hour before riding.
- **Real-Time Style**:
  A passenger can make a request when she wants to ride: that is, she simply calls the control center when she wants a ride.

This study presumes, we suppose the **real-time** service because it can be applied more generally to various conditions that include the usage of fixed-route systems.

Bus routing policy also has some variations. For example, here are two typical policies:

- **Basic-Route with Optional Detour Routes**:
  A bus mainly follows a basic route; it turns onto predefined optional detour routes according to passengers' requests. A passenger can embark or disembark at anywhere along these routes.
- **Free-Routing**:
  A bus can runs on any road in a certain area. A passenger can embark or disembark anywhere in the area.

We focus on **free-routing** In these policies, because it provides the most important service of the dial-a-ride system.

2.2 Usability and Profitability

As stated in Section 1, the purpose of the simulation is to compare usabilities and *profitabilities* of dial-a-ride and fixed-route systems. Generally, the evaluation of such criteria is difficult because usabilities depend on subjective factors and profitabilities may change according to social conditions. In order to avoid these difficulties and to enable such evaluation by simulation, we simplify usabilities and profitabilities in order to allow them to be handled quantitatively as follows.

For *usability*, we focus on the primary purpose of a bus system, that is, to provide a way for a passenger to get to his/her destination as quickly as possible. From this point of view, *usability* can be defined as follows:

   Usability: average elapsed time from when a demand is told to the bus center until the demand is satisfied.

---

[1] We call the passenger's request to ride from somewhere to another place as a *demand*.

Note that we use the time when the request is made instead the time when the passenger departs, because we need to compare dial-a-ride and fixed-route systems under the same conditions. In the case of a fixed-route system, a passenger goes to a bus-stop when he/she needs a ride. This means that the elapsed time is measured from then. Thus, we use the same measure in the case of a dial-a-ride system.

In addition, we suppose that a passenger never transfers buses. The first reason is that it is difficult to measure physical and mental costs of the transfers. People may use a slower bus route instead of a faster one when the latter one requires many transfers. This implies that we need to interpret such costs in *usability*, which by definition is measured in term of time. To avoid such complexity, we do not consider cases in which a passenger transfers buses.

Profitability is formalized as follows. The profit (or deficit) of a bus company depends on maintenance, fuel and labor costs, and fare incomes, which vary in terms of social and economic conditions. In addition, fare-pricing causes secondary social effects by which the number of passengers changes. Therefore, it is difficult to directly quantify *profitability*. Instead, we simplify it as a balance between fare revenue and cost, where revenue and cost change in proportion to the number of passengers and buses, respectively. In other words, *profitability* is defined as follows:

> **Profitability**: the number of demands that occur in a unit period per one bus.

2.3   Virtual Town

In order to prepare field for the simulation, we compose a virtual town as follows:

- Streets in the town are arranged in a grid pattern as in Kyoto and New York City.
- The town shape is a square.
- All stops are at the crossings.
- There are no traffic jams.
- A bus goes through, turns left or right at a crossing with the same duration.
- There are no limitations in the passengers capacity per bus.
- Getting on and off buses requires no time.

In this virtual town, demands occurs under the following conditions:

- Demands occur at a constant frequency.
- Departure and destination points are decided randomly. (All positions of crossings in the town have the same probability of being departure or destination points.)
- If a passenger can reach his/her destination on foot faster than riding a bus, the passenger refuses to use a bus. In this case, the time to walk is treated as the elapsed time to satisfy the demand.
- A passenger does not transit buses.

3   Simulation Setup

3.1   Fixed-Route Systems

The usability of a fixed-route systems varies according to bus-routes. It is difficult
to find the optimal set of routes to cover a town theoretically because it is affected
by many factors such as number of buses, average bus speed, number of routes,
the shape of the town, and so on. Therefore, we apply a genetic algorithm (GA)
in order to determine a semi-optimal set of routes.

Individual of Fixed-Route Systems In this simulation, an individual of GA
consists of a set of bus-routes. We suppose that the number of routes is fixed, and
that just one bus runs on one route. Therefore, the number of buses is equal to
the number of routes. There are two route types: *normal* routes and *loop* routes.
On a *normal* route, a bus runs back and forth between two terminals. On a *loop*
route, a bus circulates in a loop.

Evaluation of Usability As mentioned in Section 2.2, usability is measured
by *average time needed to satisfy a demand* (ATCD). When a passenger decides
which route to use, the ATCD (T_{demand}) can be calculated as.

$$T_{\text{demand}} = (L_{\text{src}} + L_{\text{dst}})/V_{\text{walk}}$$
$$+L_{\text{route}}/(M_{\text{bus}} \times V_{\text{bus}})$$
$$+L_{\text{bus}}/V_{\text{bus}}, \tag{1}$$

where L_{src}, L_{dst}, and L_{bus} are distances between a departure-point and
an embarkation stop, between a disembarkation stop and a destination point,
and between the two stops, respectively. L_{route} is the length of the whole
route. V_{walk} and V_{bus} are walking speed and bus speed; M_{bus} is the number of buses per a route[2]. In the equation, the first, second, and third terms of
the right-hand side indicate "walking time", "average waiting time at bus stop",
and "riding time on bus", respectively.

Because we evaluate the best performance of an individual (a set of bus-
routes), the individual searches for the best route from a set of routes and determines the best combination of stops to embark and disembark for a given demand. Note that evaluation includes ATCD of the case where a passenger chooses
to walk the whole journey to the destination because walking is faster than using
a bus. In this case, L_{route} and L_{bus} are assumed to be zero; $L_{\text{src}}+L_{\text{dst}}$ is equal
to the distance between the departure-point and the destination-point.

---

[2] As mentioned above, M_{bus} is fixed to be 1 in this simulation.

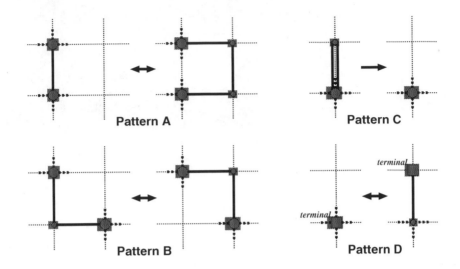

Fig. 1. Mutation pattern

Alternation of Generations A generation consists of 100 individuals. Each individual is evaluated by calculating average ATCD based on Eq. 1 using 50 randomly generated demands. Then, the top 10 individuals are selected and survive to the next generation. The next generation consists of 10 survivors, 70 descendants generated from the survivors (7 descendants per a survivors), and 20 new randomly-generated individuals.

Individuals in the last population (and in the initial generations) are generated as follows:

1. Two terminal points are chosen from all crossings in the town randomly.
2. A type of route is chosen from *normal* and *loop*.
3. When the route is the *normal* type, then the route connects the two terminals by 'L'- and 'Γ'-shape paths. When the route is the *loop* type, the route forms a rectangle whose two diagonal apexes are the two terminals.

Descendants are generated by mutation and cross-over described as follows;

Mutation We restrict mutation within the following four patterns to guarantee that a mutated bus route is a valid route.

Pattern A (Fig. 1-A) : If a route connects two adjoining crossings by a direct edge, replace the edge is replaced by a detour of three edges (and its inverse transformation).

Pattern B (Fig. 1-B) : If a route connects two diagonal crossings of a block by two edges, the two edges are replaced by other two edges of the block.

Pattern C (Fig. 1-C) : If a route has a branch that goes between two adjoining crossings directly, the branch is shortened.

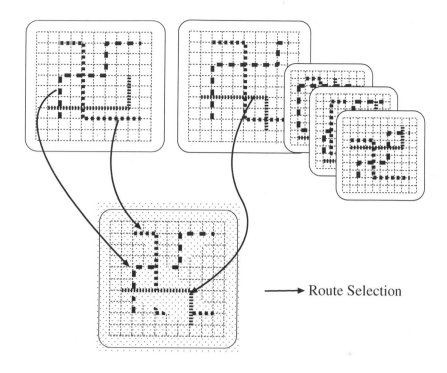

Fig. 2. Cross-over

Pattern D (Fig. 1-D) : In the case of a *normal* route, a terminal is
moved to on an adjoining crossing and extends/shortens the route.

When a descendant is generated from a parent individual, up to one mutation
occurs per route[3].

Cross-Over Cross-over is realized by exchange routes between survivors' descendants as shown in Fig. 2. Note that the cross-over changes only the combination
of routes, not routes themselves.

Acquired Routes Figure 3 shows examples of routes acquired by GA. These
examples are the best individuals of the 10,000th generation, where the number
of routes is 3 and the ratio of bus and walking speed varies from 8 to 256.
Figure 3 shows that the town is roughly covered by three 'L'-shape routes when
the bus speed is slow, while the routes come to cover almost all crossings when
the speed increases. These results indicate that the proposed GA method can
yield reasonable semi-optimal routes for a given condition.

---

[3] Because most mutations change the usability for the worse, the probability of improving usability becomes very low when we apply multiple mutations per route.
Therefore, we restrict the number of mutations to one per route.

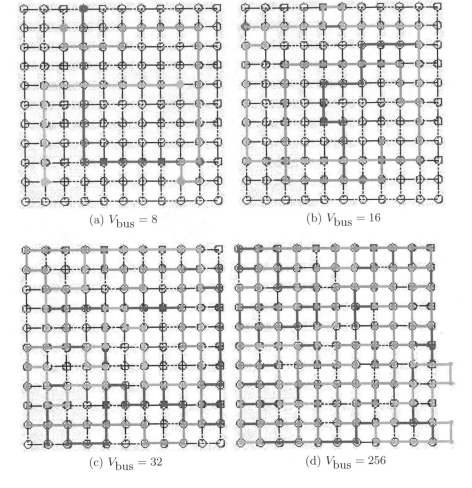

(a) $V_{bus} = 8$ (b) $V_{bus} = 16$

(c) $V_{bus} = 32$ (d) $V_{bus} = 256$

Fig. 3. Semi-optimal fixed-routes acquired by GA

3.2 Dial-a-Ride System

For simulation of a dial-a-ride system, we must solve the problem of how to assign a new demand to buses and to re-plan a path for each bus. This is a kind of dynamic traveling salesman problem. Moreover, the problem includes more complex constraint in which each demand is refused when the expected arrival time is overdue for its deadline[4]. Therefore, it is hard to find the optimal assignment in a reasonable time. Instead, we take a way to find a semi-optimal

---

[4] Deadline of a demand is defined as the latest time the demand should be completed. In our simulation, the deadline is the time when the demand will be completed if the passenger walks me entire distance to his/her destination.

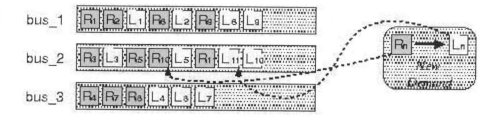

Fig. 4. Successive best insertion

assignment by using an approximation method called *successive best insertion* (Fig. 4) described as follows:

1. Each bus stores assigned demands in a via-point queue, in which an assigned demand is divided two way-points: the departure point and destination point, which are inserted at appropriate positions. The bus always runs toward a way-point at the top of the queue, and removes it from the queue upon arrival. We suppose that the order in the queue is not changed after the assignment.
2. Each bus also satisfies its expected time to complete each assigned demand. The expected time is calculated by supposing that the bus will run according to the *current* queue of via-points.
3. When a new demand occurs, each bus searches for the best positions to insert two via-points of the demand, which minimizes the cost, that is, the sum of the total delay of existing demands and expected time to complete the new demand. If the deadline of an existing or new demand expires by the insertion, the bus reports it has *no solution*.
4. The bus control center assigns the demand to a bus whose cost is the minimum of all buses. When all buses report *no solution*, then the demand is refused.

4 Simulation Result

We conducted various simulations of both bus systems using the following parameters: The size of the town is 11×11, and the ratio of walking and bus speeds is $1 : 8$.

4.1 Case 1: Fixed Number of Buses

In the first simulation, we evaluate the case in which a fixed number of buses are used in both systems. Figure 5 shows changes of ATCD of both systems using three buses when the number of demands per unit time increases. In this figure, a strait horizontal line indicates the ATCD of the fixed-route system. The ATCD

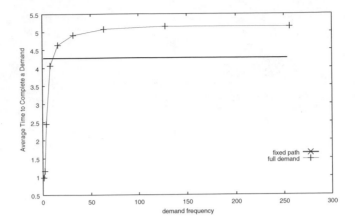

Fig. 5. Changes of average time needed to satisfy a demand in the case of three buses

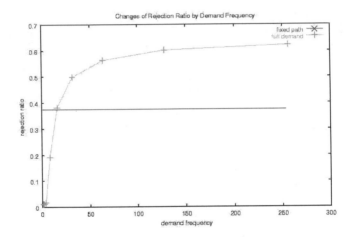

Fig. 6. Changes of ratio to refuse demands in the case of three buses

of the fixed-route system does not change according to the number of demands because we do not consider time to get on and off.

On the other hand, the ATCD of the dial-a-ride system starts with a small value in the case of few demands and increases immediately over the fixed-route system. This means that usability of the dial-a-ride system with the fixed number of buses quickly decreases when the number of demands increases. The reason for this change for the worse in the dial-a-ride system is that most of the demands are refused when many demands occur. Figure 6 shows changes in the ratio of refused demands. As indicated in this graph, the refusal ratio of the dial-a-ride system decreases more quickly than that of the fixed-route system.

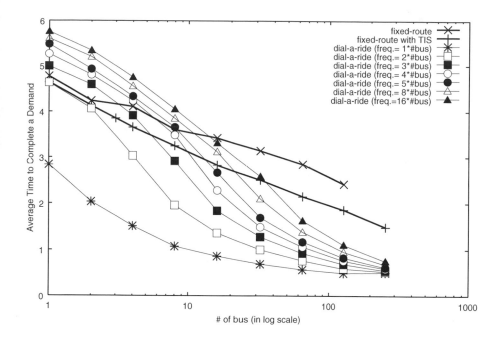

Fig. 7. Changes of average time to complete a demand when the profitability is fixed (the number of buses increases constantly according to the number of demands)

4.2 Case 2: Fixed Profitability

In the second simulation, we evaluate the case in which profitability of the systems is fixed. As defined in Section 2.2, profitability is the number of demands occurring in a unit period per bus. Therefore, in this simulation, we increase the number of buses according to the number of demands while maintaining a certain ratio of demands and buses.

Figure 7 shows the simulation results. In the figure, two thick lines indicate performance of the fixed-route systems. The upper thick line shows the case of a normal fixed-route system in which a passenger decides a route according to the expected ATCD of each route. The lower thick line is the case of a TIS(Traffic Information System)-supported fixed-route system. This case is discussed later. Other thin lines indicate performances of dial-a-ride systems with various profit-abilities. The profitability varies from $\langle$# of demands in unit period$\rangle / \langle$# of buses$\rangle = 1$ to 16. The graph plots changes of ATCD in each case by the number of buses. This figure shows that the usabilities are improved in each case. In Addition, improvement of dial-a-ride systems comes more quickly than fixed-route systems. In both systems, the usabilities are improved because a passenger is provided many choices in reaching his/her destination. In addition, because the dial-a-ride system provides more flexibility to fit passenger's demands, the improvement is greater than that of the fixed-route system.

4.3   Case 3: Comparison with TIS-Supported Fixed-Route Systems

In the previous simulation, we assume that a passenger decides a route according only to the expected ATCD of routes in a fixed-route system. This is a reasonable assumption when a passenger does not know when the next bus of each route will come. However, the usability of this fixed-route system can be improved using recent TIS. Suppose that there are many possible routes that provide similar ATCDs for a demand and that a passenger can know the exact time for the next bus of each route at any stop by TIS. In this case, the passenger can calculate a more accurate time to satisfy his/her demand for each route instead of the average one. Using the accurate value, he/she can choose a more appropriate route.

The lower thick line in Fig. 7 indicates performance of this case. As shown in the graph, usability is improved by the TIS support. This improvement becomes obvious when the number of buses increases. Nevertheless, the usability of the dial-a-ride system offers an advantage when the number of buses is large.

4.4   Case 4: Fixed Profitability with Converged Demands

In the previous three cases, we assumed that demands occur uniformly in any place in the virtual town. This is, however, not realistic because a town generally has several centers such as a train station and a shopping center, where demands converge. We conducted a simulation using converged demand to reflect such a condition in the simulation.

In the simulation, we assume that there is a center of convergence of demands in the middle of the town. When a demand is generated, one of departure point or destination is the center in a certain ratio, called *convergence ratio*.

Figure 8 shows results of the simulation when the convergence ratio is (a) 0.5 and (b) 0.9. Compared these graphs and Fig. 7, we can see that the advantage of dial-a-ride systems in the usability becomes more obvious when the convergence ratio is high. For example, when a dial-a-ride system supposes profitability ($\langle$# of demands in unit period$\rangle/\langle$# of buses$\rangle$) is 16, its usability becomes better than the fixed-route system with TIS at the number of buses is 64 in Fig. 8 and 16 in Fig. 7-(b).

5   Discussion and Conclusion

In conclusion, we can summarize features of a dial-a-ride system compared with a fixed-route system from simulations in previous section, as follows:

- When the number of buses is fixed, the usability of the dial-a-ride system degrades quickly when the number of demands increases. On the other hand,

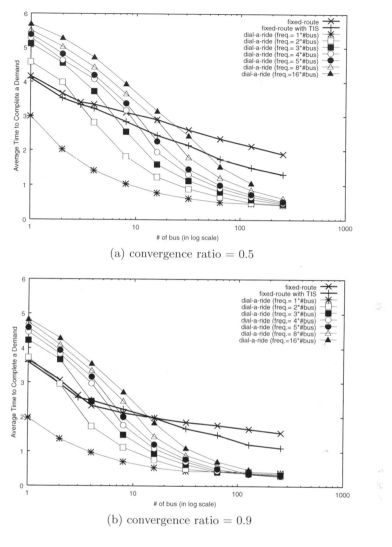

(a) convergence ratio = 0.5

(b) convergence ratio = 0.9

Fig. 8. Changes of average time to complete a demand when the profitability is fixed with converged demands

usability of the fixed-route system is stable against changes of the number of demands until buses become full. For usability, in other words, we can choose the dial-a-ride system with a fixed number of buses only when frequency of demands is very low. This is bad news for the dial-a-ride system because it is difficult to keep usability at a reasonable level by the dial-a-ride system, while more and more demands are required for profitability. It is, therefore, not true that "dial-a-ride systems will be profitable when we have sufficient demands".

– When the number of buses increases with the fixed profitability, usability of the dial-a-ride system is improved more quickly than the fixed-route system. Therefore, even if the case where usability of the dial-a-ride system is worse than the fixed-route system in the case of low frequent demands because of keeping the high-profitability, it gets better when the demand frequency increases.

The following open issues about the simulation remain:

– **Correspondence with Real Values**: Parameters in simulations shown in this article are abstracted so that it is difficult to make a correspondence with realistic values of actual phenomena. For example, we need to investigate the ratio of bus and walking speeds, and to use an actual town map in which is complicated compared with grid pattern town.
– **Collaboration with other Transportation**: In the actual transportation in urban areas, we use several transportations at the same time. Usability of a bus system should be evaluated in conjunction with other systems like trains.
– **Comparison between Transferable Bus System and Dial-a-Ride**: In this simulation, the assumption that passengers cannot transfer buses is applied. If passengers can transfer the buses, can the usability of fixed route systems become better than that of dial-a-ride systems? Furthermore, from the point of view of applying dial-a-ride systems to real world, the combinational systems of dial-a-ride and fixed route systems may be required actually.
– **Inconstant Demands**: The simulation described here evaluate systems only under the condition where demands occur constantly. Inconstant and intermittent occurrence of demands like 'rush-hours' are general phenomena for transportation systems. In such cases, a simulation must address a framework to switch bus systems.

References

[1] Krumke, S.O., de Paepe, W.E., Poensgen, D., Stougie, L.: News from the online traveling repairman. Lecture Notes in Computer Science **2136** (2001) 487–496 106
[2] Bianco, L., Mingozzi, A., Riccaiardelli, S., Spadoni, M.: Exact and heuristic procedures for the traveling salesman problem with procedence constraints, based on dynamic programming. In: INFOR. Volume 32. (1994) 19–31 106
[3] William A. Bailey, J., Thomas D. Clark, J.: A simulation analysis of demand and fleet size effects on taxicab service rates. In: Proceedings of the 19th conference on Winter simulation, ACM Press (1987) 838–844 106
[4] Savelsbergh, M.W.P., Sol, M.: The general pickup and delivery program. Transportation Science **29** (1995) 17–29 106
[5] Bodin, L.D., Golden, B.L., Assad, A., Ball, M.O.: Routing and scheduling of vehicles and crews: the state of the art. Computers and Operation Research **10** (1983) 63–211 106

[6] Ruland, K.S., Rodin, E.Y.: The pickup and delivery problem: faces and branch-and-cut algorithm. Computers Math. Applic **33** (1997) 1–13 106

[7] Li, H., Lim, A.: A metaheuristic for the pickup and delivery problem with time windows. In: IEEE International Conference on Tools with Artificial Intelligence. Volume 13. (2001) 160–167 106

[8] Healy, P., Moll, R.: A new extension of local search applied to the dial-a-ride problem. European Journal of Operations Research **83** (1995) 83–104 106

[9] Cordeau, J.F., Laporte, G.: A tabu search heuristic for the static multi-vehicle dial-a-ride problem. Transportation Research Part B: Methodological (2003) 106

[10] Silesia, Z.C.: Parallel simulated annealing for the delivery problem. In: The 9th Euromicro Workshop on Parallel and Distributed Processing. (2001) 219–226 106

[11] Silesia, Z.C.: Parallel simulated annealing for the set-partitioning problem. In: The 8th Euromicro Workshop on Parallel and Distributed Processing. (2000) 343–350 106

[12] Hauptmeier, D., Krumke, S.O., Rambau, J., Wirth, H.C.: Euler is standing in line dial-a-ride problems with precedence-constraints. Discrete Applied Mathematics **113** (2001) 87–107 106

[13] Feuerstein, E., Stougie, L.: On-line single-server dial-a-ride problems. Theoretical Computer Science **268** (2001) 91–105 106

[14] Psarfatis, H.N.: Analysis of an $o(n^2)$ heuristic for the single vehicle many-to-many euclidean dial-a-ride problem. Transportation Research **17B** (1983) 133–145 106

[15] Psarfaits, H.N.: A exact algorithm for the single vehicle many-to-many dial-a-ride problem with time windows. In: Transportation Science. Volume 17. (1983) 315–357 106

[16] Psarfaits, H.N.: A dynamic programming solution to the single vehicle many-to-many immediate request dial-a-ride problem. In: Transportation Science. Volume 14. (1980) 135–154 106

[17] Grotschel, M., Hauptmeier, D., Krumke, S., Rambau, J.: Simulation studies for the online dial-a-ride-problem (1999) 106

[18] Hauptmeier, D., Krumke, S.O., Rambau, J.: The online dial-a-ride problem under reasonable load. Lecture Notes in Computer Science **1767** (2000) 125–133 106

[19] Ascheuer, N., Krumke, S.O., Rambau, J.: Online dial-a-ride problems: Minimizing the completion time. Lecture Notes in Computer Science **1770** (2000) 639–650 106

[20] Grotschel, M., Krumke, S.O., Rambau, J.: Online optimization of complex transportation systems (2001) 106

[21] Horn, M.E.T.: Multi-modal and demand-responsive passenger transport systems: a modelling framework with embedded control systems. Transportation Research Part A: Policy and Practice **36** (2002) 167–188 106

[22] Haghani, A., Banihashemi, M.: Heuristic approaches for solving large-scale bus transit vehicle scheduling problem with route time constraints. Transportation Research Part A: Policy and Practice **36** (2002) 309–333 106

[23] Lipmann, M., Lu, X., de Paepe, W.E., Sitters, R.A., Stougie, L.: On-line dial-a-ride problems under a restricted information model. Lecture Notes in Computer Science **2461** (2002) 674–685 106

Effects of Conflict between Emergent Charging Agents in Social Dilemma

Keiji Suzuki

Future University - Hakodate
Kameda-Nakano 116-2, Hakodate City, 041-8655, Japan
suzukj@fun.ac.jp

Abstract. This paper shows the agent based simulation with changing roles in the social dilemma game, that is, the Tragedy of the Common. The Tragedy of the Common is known to treat the problem that is how to manage the limited common resource. To control the usage of a common resource, the levy based control strategy is employed. The role of the charging-agents are introduced to charge the levy to other agents in the proposed simulation. The levy based control strategy can be expected to avoid the dilemma situations even if the agents obey the individual rationality. However, to introduce the charging-agents, it should be considered that who became the charging-agents and how to make the charging plan as the levy against the activities of the agents. To solve the problems, it is proposed that the agents have both activities as the normal players and the charging role. The agents in the game can play the both roles. Namely, the proposed agents can change the role between the normal player and the charging-agent autonomously according to the situations. Concerning to adjusting the charging plan, the plan is created by the GA based on the proposed evaluation methods. The evaluation methods include the effects of the conflict between the charging-agents to prevent the selfish behavior. Throughout the experiments, the effects of the changing roles and the formation of the charging plan are examined.

1 Introduction

Agent based social behavior simulations are research field that treats complex game situations and examines artificial intelligence [1] [2]. Social dilemmas are one of the complex game situations and suite to examine the intelligence of agents [3]. In this paper, the Tragedy of the Common [4], which is one of the social dilemmas, is treated in the agent-based simulation. In this game, players use common limited resources to get the reward. If players behave based on the individual rationality, all players will face to tragedies loosing higher payoff. To avoid such tragedies, players have to make the relationship between other agents to prevent the selfish behaviors or change the problem structure, for example, changing the payoff functions. In the simulations of the Prisoner's Dilemma and the n-persons dilemma game, to avoid the selfish behavior, extended agent's abilities and several social norms were introduced [5]. The results of these approaches will be enough to avoid the dilemma situations if almost agents in the societies can possess the assumed abilities and norms. However, the simulated societies become more complex, that is, the properties of the agents become more heterogeneous, we should be prepare the another types of approach to avoid the dilemma situations. The changing problem structure can be thought as one of such other approaches. In this paper, to avoid the dilemma situations, the approach of the changing problem structure is employed. That is, the charging-agents are introduced to control the levy that changes the received rewards of the players [5].

Because it is important who acts the role of the charging-agents in real society, the agents in the social simulations should possess the decision mechanism that includes the selection of the role. Therefore, it is proposed that role of the charing-agent is treated as one of the activities of the players. Namely, the player will select the role of the charging-agent if the expected revenue exceeds than the expected rewards when the agent acts as the player. Another problem for introducing the charing-agent is how to set the plan of the levies charged to the activities of the players. To acquire the levy plan, the Genetic Algorithm is applied. Based on the evolutionary acquisition of the levy plan and the decision mechanism including the selection of the role, the effects of the interactions between the charing-agents and the agents are examined in the Tragedy of the Common game. In the next section, the problem structure of the Tragedy of the Common is introduced. Then the proposed approach is described.

2   The Tragedy of the Common

The Tragedy of the Common [4] is famous game problem as one of the n-persons social dilemmas [6]. This game enables for us to analyze the behaviors of players sharing common limited resources. Owing to the common resources are limited, higher activity of agents to get the higher payoff will become to bring lower payoff. The one of the general form of the payoff function in the Tragedy of the Common [4] is as follows;

$$Payoff(a_i, TA) = a_i(|A| \times N - TA) - 2a_i \qquad (1)$$

where, $Payoff(a_i, TA)$ is the payoff of agent i. a_i denotes the degree of activity of agent i. TA is the total activities, $\sum_j^N a_j$. A is the set of the activities. N is the number of the agents.

The example of the payoff function [7] is shown as follows;

$$Payoff(a_i, TA) = a_i(16 - TA) - 2a_i \qquad (2)$$

where, $TA = a_1 + a_2 + a_3 + a_4$. Here, 4 agents participate and 4 degrees of the activities, $a_i \in \{0, 1, 2, 3\}$, is supposed. The payoff values based on the function becomes like as Table 1.

Let's consider the game in which the player decides own activity based on the individual rationality. The game assumes the activity of agents consuming the limited common resources. Therefore, the payoff becomes will decrease when

Table 1. Example payoff table of the Tragedy of the Common

Total activities of the agents except agent i

	0	1	2	3	4	5	6	7	8	9
a^i 1	13	12	11	10	9	8	7	6	5	4
2	24	22	20	18	16	14	12	10	8	6
3	33	30	27	24	21	18	15	12	9	6

total activities increase. However, the agent i will increase the activity against any total activity of other agents, because the agent i can increase own payoff until the total activity of the agents reaching 11 in the example. Namely, the strategy of higher activity always dominates the strategy of lower activity. Thus all players will decide to increase their activities based on the individual rationality. Thus the decisions based on the individual rationality will cause the limited common resources being exhausted and the payoffs will become decrease accroding to the total activities. Finaly, the agents will be face to the tragedy. In the example, the tragedy arises when total activities reached 12. That is, the payoff can't incease even though the agent i increases the activity from 2 to 3.

The characteristic of the game is known that no technical solution exists. Therefore, to solve this game, players should change the individual rationalities to other types of rationality or problem structures should be changed to payoff function. One of the objectives of the agent-based simulations is examined what kinds of rationalities and extended problem structures can avoid social dilemmas like as the tragedies. In this paper, the architecture of the proposed simulation method is belonging to the extension of the problem structure. Namely, the

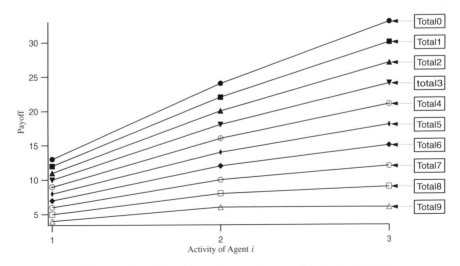

Fig. 1. Graphical view of example payoff value in Table1

charging-agent is introduced to prevent the agents causing the tragedy. The detail of the proposed approach is described in next section.

3 Approach

To solve the social dilemma, the levy based control strategy is introduced (Fig. 2). In this strategy, the property of the levy plan is important. Apparently, it will be enable to fix the suitable levy plan by analyzing the game properties. Then the plan can be embedded in the simulation beforehand. However, one of the purposes of the agent-based simulations is the examination of the autonomous property of the agents in social environments. Therefore, the autonomous acquisition of the suitable levy plan is desirable. To acquire and control the levy plan according to the situations, the role of charging-agent is introduced. It is defined that the charging-agent can broadcast the levy plan and get the revenue by charging the levies to the activities of the agents. To realize the social simulation based on the charging-agent approach, we have to treat two problems, that is, who becomes the charging-agents and how to manage the levy plan. To treats the problems, it is proposed that the decision making includes not only the selection of the activity but also the selection of the role of the charging-agent. Therefore, it is expected to emerge the role of the charging-agents autonomously according to the situations. To adjust the levy plan, the GA is used to modify the plan in each agent. The evaluation function for the GA reflects the competition between the charging-agents. The simple rule to create the competition between the charging-agents is proposed to prohibit the charging-agent behaving selfishly and adjust the levy plans. The details of the architecture of the agents are described in the following subsections.

3.1 Architecture of Agents

The group of agents is represented by N. $N = \{1, 2, \ldots, n\}$. The activities of the agent is represented by $A = \{a^1, a^2, \ldots, a^k, a^{ch}\}$. It is assumed a^{i+1} is higher activity than a^i in the Tragedy of the Common game. The element of the activity, a^{ch}, means the agent acts as the role of the charging-agent. Namely, the agent can select the role of the charging-agent as one of the activities.

The decision making for selecting the role of the charging-agent is based on the levy plan. Each agent prepares the levy plan for becoming the charging-agent. Using the own levy plan, the agent evaluates the expected revenue for deciding the agent should become the charging-agent or not. If the agent selects the charging-agent role, the levy plan is broadcasted to other agents. According to the possible activities as the normal agent, the agent evaluates the expected payoffs by referring the broadcasted levy plans and the payoff function. After the evaluations, the decision-making for selecting the activity carries out to maximize the expected incoming among the expected rewards and revenue. The details of the levy plan are described in the next subsection. The decision-making method are mentioned later.

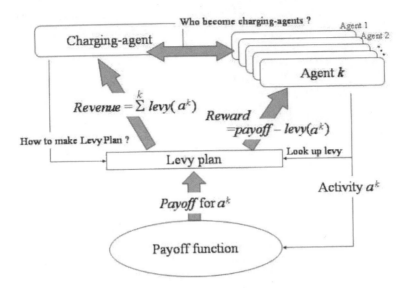

Fig. 2. Schematic view of the levy based control strategy

3.2   Levy Plan and Charging Rule

The levy plan consists of the values of levies, $\{Lv^1, Lv^2, \ldots, Lv^k\}$, corresponding to the activities, $\{a^1, a^2 \ldots, a^k\}$. Namely, the levy, Lv^i charges to the payoff of the activity, a^i.

The levies can change the rewards of normal agents by charging the original payoff values. The received reward becomes the difference between the payoff value and the charged levy. Therefore even if the agents decide their activities based on the individual rationality, the suitable levy plan will be possible to prevent the activities exhausting the limited common resources. However, it is remained that the problem is how to set the suitable levy plan. The issue is connected to the planning policy of levies. In this approach, the individual rationality is employed for the planning policy. Namely, the objective of the charging-agent is to maximize the revenue. The reason of adopting the individual rationality is simplicity. The policy doesn't ask the charging-agent to have a specific cooperative rationality. However, the policy of the charging-agent is afraid to increase the levies selfishly. To inhibit the selfish behavior of the charging-agent, the simple rule for charging the levy is introduced. The charging agent can receive the levy value against an activity if the applied levy value becomes the lowest levies among the other charging-agent's levies and the lower than the payoff value for the agents. Otherwise, the received value become 0. It means that only one charging-agent can receive the levies against an activity. Thus simultaneously emerged charging-agents have to compete each other to get the levy values by setting the low levy values. This simple rule can be expected to inhibit the selfish behavior of the charging-agent.

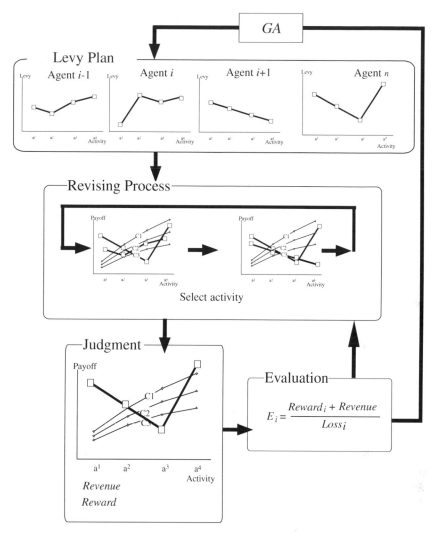

Fig. 3. Proposed agent-based simulation process

To search the suitable levy plan, the genetic algorithm is applied. The details of the evolution of the levy plan are mentioned later.

3.3   Decision Making and Revising Process

To determine the activity of the agent, the revising process is prepared. In this game, the payoff is varied by the other agent's activities, that is, TA. Therefore, it is difficult to determine the activity without the information of the other agent's activities. Instead of the decision simultaneously among the agents, the process for deciding the activities in turn is introduced. The process is named the revising process. The revising process consists of the fixed length of steps. In each step, one of the agents randomly selected. The selected agents can decide the activity referring the other agent's activities and the broadcasted levy plans. To decide the activity, the agent calculates the expected rewards and the expected revenue. The expected rewards corresponding the activity, a^i can be obtained from the following equation.

$$Reward(a^i) = Payoff(a^i, TA) - Lv_{min}^i \tag{3}$$

Where, Lv_{min}^i is the minimum levy value among the broadcasted levy values. Namely, in the proposed method, more than one agent can become the charging-agent. Therefore, some levy plans are simultaneously broadcasted. For example, the levy plans, Lv_k and Lv_h, are broadcasted from the agent k and h respectively. Among the several levy values corresponding the activity a^i, it is supposed only the minimum levy value can be charged to the activity and only the proposed agent of the levy value receives the incoming levy. For example, if $Lv_k^i \in Lv_k$ is smaller than $Lv_h^i \in Lv_h$, the agent k can receive the incoming levy Lv_k^i. If no charging-agent exist, Lv_{min}^i is treated as 0. The competition between the charging-agents is also expected to prohibit the selfish behavior among the charging-agents.

Concerning the expected revenue, $Revenue_k$, of the charging-agent, k, the value can be obtained from the following equation.

$$Revenue_k = \sum_i L'v_k^i |A^i|, \tag{4}$$

$$where \quad L'v_k^i = \begin{cases} Lv_k^i \text{ if } Lv_k^i = Lv_{min}^i \\ 0 \text{ otherwise} \end{cases}$$

In the above equation, $|A^i|$ means the number of agents taking the activity a^i.

Because the competition between the charging-agents, the expected revenue will be increased if the prepared levy value, Lv^i, becomes Lv_{min}^i.

Throughout the calculations for the expected rewards and the expected revenue, the activity is selected to maximize the incoming value. If the expected revenue exceeds the expected rewards, the agent selects the role of the charging-agent. Otherwise, the agent acts as the player selecting the activity corresponding the maximum expected reward.

After the one agent decides the activity, another agent, that is selected randomly, will decide the own activity based on the determined other's activities in the revising process. The length of the revising process is assumed to be enough for that one agent can revise the own decision in several times. When the revising process is over, the final decisions of the agents are applied to the game. Then the rewards and the revenue are decided. To avoid the tragedy situations, it is required that the suitable levy plans are broadcasted in the revising process. To acquire the suitable levy plan, the genetic algorithm is applied.

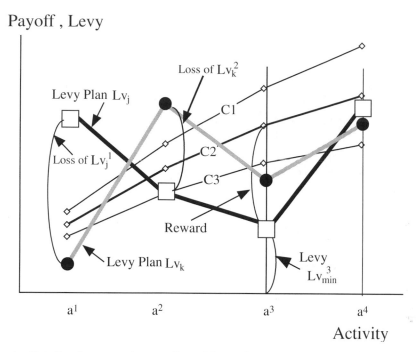

Fig. 4. Relation between the payoffs and levy plan concerning reward, levy and loss

3.4 Evolution of Levy Plan

To make the suitable levy plan, the genetic algorithm is applied. Each agent has the population of the chromosomes and the genetic algorithm works in each agent. The chromosome consists of the blocks. Each block is decoded to the value of levy in the levy plan. In the following simulation, the value of the levy is encoded by binary representation in the block. A levy plan decoded from one of the chromosome is used in the game. After the game, the agent using the levy plan will get the reward and revenue. The evaluation of the levy plan is based on the reward, revenue, and the following loss value. Here, the genetic operations will work the chromosomes to increase the incoming values. The evaluation strategy includes the competitiveness with other charging-players. That is the loss value. The loss ,$Loss_i$, of agent i is determend as follows:

$$Loss_i = \sum_j (Lv_i^j - Lv_{min}^j)|A^j| \tag{5}$$

Using the reward, the revenue and the loss, the evaluation of the chromosome, which generates the levy plan, is defined as follows.

$$E_i = \frac{Reward(a_i) + Revenue}{Loss_i} \tag{6}$$

In this evaluation, the loss value represents the inferiority of the levy value comparing to the minimum levy. If the other charging-agent sets the lower levy value than the value of one agent against an activity, the agent can't receive the levies even if the agent becomes the charging-agent. Therefore, the agent having higher value of the loss will lost the chance to become the charging agent. The loss value in the evaluation function is expected to make the chance to become the charging agent role for several agents.

To increase the score of the evaluation function, the lower loss value is required. However, the lower loss value means that the revenue becomes small. Thus, it isn't easy to make the suitable levy plan to increase the evaluation function. Some kind of the strategic plan will be required. For example, even if the revenue become small corresponding to an activity, the sum of the total levy as the revenue will become large when the number of the normal agents selecting the activity is increased, To realize the such situation, the levy plan must have the property to collect the selection of agents against a specific activity.

In the simulations, the game is iterated in several times against to the same levy plan, because the averaged evaluation value would like to be considered.

After the evaluation values are fixed for all of the chromosomes, the genetic operations are applied. Namely, the crossover, the mutation and reproduce are applied in turn.

4   Simulation

To confirm the effectiveness of the proposed methods for avoiding the tragedy situation in the social dilemmas, the simulation is executed. The payoff function is set as follows;

$$Payoff_i = a^i(|A| \times N' - \sum_{j}^{N'} a^j) - 2a^i \qquad (7)$$

where N' is the number of agents excepting the number of charging-agents.

Two cases of the number of agents, 12 agents and 30 agents, are simulated, The activities for each agent are 5 for 12 agents, 6 for 30 agents and a^{ch}. Each agent has 30 chromosomes. According to the decoded plan, the game, The tragedy of the common, is iterated 10 times for averaging the rewards and revenues. In each game, 4 times for revising chances are given for each agent. The averaged evaluation values in the iterated games are given as fitness of the chromosomes. The crossover and mutation are applied the chromosomes. The crossover rate is 1.0 and the mutation rate is 0.05. Under these parameters, the evolution of the levy plans in the agents are proceeded until 50 generations. The calculation time is about 8 hours for one simulation with Pentium 4, 1.5 GHz.

The example of the evolution process with 30 agents are shown in Fig. 6, Fig. 7 and Fig. 8. Fig. 6 is the progress of the averaged score value corresponding the equation.6. The score value is relatively increased according to increarsing the

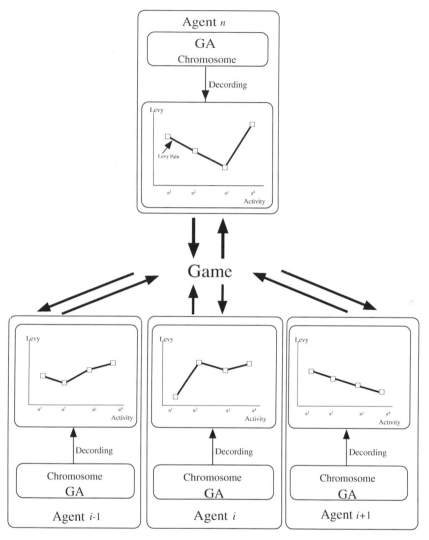

Fig. 5. Each agent applies genetic algorithms to acquire suitable levy plan

averaged reward (Fig. 7) and suppressing the fractuation of the averaged loss value (Fig. 8).

The examples of the aquired levy plans are shown in Fig. 9 in the case of 12 agents and Fig. 10 in the case of 30 agents.

In Fig. 9, the bold line represents the levy plan of the major agent becoming the charging-agent. The major levy plan has one specific point to become lowest levy value. Other values are relatively high. Therefore, the plan has the property to collect the selection of the normal agents in the specific activity. The plan can

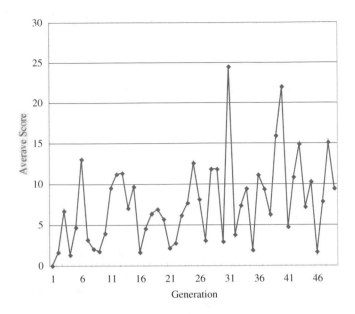

Fig. 6. Progress of averaged score with 30 agents

get the higher revenue by the multiplication of the small levy and the number of gathered agents.

The same type of properties can be observed in the acquired plans in the case of 30 agents. In the Fig. 10, the bold lines are the major agents to become the charging-agents. The plans represented the bold lines have the specific point set up the lower levies. When the agents becomes the charging-agents, they will get the higher revenues from the specific points by gathering the selection of other agents.

It is interesting that the emergent properties of the levy plans are acquired throughout the competition between the emergent charging-agents. The acquired strategy in the levy plans can be observed in the result of the selection rates in Fig. 11. In this graph, the selection rates according to the activities includes the activity as the role of the charging-agent, *a-ch*, are shown in the cases of 6 agents, 12 agents and 30 agents. If the charging-agent doesn't exist, it is obvious that all agents will select the highest activity. The simulated results show that the rate of the highest activity are suppressed and selection rates are gathered in 2nd higher activity. Namely, the worst tragedy situation can be avoided. The selection rates of the charging-agent are varied according to the size of agents. The rate becomes higher when the size of agents decrease. The reason can be considered as when the size of the agents becomes large, the difficulty of the acqisition is inceased in each agent.

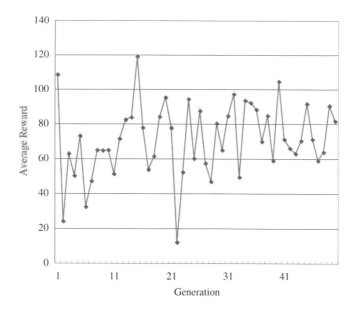

Fig. 7. Progress of averaged reward with 30 agents

Another interesting phenomena can be observed in the revision process. The example of the revision process is shown in Fig. 12. In this figure, *Charge* means that the agent selects the role of the charging-agent and others are quantity of the activity for the normal agents. In the decision process, at first, two agents select the highest activity because no charging-agent exists. When one agent selects the role of the charging, after all agents select 2nd higher activity because the highest activity is charged huge levy. When the decision turn of the charging-agent comes, the agent tries to select the highest activity. The behavior is just the free-rider. However, another agent becomes the charge role, then the free-rider agent is abandon to change 2nd higher activity. The levy plan of the current charging-agent may be inferior. Two agents select the role of the charge. Three agents compete each other as the charging-agents. Finally, two agents remain as role of charge but one charging-agent is abandon. From this result shows that the charging-agents emerged autonomously according to the situation to suppress the free-rider and selecting the highest activity.

The remaining problem is that the selfish behavior of the charging-agents are suppressed or not. In Fig. 13, the averaged revenue of the charging-agents and the averaged rewards of the agents are compared in the case of 30 agents. The result is showm that the both values become same value. Namely, the selfish behavior of the charging-agent perfectly suppressed by the competition between agents.

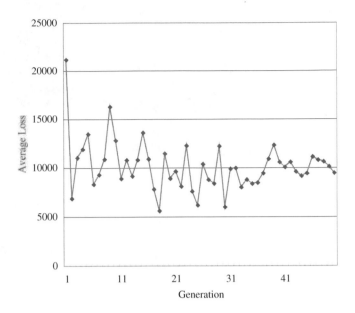

Fig. 8. Progress of averaged loss with 30 agents

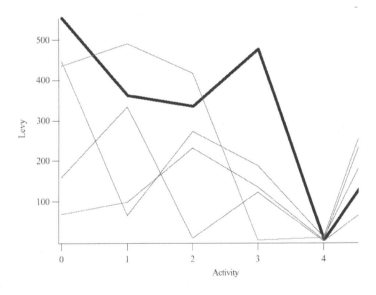

Fig. 9. Example of aquired levy plans in case of 12 agents. The bold line represents the plan of a major agent becoming the charging-agent

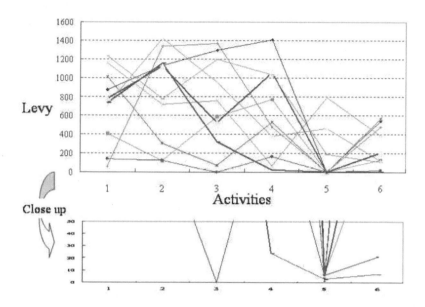

Fig. 10. Example of aquired levy plans in case of 30 agents. The bold lines represent the plans of major agents becoming charging-agents

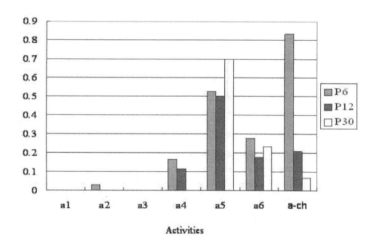

Fig. 11. Selection Rates of the activities. P6 is the case of 6 agents. P12 and P30 are the cases of 12 agents and 30 agents respectively

5   Conclusion

This paper shows the agent based simulation with changing roles in the social dilemma game, the tragedy of the common. To control the usage of a com-

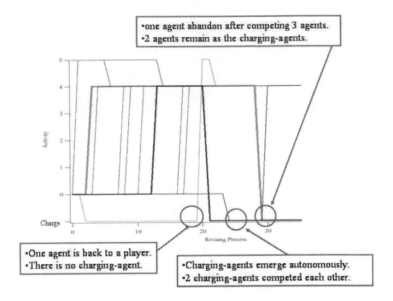

Fig. 12. Example of the revising process in 6 agents

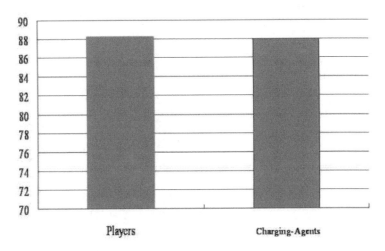

Fig. 13. Comparison ofbetween the averaged rewards of the players and the averaged revenues of the charging-agents

mon resource, charging-agents are introduced in the game. The objective of the charging-agents is to get the revenue from the agents according to their activities. To introduce the charging-agents, it should be considered that who became the charging-agents and how to make the charging plan of levies against the activities of the agents. Therefore, it is proposed the decision making of the agents that includes the role of the charging-agent. Namely, the agents can select one activity from the role of the charging-agent and the activities for the normal agent. The selection is obey the individual rationality. The agent selects the extended activities to maximize the incoming value among the revenue and rewards. If the agent selects the role of the charging-agent, the levy plan of the agent is broadcasted. The broadcasted plans are influenced to the selections of the other agents. To select the role of the charging-agent, there is no restriction. Thus, some charging-agents can coexist simultaneously. Such simultaneously existing charging-agents compete each other to get the levies based on the introduced rule. The rule is introduced to prevent the selfish behavior of the charging-agents. Namely, the rule is that only a charging-agent agent setting a minimal levy value can get the levies form the normal agents. Thus, the agents trying to become the charging-agent make the suitable levy plan by GA to get the higher revenue even if the levy values in the plan keep the minimal value against the other agents. Throughout the simulations, the acquired levy plans have the strategy to collect the small levy values effectively. That is, only a specific activity point is set the levy to minimal value and others are relatively set higher values. Then the charging-agent can effectively collect the levy from the specific activity. The effect of the strategy influences to avoid the worst tragedy situation. It is interesting that the property of the strategy in the acquired levy plan emerged from the interactions between agents based on the simple rule concerning the competition.

Another interesting point is observed in the process of the decision making. In this simulation, the revising process is introduced. In the revising process, the role of the charging-agents are emerged autonomously according to the situation. Ordinarily, in the revising process, the charging-agents compete each other. From the simulation result, it can be observed the interesting phenomena that one agent try to become the free-rider using the property of the levy plan. Namely, at first, one charging-agent suppress the other agent's activities to lower. After all of the other agents suppressed to lower activities, the charging-agent gets the chance to receive the highest reward by being back to the normal agent and selecting the highest activity.

Concerning this simulation model, The last question may be related to which roles has advantage to receive the incoming value. The examination result to compare the incoming values between the normal agents and the charging-agents, the incoming values becomes just same value. Namely, there is no advantage existing concerning to the roles. the result can be considered to be made by the competition between the charging-agents.

In this paper, it is shown that one of the simulation model based on the changing structure of the game and the results of the proposed mechanism to change the game structure by agents itself. The proposed mechanism can be consider the approach to extend the ability of the agent based simulations.

References

[1] Suleiman, R., Troitzsch, K. G., Gilbert, N. eds. :Tools and Techniques for social Sience Simulation, (2000) *Springer.* 120

[2] Namatame, A., Terano, T., Kurumatani, K., eds.: Agent-Based Approaches in Economic and Aocial Complex Systems, (2002)*IOS Press.* 120
[3] Conte, R., Hegselmann, R., Terna, P. eds.: Simulating Social Phenomena,(1997)*Springer.* 120
[4] Hardin, G.: The Tragedy of the Commons, *Science* 162:1243 (1968) 120, 121
[5] Yamashita, T., Suzuki, K., Ohuchi, A.: Distributed Social Dilemma with Competitive Meta-players, *Int. Trans. in Operational Research* Vol.8, No.1:75–88 (2001) 121
[6] Yao, X. : Evolutionary stability in the N-person prisoner's dilemma,*BioSystems,* **37**, (1996) 189–197. 121
[7] Suzuki, M.: New Geme Theory,(1994)*Soukei-Shobou* (in Japanese) 121
[8] Liebrand, W., Messick, D. eds.: Frontiers in Social Dilemmas Research, (1996) *Springer.* 120

Investigation of Mutual Choice Metanorm in Group Dynamics for Solving Social Dilemmas

Tomohisa Yamashita[1], Robert L. Axtell[2], Koichi Kurumatani[1], and
Azuma Ohuchi[3]

[1] Cyber Assist Research Center (CARC)
National Institute of Advanced Industrial Science and Technology (AIST)
Aomi 2-41-6, Koto-ku, Tokyo 135-0064, Japan
tomohisa@carc.aist.go.jp
k.kurumatani@aist.go.jp
[2] Center on Social and Economic Dynamics, Brookings Institution
1775 Massachusetts Ave., N.W., Washington, D.C. 20036, U.S.A
raxtell@brookings.edu
[3] Research Group of Complex Systems, Hokkaido University
North 13, West 8, Kita-ku, Sapporo 060-8628, Japan
ohuchi@complex.eng.hokudai.ac.jp

Abstract. In this research, we propose group dynamics that promotes
cooperative behavior in the so-called Social Dilemmas and enhances the
performance of systems. If cooperative behavior among self-interest individuals is established, effective distribution of resources and useful allocation of tasks based on coalition formation can be realized. In order to
realize group dynamics, we extend the partner choice mechanisms for 2-
IPD to that for N-person Dilemma game. Furthermore, we propose group
split based on metanorm. As a result of simulations with an evolutionary
approach, we confirm i) the establishment and maintain of cooperation,
and ii) the enhancement of the performance of the systems consisting of
self-interest players by group dynamics based on mutual choice in the
Social Dilemmas.

1 Introduction

In this paper, we propose in group dynamics that enhance the performance of
systems consisting of self-interest individuals in Social Dilemmas.

The question of how cooperative behaviors among self-interest individuals
are established without central authority has been taken up by the researchers
in many fields, e.g. economics, politics, sociology, social psychology, computer
science and so on [ ]. In a group (a gathering of individuals without a binding
agreement), is cooperative behaviors of self-interest individuals always promised?
It is difficult to promote cooperative behaviors in the case that an individual can
always acquire a higher payoff by non-cooperative behaviors to the group regardless of other members' behavior although cooperative behaviors of all individuals
for the group maximizes the payoff of all members [ ]. This situation is generally

K. Kurumatani et al. (Eds.): MAMUS 2003, LNAI 3012, pp. 137–153, 2004.
© Springer-Verlag Berlin Heidelberg 2004

called the Social Dilemmas [ ], where free-riders who choose non-cooperative behaviors decrease the total reword in the group. A lot of researchers have used the
Iterated Prisoner's Dilemma (IPD) as the model of Social Dilemmas to explore
the potential emergence of mutually cooperative behaviors among non-altruistic
individuals. In the society, this problematic situation is often observed in resource distribution and task allocation without central authority. Self-interest
individuals do not take cooperative behaviors for maximizing the payoff of the
group because they prefer the individually best outcome to the collectively best
outcome.

Because generally institutional approach, e.g. the introduction of sanctioning
systems, provides second-order dilemmas, it is not an adequate solution of the
original dilemma [1 , 1]. Therefore, in this research we consider the solution
of social dilemmas that don't cause second-order dilemmas. Therefore, if some
mechanisms without central authority prevent free-riders from joining cooperative groups, the total reword in the group can be increased and the performance
of the systems can be enhanced. In this context, group dynamics, which does
not require the existence of central authority, is one of the most important interactions in order to promote cooperation.

In this paper, in order to realize effective group dynamics in dilemma situation, we use the mutual choice mechanisms [1] as the basic interaction for group
dynamics, which is the matching mechanism of game opponents in a multiple 2-
person Prisoner's Dilemma (2-PD). The conventional partner choice mechanisms
for matching two persons are extended to that for matching N persons. As the
dilemma situation in each group, an N-person dilemma game is used. Furthermore, we propose a group split rule based on mutual choice metanorm [ ]. The
effect of our proposed group dynamics on the establishment of cooperation and
the enhancement of system performance is confirmed through an agent-based
simulation with evolutionary approach.

2   Partner Choice Mechanisms

A lot of studies on the Social Dilemmas assumed that individuals have no control over which opponents they play. However, if one individual keeps choosing
a defect, the others may cease maintaining their relationship with that individual rather than keep choosing a defect against his defect. It is important for an
individual to choose not only to cooperate or defect but also with whom to play
the game [, 1]. Actually, social interactions are also often characterized by
choosing partners. Examples of partner choice are easy to find in the real world;
the establish and rupture of diplomatic relations in international society, the beginning and suspension of business transactions in the corporate community, and
the connecting and breaching of relationships in human relations. Partner choice
is an endogenous matching mechanism, where players can choose the partners by
themselves. On the other hand, if an exogenous matching mechanism is applied,
partners are determined by round robin, random matching and grid neighborhood among other methods. Although there are many kinds of partner choice

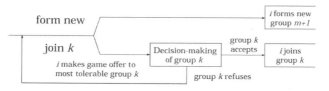

Fig. 1. Outline of decision-making of player i in group formation based on mutual choice

mechanisms, in this research we take up unilateral choice and mutual choice to realize group dynamics.

2.1   Unilateral Choice

In unilateral choice, the PD game has to be played if at least one partner chooses to play the PD game [9]. Hauk and Nagel [9] found with the unilateral choice setup that intending defectors are more likely to try to avoid a match than intending cooperators.

2.2   Mutual Choice

In mutual choice applied as partner choice, the PD game is played between two individuals only if both individuals mutually agree to play the game [1, 12, 13]. Stanley et al. [12] confirmed that, although full cooperation is the most frequently observed population structure may arise where, several other population structures everyone is inactive.

There are various partner choice mechanisms besides unilateral and mutual choice, e.g. ostracism [10] and exit option (opt-out)[6]. These mechanisms are also suitable for the establishment of cooperation. In ostracism, each individual decides whom to exclude from the group, and in exit option, each individual decides whether to leave the group. However, these mechanisms cannot realize group dynamics, including group split, because they only represent the relationship between an individual and a group.

3   Group Dynamics

Group dynamics in the dilemma situation is modeled as a two stage game. The first stage is group dynamics, where players choose group members. The groups are determined through group dynamics, i.e., the population of all players is partitioned. A group is defined as a subset of the overall player set. Each player can join only one group at the same time. The order of decision-making for group dynamics is set as random. According to this order, the players make decisions for group dynamics one by one, and then groups are gradually formed. The second stage is the dilemma game. In groups consisting of two or more players, players play the dilemma game with their group members. The result of the dilemma game in a group is independent of the players in other groups. In groups consisting of a single player, the player acquires a fixed payoff.

3.1   Group Formation Based on Unilateral Choice

The alternatives of each player in group formation based on unilateral choice are forming a new group or joining an existing group. The procedure of group formation based on unilateral choice is as follows.

1. Let $N = \{1, .., i, .., n\}$ be the player set. The first player in the decision-making of group formation cannot join an existing group but has to form a new group. The players make decisions after the first player chooses one group k out of the group set $G = \{G_1, .., G_k, .., G_m\}$, where G_k is the set of the players that have already made a decision on group dynamics. Player i chooses one group, and then player i makes an offer to group k that is most tolerable for player i. How to decide the most tolerable group of player i is taken up in next section. Player i can join group k surely because group formation is based on unilateral choice. Player i is added to group k as $G_k \cup \{i\}$, which is the new group k.

   If there is no tolerable group for player i, player i does not make an offer but forms a new group, $G_{m+1} = i$. New group $m + 1$, which includes only player i, is added to group set G, and then group set G is modified as $G = \{G_1, .., G_k, .., G_m, G_{m+1}\}$.

2. After the decision-making for group dynamics, the players in groups of more than two players play the dilemma game with the players in the same group. Because a player in a group that only includes itself after group dynamics cannot play the dilemma game, such a player acquires the fixed payoff for lone players, $P_{reservation}$, instead of the payoff of the dilemma game.

3.2   Group Formation Based on Mutual Choice

In group formation based on mutual choice, the player making an offer and the group receiving the offer form a new group both only if the group and the individuals mutually agree. Therefore, refusing or accepting the offer of a group in group formation based on mutual choice is added as a new alternative to the alternatives of unilateral choice. The procedure of group formation based on mutual choice is as follows.

1. The first player in the decision-making of group dynamics cannot join an existing group and has to form a new group. In the same way as group formation based on unilateral choice, player i chooses one group, and then player i makes an offer to group k, which is most tolerable for player i. If there is no tolerable group for player i, player i does not make an offer.

2. After the group choice of player i, the group k chosen by player i decides to refuse or accept the offer of player i. How group k decides whether to refuse or accept the offer of player i is taken up in the next section. If group k accepts the offer of player i, player i joins group k. Player i is added to group k as $G_k \cup \{i\}$. If group k refuses player i, player i makes an offer to the second most tolerable group l. Player i continues making game offers until a group accepts its offer or until all tolerable groups refuse. If player i is refused by all tolerable groups, player i forms a new group, G_{m+1}. New group $m+1$, which only includes player i, is added to group set G, and then group set G is modified as $G = \{G_1, .., G_k, .., G_m, G_{m+1}\}$.

3. After the decision-making for group dynamics, the players in groups of more than two players play the dilemma game with the players in the same group.

An outline of the decision-making process for player i on group formation based on mutual choice is shown in Fig. 1.

3.3 Group Split

Here, we propose group split based on mutual choice metanorm.

According to Axelrod [2], if there is a certain norm, a metanorm is one "punishes not only against the violators of the norm but also against anyone who refuses to punish the defectors." The existence of a metanorm is a powerful way to establish a norm. In this research, a norm based on mutual choice is one that "doesn't choose defectors as group members." A metanorm based on mutual choice is one that "refuse not only defectors but also anyone who chooses defectors as group members." This metanorm realizes group split by dividing all players into one group of players agreeing to accept a player (agreeing players) and another group of players opposing the acceptance of that player(opposing players). ¿From the point of view of the opposing players, agreeing players violate the metanorm because they choose a player that opposing players consider a defector. In order to not choose the players who choose defectors as group members, opposing players leave from the group. The group split rule is applied as follows.

1. When player i makes an offer to group k, group k decides whether to accept or refuse player i. If group k accepts player i, the players opposing the acceptance of player i consider the players agreeing the acceptance of player i as players choosing a defector. In group k, the players agreeing to the acceptance of player i are defined as G_k^{agree}, and the players opposing the acceptance of player i are defined as G_k^{oppose}, where $G_k = G_k^{agree} \cup G_k^{oppose}$ and $G_k^{agree} \cap G_k^{oppose} = \phi$.

2. The members of G_k^{oppose} leave from group k and form a new group. The new group formed by G_k^{oppose} is assigned to G_{m+1}, and G is modified as $G = \{G_1, .., G_k, .., G_m, G_{m+1}\}$. Then, player i joins group k ($G_k = G_k^{agree} \cup \{i\}$).

3.4   Re-offering

Finally, we propose a re-offering after group split. By the introduction of group split, the size of groups may decrease. Re-offering is proposed to increase the chance of forming groups with several players as soon as possible. Re-offering is used after a player opposing the acceptance of a player leaves from group k and forms the new group G_{m+1}. If G_{m+1} includes only player j, player j makes an offer to the most tolerable groups in the same way as the above-described unilateral choice.

4   Dilemma Game

In this model, we use a more general dilemma game than the N-person Dilemma (N-PD) in a strategy set [14]. After group dynamics, the players in each group play the dilemma game with group members if the players are in groups of more than two players. Otherwise, a player in a group that only includes itself acquires the fixed payoff for lone players, *reservation payoff* $P_{reservation}$, instead of the payoff of the dilemma game [1, 12, 13].

Each group member decides the degree of contribution to his group, and then the profit taken from the amount of contribution of all members is redistributed equally to the group members. Each player i in group k contributes some amount, $x_i \in \{0, 1\}$, to group k as the strategy and has a payoff function, F_i. The total contribution of all players in group k amounts to $X \equiv \sum_{i \in G_k} x_i$; $X_{\sim i} \equiv X - x_i$. The payoff function of player i in group k can be written as

$$F_i(x_i; X_{\sim i}, |G_k|) = a \, \frac{x_i + X_{\sim i}}{|G_k|} + b(1 - x_i), \tag{1}$$

where $|G_k|$ is the size of group k, and a and b are positive constants.

The payoff function satisfies the condition that the payoff of player i increases linearly as total contribution in group k increases. The payoff depends on the average contribution of group members and the contribution of player i and does not depend on the size of the group [20]. The Nash equilibrium of this dilemma game is that none of the members contribute at all, i.e., $x_i = 0$ ($i \in G_k$), because the dominant strategy of player i is no contribution, $x_i = 0$. Evaluating the collective outcome in the payoffs of all members in group k, the collective outcome is the best when all members contribute completely, $x_i = 1.0$. Therefore, the Nash equilibrium of the dilemma game is not Pareto optimal. Some basic structure of this dilemma game is similar to the N-PD, e.g., the dominant strategy is defective strategy, the payoff increases monotonically as the amount of contribution in the group increases, the payoff when all members contribute completely is more than that when none of the members contribute at all.

5   Agent-Based Modeling

In order to measure the effect of the proposed group dynamics to the establishment of cooperation and the enhancement of system performance, we use agent-based simulation. In this section, we discuss how a player and a group make decisions in group dynamics and the dilemma game.

5.1   Architecture of Agent

In this section, we explain how players and groups make decisions. For the analysis of the player's behavior, we don't use the game theoretical assumption, i.e., rational behavior. Therefore, in undertaking an analysis of group dynamics and cooperative behavior in a changing environment, we adopt an evolutionary approach as a social learning mechanism. The details of this evolutionary approach are explained in the next section. In order to construct an agent-based simulation with evolutionary operations, we utilize bounded rational decision-making. Furthermore, because an iterated game of our proposed game is used in the simulation, the decision-making mechanism is based on the assumption of iteration.

The strategy of a player in our proposed game can be represented in two dimensions [ ]. The strategy of player i has cooperativeness C_i and vengefulness V_i, where both C_i and V_i are real numbers from 0.0 to 1.0. Cooperativeness C_i represents player i's degree of contribution in the dilemma game. The value of C_i is directly considered as contribution x_i in each round of the dilemma game. Vengefulness V_i represents player i's degree of vengefulness toward defection associated with the other players. The higher the vengefulness of player i is, the more player i refuses to forgive the defection of the others.

In the previous researches on the 2-IPD with evolution, a finite state machine and an automaton have been often used for the strategy of the 2-IPD, which decides whether to cooperate or defect in each round of the iterated game. Because a finite state machine and an automaton with evolution can establish cooperative behavior, it is difficult to distinguish whether group dynamics or evolutionary automata is the cause of the behavior's establishment. For example, if the strategies of all players are Tit-for-Tat from the beginning of the evolution of group dynamics, cooperation can be established regardless of whether group dynamics is applied. Therefore, in this research the strategy of players is described in real numbers.

Player i makes decisions to make offers and re-offers based on vengefulness V_i and the *contribution record* of the opponents in past dilemma games. Group k decides to refuse or accept an offer and also whether to split. The decision of group k occurs through a majority vote of the group members. Player j in group k votes based on vengefulness V_j and *contribution record*. In the following, the procedures for these decisions are explained. At first, we explain *contribution record* and the way of updating it.

5.2   Updating *Contribution Record*

In the initial iteration of group dynamics, all players have the same *initial contribution record* π_0 for each player. The *contribution record* is updated after each dilemma game is played. Considering any player in group k, if player j is in group k that includes player i in iteration t, player j can know *contribution* x_i, and *contribution record* $\pi(i|j)$ can be updated. If player j is not in group k, *contribution record* $\pi(i|j)$ cannot be updated.

5.3   Making an Offer

At the t-th iteration of group dynamics, player i estimates existing groups based on *contribution record* $\pi(i|j)$ with player $j(\in N)$. This history is used to decide which group is the most tolerable for each player. Given any player i in group k, group k is tolerable for player i in iteration t only if

$$\frac{\sum_{j\in|G_k|}\pi_t(i|j)}{|G_k|} \geq V_i. \tag{2}$$

The groups satisfying condition (2) are defined as *tolerable groups* for player i. The most tolerable group is defined as the group with the highest average *contribution record* for player i. Player i makes an offer to the most tolerable group k. If the most tolerable group refuses player i, player i keeps making offers in descending order of average *contribution record* until a tolerable group accepts player i, or until all tolerable groups refuse.

5.4   Refusing and Accepting an Offer

After receiving the offer of player i, group k decides whether to refuse or accept the offer of player i. In order to decide this, a majority vote is held. Player j in group k agrees to accept player i only if $\pi(j|i) \geq V_j$ because player j doesn't consider player i a defector. Otherwise, player j opposes the acceptance of player i because player j considers player i a defector. If the majority of players agree to accept player i, group k accepts the offer of player i and then player i joins group k. Player i is added to group k as $G_k \cup \{i\}$.

5.5   Splitting Group

After the majority vote in group k, if the number of players agreeing to the acceptance of player i is more than that opposing it, player i joins group k. G_k^{oppose}, consisting of the players opposing the acceptance of player i (player j $(\in G_k^{oppose})$), satisfies condition $\pi(j|i) \leq V_j$ and leaves from group k and to form new group $m+1$. [1] An example of group split is shown in Fig. 2.

5.6   Re-offering

After splitting group k, if G_k^{oppose} is composed only of player j, player j makes an offer to the most tolerable group again in the same way as making an offer.

---

[1] This decision-making is a kind of myopic "best reply" in the sense that the "agree" players might wish to compare their payoff with and without group split, since truly strategic players would condition their vote on their beliefs about what others will do, i.e., the voting is non-strategic.

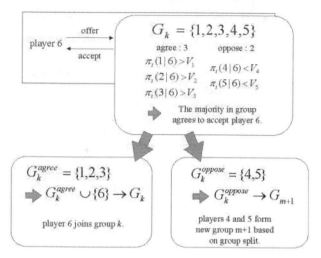

Fig. 2. Example of group split; There are five players (players $1 \sim 5$) in group k. Player 6 makes an offer to group k. Players 1, 2 and 3 agree to the acceptance and players 4 and 5 oppose it. As a result of majority vote, group k accepts player 6. Players 4 and 5 leave group k and form new group $m + 1$ based on the metanorm

6   Simulation Setup

6.1   Evolutionary Approach

In our simulations, a genetic algorithm is applied to evolve the player's strategies. The genetic algorithm is a model of machine learning that derives its behavior from a metaphor of the processes of evolution in nature. The dynamic behavior of agent-based modeling with a genetic algorithm is regarded as a powerful method for modeling social learning.

In implementing the encoding of the chromosomes, the strategy of an individual player is represented by a binary bit string. The two dimensions of a strategy, cooperativeness C_i and vengefulness V_i, are each divided into $2^x - 1$ equal levels, from 0.0 to 1.0. Because $2^x - 1$ levels are represented by x binary bits, a player's strategy needs a total of $2x$ bits: x bits for cooperativeness C_i and x bits for vengefulness V_i.

Each simulation is initialized with a population of all players. Each generation consists of an iteration of group formation and split, and then the Dilemma game. At the beginning of the genetic phase, each player's strategy in a population is assigned a fitness equal to its average payoff given per payoff received. A partner for crossover is selected by means of a tournament selection. Uniform crossover is accomplished between the strategies of a player and a partner to obtain a new strategy for one offspring if the fitness of the partner is better than that of the player in tournament selection.

After that, the strategy of this offspring is subjected to mutation, where each bit is flipped one bit with a certain probability.

Table 1. Common parameters in the simulations of group dynamics

Number of players	50
Number of generations	5000
Number of group dynamics per generation	200
Coefficient of payoff function a	1.0
Coefficient of payoff function b	0.6
Payoff for lone player $P_{preservation}$	0.1
Initial value of expected cooperation π	1.0
Initial value of Cooperativeness C_i	0.0
Initial value of Vengefulness V_i	0.0
Mutation rate	0.05
Binary bits for C_i and V_i (total bits)	10

6.2 Parameter Setting

In this paper, because our purpose is to examine whether group dynamics can promote cooperative behavior of players and enhance the performance of systems, we pay attention to the transition of players' strategies and the average payoff of all players. In order to confirm the effect of the proposed group dynamics, we compare four settings: case 1) only group formation based on unilateral choice, case 2) only group formation based on mutual choice, case 3) group formation based on mutual choice and group split, and case 4) group formation based on mutual choice, group split and re-offering.

It is impossible to keep such a state constant due to the high mutation rate of 0.05. We define the establishment of cooperation as the condition where both average cooperativeness of all players ($\overline{C}$) and average vengefulness ($\overline{V}$) are bigger than 0.8 because it is impossible to keep the state, $V_i = 1.0$ and $C_i = 1.0$ ($\forall i \in N$), due to high mutation rate 0.05.

The other important parameters and the payoff function of the dilemma game are shown in Table. 1. Under these conditions, we examine whether group dynamics accelerate cooperative behavior and what rules of group dynamics are effective for enhancing the performance of systems.

Table 2. Number of times cooperation is established in 40 trials of four cases

case 1	0/40
case 2	4/40
case 3	12/40
case 4	40/40

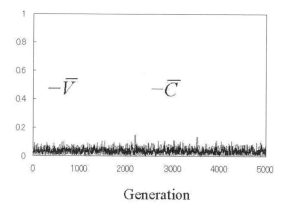

Fig. 3. Example of the failure of the establishment of cooperation in case 1: the transition of the average cooperativeness $\bar{C}$ and vengefulness $\bar{V}$ from 0 to 5,000 generations

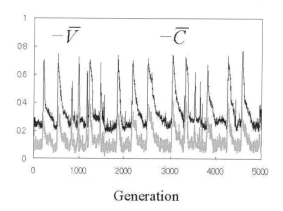

Fig. 4. Example of the failure of the establishment of cooperation in case 2 and 3: the transition of the average cooperativeness $\bar{C}$ and vengefulness $\bar{V}$ from 0 to 5,000 generations

7   Simulation

The number of times cooperation is established in 40 trials of four cases is shown in Table. 2. In regard to these results, we take up the average cooperativeness ($\bar{C}$) and vengefulness ($\bar{V}$) of all players after 5,000 generations and the average payoff of all players. Three typical transitions of the average cooperativeness and vengefulness of all players are shown in Figs. 3, 4, and 5. In these graphs, the horizontal axis represents the generation, and the vertical axis represents the average cooperativeness and vengefulness of all players. The transition of the average payoff of four cases is shown in Fig. 6. In these graphs, the x-axis is the generation, and the y-axis is the average payoff of all players.

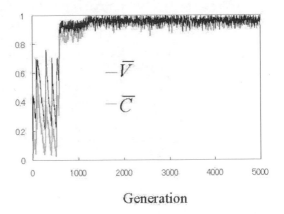

Fig. 5. Example of the establishment of cooperation in case 2, 3, 4: the transition of the average cooperativeness $\bar{C}$ and vengefulness $\bar{V}$ from 0 to 5,000 generations

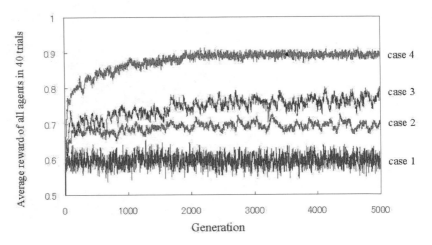

Fig. 6. Transition of the average payoff of all players in 40 trials of four cases of group dynamics

7.1   Establishment of Cooperation

In all trials of case 1, there were little cooperativeness and vengefulness, i.e., cooperation was not established at all within 5,000 generations. The typical behavior of $\bar{C}$ and $\bar{V}$ in case 1 for 5,000 generations is shown in Fig. 3. Throughout the generations, $\bar{C}$ and $\bar{V}$ fluctuated in the range of 0.0 to 0.1. In 36 trials of case 2, cooperation was not established within 5,000 generations. In the remaining 4 trials, there were great deal of cooperativeness and vengefulness, i.e., cooperation was established. In 28 trials of case 3, cooperation was not established within

5,000 generations. In the remaining 12 trials, cooperation was established. In all trials of case 4, cooperation was established.

The typical behavior of $\bar{C}$ and $\bar{V}$ in case 2 and 3 when cooperation was not established within 5,000 generations is shown in Fig. 4. Usually, $\bar{C}$ remained in the range of 0.0 to 0.2 and $\bar{V}$ remained in the range of 0.2 to 0.4. However, occasionally $\bar{C}$ rose to 0.4 and $\bar{V}$ fell to 0.3, and then $\bar{C}$ and $\bar{V}$ returned to their initial states. This fluctuation was repeated throughout the generations.

The typical behavior of $\bar{C}$ and $\bar{V}$ in case 2, 3, 4 when cooperation was established within 5,000 generations is shown in Fig. 5. At first, $\bar{C}$ fluctuated in the range of 0.6 to 0.8 and $\bar{V}$ fluctuated in the range of 0.4 to 0.8, $\bar{C}$ and $\bar{V}$ became about 1.0 in the end. Once $\bar{C}$ and $\bar{V}$ reached 1.0, this state continued to remain there and did not transfer to another state.

7.2   Transition of Average Payoff

The average payoffs of all players in 40 trials of four cases are ranked in descending order as case 4, 3, 2, 1. In the graph of Fig. 6, throughout all generations, the average payoff of unilateral choice continued to fluctuate near 0.6. The average payoff of mutual choice also continued to be near 0.7. The average payoffs of mutual choice with the split rule continued to slightly rise from 0.7 to 0.8. The average payoffs of mutual choice with the split rule and re-offering rose to 0.9 until 2,000 generations. After 2,000 generations, it seldom changed.

8   Discussion

We discuss the establishment of cooperation based on the strategy (C_i and V_i) in four cases and the enhancement of systems' performance based on the average payoff of all players. In the following discussion, a player with a high level of cooperativeness is represented as C_{high}, and a player with a low level of cooperativeness as C_{low}. In the same way, a player with high and low levels of vengefulness are represented as V_{high} and V_{low}, respectively.

8.1   Establishment of Cooperation

Case 1 In all trials of the group dynamics in case 1, why did the establishment of cooperation fail? A player with low cooperativeness by mutation, i.e., a player with C_{high}, cannot acquire a higher payoff than the players with C_{low}. The reason is that the players with C_{high} cannot refuse an offer from the players with C_{low} in group dynamics based on unilateral choice, and the players with C_{low} have a free-ride on the players with C_{high}. Accordingly, the players with C_{high} do not increase in the next generation. Therefore, cooperation is never established.

Case 2 In 36 trials of the group dynamics in case 2, why did the establishment of cooperation fail? We analyze the factors leading to the failure of cooperation based mutual choice.

First, we assumed that there was only one player with C_{high} and V_{high}. Mutation decreases cooperativeness or increases vengefulness because the initial condition is $V_i = 0$ and $C_i = 0$ ($\forall i \in N$). A player with cooperativeness decreased by mutation, i.e., a player with C_{high}, cannot acquire a higher payoff than the players with C_{low} because the players with C_{low} have a freeride on the players with C_{high}. Accordingly, the players with C_{high} do not increase in the next generation. A player with vengefulness increased by mutation, i.e., a player with V_{high}, cannot acquire a higher payoff than the players with C_{low} because players with V_{high} do not join a group consisting of players with C_{low}. Therefore, one player with C_{high} and V_{high} by mutation cannot acquire a higher payoff than the players with C_{low} and V_{low}. Consequently, the player with C_{high} and V_{high} is not selected in genetic operation, and it then perishes.

Next, we assumed that there were several players with C_{high} and V_{high}. If a group consists of only players with C_{high} and V_{high}, the group refuses the offers of players with C_{low}. If a group consists of both players with C_{high} and V_{high} and players with C_{high} and V_{low}, it is possible that a player with C_{low} would join this group and have a free-ride. The player with C_{low} can join the group because, while the players with C_{high} and V_{high} oppose the acceptance of his/her game offer, the players with C_{high} and V_{low} agree to it. If the players with C_{high} and V_{low} win the majority vote over the players with C_{high} and V_{high}, the player with C_{low} can join the group. In such a group, the players with C_{low} have a free-ride on the players with C_{high}. The players with C_{high} and V_{high} are not selected in the genetic operation and then perish because they cannot acquire higher payoffs than the free-rider. Although there are plural players with C_{high} and V_{high}, the players with C_{low} and the players with C_{high} and V_{low} prevent the establishment of cooperation. The players with C_{low} directly prevent the establishment of cooperation because they have a free-ride on the players with C_{high} and V_{high}. On the other hand, the players with C_{high} and V_{low} indirectly prevent the establishment of cooperation because they accept offers from the players with C_{low} who have a free-ride on the players with C_{high}. In group dynamics based on mutual choice, Therefore, the establishment of cooperation often fails.

On the other hand, in the remaining 4 trials, why did the establishment of cooperation succeed? Here, we analyze the factors leading to the establishment of cooperation in group dynamics based on mutual choice. The reason for the establishment of cooperation was that a player with C_{low} can join the group consisting of both players with C_{high} and V_{high} and players with C_{high} and V_{low}. If there are players with C_{high} and V_{high} but no player with C_{high} and V_{low}, the player with C_{low} cannot join the group, and then the players will defect from each other. As a result, the player with C_{low} acquires a lower payoff than the players with C_{high} and V_{high} who cooperate with each other. If the number of players with C_{high} and V_{high} increases, and the players predominate in the population for a few generations before the number of players with C_{high} and V_{low} increases by crossover or mutation, cooperation becomes established. Therefore, since the simulation results show that cooperation was established in 4 out of 40 trials, we can conclude that it is not impossible but difficult to realize the establishment of cooperation in group dynamics based on mutual choice.

Case 3 In 12 trials of group dynamics in case 3, why did the establishment of cooperation succeed? In case 3, the establishment of cooperation fails because the players with C_{high} and V_{low} accept the offer of the players with C_{low}. Here, we analyze the factors leading to the establishment of cooperation in group dynamics based on mutual choice with the split rule.

In group dynamics based on mutual choice with the split rule, if the players with C_{high} and V_{low} agree to accept the offer of a player with C_{low}, and the group as a whole also accepts it, the players with C_{high} and V_{high} leave the group based on the split rule; they refuse to play the dilemma game with those who play with defectors. The split rule prevents the player with C_{low} from having a free-ride on the players with C_{high} and V_{high}. This is because if the player with C_{low} joins the group, the players with C_{high} and V_{high} leave. As a result, if there are some players with C_{high} and V_{high}, they can form a group without the player with C_{low}. The players with C_{high} and V_{high} can acquire higher payoffs because they cooperate with each other. Throughout this process, the number of players with C_{high} and V_{high} increases and they predominate in the population. Therefore, cooperation becomes established.

Case 4 In all trials of group dynamics in case 4, why did the establishment of cooperation succeed? Based on group formation based on mutual choice and group split, a player with C_{high} and V_{high} sometimes leaves from the group and then joins a group consisting of only itself. In this case, the player with C_{high} and V_{high} acquires the payoff of the loner, which is lower than that in a group. If the player with C_{high} and V_{high} has a chance of re-offering, the player leaving from one group may be able to join another group. The player with C_{high} and V_{high} can avoid acquiring a lower payoff by mutual cooperation if another group consists of many players with C_{high}. The re-offering of a player leaving from a group increases the chance for players with C_{high} and V_{high} to acquire a higher payoff. Accordingly, the establishment of cooperation increases because the players with C_{high} and V_{high} do not decrease in the next generation.

8.2   Comparison of Average Payoffs

In this research, we compare the effect of the proposed group dynamics by the average payoff because the average payoff can be considered as a measure of the system performance. Based on the comparison of the average payoffs, the effect of four cases is ranked in descending order as case 4, 3, 2, 1. ¿From the transition of the average payoffs, we can acquire the following results of group dynamics. In relatively early generations, the effect of the split rule doesn't provide good results for the establishment of cooperation because there is not a great difference between case 3 and 4.

152   Tomohisa Yamashita et al.

9 Conclusions

In this paper, in order to enhance the performance of systems consisting of self-interest players, group dynamics was proposed. The partner choice mechanisms for the multiple 2-PD were extended to that for a multiple N-person dilemma game to realize group dynamics. Four kinds of group dynamics, case 1) only group formation based on unilateral choice, case 2) only group formation based on mutual choice, case 3) group formation based on mutual choice and group split, and case 4) group formation based on mutual choice, group split and re-offering were proposed based on the partner choice mechanisms. In order to measure the effect of the proposed group dynamics on the establishment of cooperation and the enhancement of system performance, an agent-based simulation was applied. Agent-based simulations with an evolutionary approach were conducted to confirm whether group dynamics with the split rule could promote cooperative behavior of players and enhance the performance of systems.

On the establishment of cooperation, the following results were confirmed: In group dynamics with only group formation based on unilateral choice, it is impossible to establish cooperation. In group dynamics with only group formation based on mutual choice, it is not impossible but difficult to establish cooperation. Similarly, in group dynamics with only group formation based on mutual choice and group formation, it is difficult to establish cooperation. In group dynamics with only group formation based on mutual choice and group formation and re-offering, it is possible to establish cooperation. Finally, it was confirmed that group dynamics has a large enough effect to increase the performance of systems if the group dynamics includes group split and re-offering.

References

[1] Ashlock, D., Smucker, S. and Stanley, A., Tesfatsion, L.: Preferential Partner Selection in an Evolutionary Study of the Prisoner's Dilemma. BioSystems **37** No. 1-2 (1996) 99–125 139, 142
[2] Axelrod, R.: An Evolutionary Approach to Norms. American Political Science Review **80** (1986) 1095–1111 138, 141
[3] Axelrod, R.: The Evolution of Cooperation. Basic Books, New York (1984) 137
[4] Axelrod, R.: The Complexity of Cooperation. Princeton University Press, New York(1997) 143
[5] Axtell, R.: The Emergence of Firms in a Population of Agents: Local Increasing Returns, Unstable Nash Equilibria, and Power Law Size Distributions. The Brookings Institution CSED Working Paper **3** (2000) 138
[6] Batali, J. and Kitcher, P.: Evolution of Altruism in Optional and Compulsory Games. Journal of Theoretical Biology **175** (1995) 161–171 139
[7] Chen, M. D., Riolo, R. L., Axelrod, R.: The Emergence of Social Organization in the Prisoner's Dilemma: How Context-Preservation and Other Factors Promote Cooperation. Santa Fe Institute Working Paper, 99-01-002, Santa Fe Institute (1999)
[8] Dawes, R. M.: Social Dilemmas. Annual Review of Psychology **31** (1981) 169–193 138

[9] Hauk, E. and Nagel, R.: Choice of Partners in Multiple Prisoner's Two-person Prisoner's Dilemma Games: An Experimental Study. Economics Working Papers, Universitat Pompeu Fabra (2000) 139

[10] Hirshleifer, D. and Rasmusen, E.: Cooperation in a Repeated Prisoners' Dilemma with Ostracism. Journal of Economic Behavior and Organization **12** 87–106 139

[11] Shussler, R.: Exit Threats and Cooperation under Anonymity. Journal of Conflict Resolution **33** (1989) 728–749

[12] Stanley, E. A., Ashlock, D. and Tesfatsion, L.: Iterated Prisoner's Dilemma with Choice and Refusal of Partners. Artificial Life **III** (1994) 131–175 139, 142

[13] Tesfatsion, L.: A Trade Network Game with Endogenous Partner Selection. Kluwer Academic Publishers (1997) 249–269 138, 139, 142

[14] Axtell, R.: Non-Cooperative Dynamics of Multi-Agent Teams. Proceedings of The First International Joint Conference on Autonomous Agents and Multiagent Systems (2002) 1082–1089 137, 138, 142

[15] Caillou, P., Aknine, S. and Pinson, S.: A Multi-Agent Method for Forming and Dynamic Restructuring of Pareto Optimal Coalitions. Proceedings of The First International Joint Conference on Autonomous Agents and Multiagent Systems (2002) 1074–1081

[16] Soh, L. and Tsatsoulis, C.:Satisficing Coalition Formation Agents. Proceedings of The First International Joint Conference on Autonomous Agents and Multiagent Systems (2002) 1062–1063

[17] Luis, J. and Silva, T.: Vowels Co-ordination Model. Proceedings of The First International Joint Conference on Autonomous Agents and Multiagent Systems (2002) 1129–1136

[18] Bicchieri, C.: Rationality and Coordination. Cambridge University Press (1993) 138

[19] Ostrom, E.: Governing the Commons. Cambridge University Press, New York (1990) 138

[20] Hauert, C., Monte, S., Hofbauer, J., Sigmund, K.: Volunteering as Red Queen Mechanism for Cooperation in Public Goods Game. Science **296** (2002) 1129–1132 142

Individual Digital Rights Management in Multi-agent Information Trading Societies

Makoto Amamiya[1], Keith Clark[2], Tadashige Iwao[3], Frank McCabe[4],
Makoto Okada[3], and Jeremy Pitt[2]

[1] Kyushu University, Fukuoka, Japan
amamiya@al.is.kyushu-u.ac.jp
[2] Imperial College London, London, UK
klc@doc.ic.ac.uk
j.pitt@imperial.ac.uk
[3] Fujitsu Kawasaki Laboratories, Tokyo, Japan
iwao@labs.fujitsu.com
okadamkt@flab.fujitsu.co.jp
[4] Fujitsu Laboratories of America, California, USA
fgm@fla.fujitsu.com

Abstract. This position statement identifies a number of future applications of multi-agent systems based on information trading economies for large-scale, file-sharing applications. To achieve mass user support, we identify the key requirement for the realisation of such applications as the representation and management of *individual* digital rights. We outline an academic-industrial, Anglo-Japanese research programme fusing a number of base platforms and technologies, whose long-term goal is the development of full-scale applications.

1 Introduction

The scale of multi-agent systems and technologies is rapidly changing and growing. On the one hand, there is so-called planetary scale computing, where a single software component can access millions of computing devices (for data and/or functionality) anywhere in the entire world. On the other, there is nanotech computing, which anticipates millions of sensors/interfaces recording and reacting to the events and devices within a single location (e.g. a home or office environment).

Our current interest is in applications somewhere in the middle of this range of possibilities. We anticipate the convergence of three new developments:

– hot spot infrastructures using IEEE 802.11b providing fast (11Mbps) wireless internet connections, affording coverage of a reasonably-sized geographical location (e.g. from a shopping mall to a city);
– lower power, high performance computing devices (PDAs) providing location-aware, context-aware, adaptive services and personalized content through a peer-to-peer distributed systems architecture;

K. Kurumatani et al. (Eds.): MAMUS 2003, LNAI 3012, pp. 154–173, 2004.

– personal user agents, collectively organized into an agent society, integrating, managing and coordinating the activities of the entities (individuals and organizations) they represent.

Thus we anticipate a rather more local configuration of data and services (personalized at the point of execution), and rather fewer, and more intelligent computing devices than merely sensors. Nevertheless, the user base is still 'massive', and this imposes a number of demands and requirements on the corresponding multi-agent computing infrastructure, if *mass user support* is to be realised in these applications.

The argument presented in this paper is as follows. We begin with some background material, first presenting a practical experiment recently deployed in Nagoya, Japan, indicating the technological feasibility for the proposed applications. Then, by contrast, we describe a theoretical model of such future computing systems called *the open agent society*. In Section 3, we outline a series of scenarios, which are both extrapolations of the experiment and instances of this theoretical model. These scenarios progressively decentralise the production and management of content, and we analyse the demands and requirements for mass user support this consequently produces. In particular, we argue that the route from practice to theory will be founded on an innovative combination of scientific and engineering methodologies, from platforms through programming languages to theoretical foundations: Section 4 discusses a number of relevant, state-of-the-art contributions. We then present, in Section 5, a description of our overall research programme, an academic-industrial, Anglo-Japanese collaboration involving the fusion of a number of base platforms and technologies based on which we aim to develop applications that satisfy the identified requirements. We make some final remarks in Section 6.

2   Background

2.1   Experiments in Mobile Technology

A large-scale experiment has been performed [15] in an underground shopping mall in the city of Nagoya (Japan) for two weeks, in which about six hundred people participated. The experiment aimed to evaluate the effectiveness of a new peer-to-peer (p2p) framework, in which agents encapsulate user and service information.

Figure 1 shows the experimental setting and a schematic of the wireless LAN access points. The size of the shopping center is about 300m x 100m, and it contains 107 shops. 802.11b was used for the wireless LAN, with ten access points connected by twenty wireless LAN repeaters. Each access point covered an area which included about ten shops. Users join the system through the registration center when they enter the mall.

Each registered user was then given a personal digital assistant (PDA, running WindowsCE). Users then get information delivered to the PDA through a wireless LAN. Typical information might be special offers or bargain prices

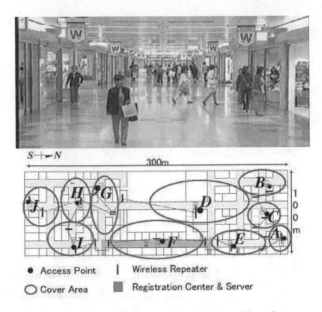

Fig. 1. Shopping Mall: A Scene for Mass User Support

from shops near the user, and so depends on the user's current location. The specific information delivered by a service depends on the user profile, including personal preferences, and the location of users and shops. The PDA then displays only information that matches the user's attributes. For example, the information in a drug store might have two pages, a cosmetics page for women and a shaving lotion page for men. When the user is a woman, or a man seeking a present for a woman, the page displayed should contain the cosmetics information.

The successful outcome of the experiment shows that it is technically feasible (and both commercially desirable and desired by the users) to integrate hot spot infrastructures with low power, high performance computing devices. This provides the foundations for mass user support, e.g. via location- and context-aware services and personalised content, using agents and their appropriate organization into an *open society*.

2.2   The Open Agent Society

We expect that to 'inhabit' future information rich applications, such as that indicated by the experiment of the previous section, will require all the usual human transactions (commerce, gossip, etc.) to be conducted in an unusual social way with new conventions, rules and habits. In particular, each and every interaction is mediated by computers and networks. People will 'meet' other people for whom they do not know the culture, values, habits, expression, and personality, etc. They will also encounter organizational representatives which are not steeped in their culture's mutual knowledge.

In addition to the new forms of human-computer interaction required for this kind of co-operation, we need new forms of computer-computer communication. For example, communication of data implies licensing digital rights with respect to conventions and contracts; some mediating third parties provisioning social order; and new models of acquaintance and reputation between the agents themselves. All of these relationships are primarily *institutional* in the sense of Searle [27, 28]: that is, they are conventionally agreed by the participating agents as part of the 'social contract'. In other words, the agents themselves will need to form a society.

In particular, that society will need to be *open*. By 'open' we mean more than mere access control, but also more than the technical definition of open systems proposed by Hewitt [14] (i.e. heterogeneous components, unpredictable environment, incomplete knowledge, local decision-making, and so on). Some of the characteristics are indicated in [2], in particular the unpredictable behaviour of self-interested agents. However, the major source for our characterisation of the open agent society originates with Popper [25], whose definition of an open (human) society included qualities such as accountability and the division of power, a market economy, the rule of law and respect for rights, and the absence of any universal truth. These qualities are reflected in our model of the open agent society as follows:

- *Accountability*: no information without representation. An information processing component (i.e. an agent) represents a human entity (whether an individual or organization), and the form of that representation needs explicit legal definition, for example in terms of liability, delegation, mandate, ownership and control ([26]);
- *Market Economy*: the content of communication between agents is information, rather than mere data [7]. Data, in itself, is a commodity, but, in electronic form, it is not just data that is traded, but implicitly, and in fact more importantly, the *right* to interpret or use that data in certain ways (that makes it information). Therefore open agent societies require an *information trading* economy;
- *Rule of Law and Respect for Rights*: a key characteristic of openness in social organization lies in the empowerment of its agents, that is in establishing how agents may create their own normative relations (permissions, obligations, rights, powers, etc.), given the existence of norm-sanctioning (both allowing and enforcing) institutions [20];
- *No Universal Truth*: in any practical implementation of an open agent society, any middleware is solely glue between the agent and the network, and not between agents (e.g. as found in the FIPA model [11]). Therefore locally consistent agents can be globally inconsistent, and decentralised models of content production, rights management, conflict resolution and regulation are required.

In the next section, we outline some scenarios which illustrate these characteristics of the open agent society, working towards the decentralisation of content production and rights management.

3   Future Scenarios

This section outlines a series of three scenarios, where we progressively decentralise the production of content and the distribution of rights. Each of these is a technological extrapolation from the practical experiments of Section 2.1, and in the concluding Section 3.5 here, we analyse how the scenarios demonstrate the requirements for information trading and individual rights as manifested in the open agent society.

3.1   Centralised Production & Rights

The first part of the scenario envisages a radio station, broadcasting to a particular geographical region. A song request is in process, which is going to be concluded by the station presented playing a particular song appropriate to the content of the request. A database search is initiated, which returns a number of possible songs and performers, together with the owners of the rights to those songs (in particular, for example, the right to broadcast in that particular geographic region). A negotiation ensues between the radio station agent and the rights manager agent to reach a contract that permits broadcast. Verification of both sides of the contract my be completed with respect to Trusted Third Party agent(s) (TTP), which verify both the identity and legitimacy of the rights holder to the radio station, and the credit rating and complicity of the radio station to the rights holder. The radio station agent then downloads the appropriate file from a data warehouse for playing on air. Note that the work of content creators (bands, orchestras, etc.) is channelled through a production company which owns the intellectual property and copyright, and lodges its digital representation with the TTP, hence both production and rights are centralised.

3.2   Decentralised Production, Centralised Rights

One course of development from the original scenario considers information trading primarily from an individual's perspective. The situation now envisaged is one in which the advances in digital technologies and treatment of information as commodities have fully materialised. We anticipate a situation where content creation is not solely preserve of professional production and publishing companies. This already happens in the case of web sites (i.e. personal home pages), but will increasingly occur for audio, video and more 'traditional' forms of content (e.g. books and plays collectively authored and 'published' over the internet). However, personal content creators may look to organizational database providers and rights managers for distribution, exploitation and protection of their content, hence the decentralisation of content production, but the centralisation of rights management.

3.3 Centralised Production, Decentralised Rights

An alternative course of development takes advantage of advances in network bandwidth and connectivity combined with low-power, high-speed device technology. This makes it technically feasible for 'radio' stations to push content in continuous datastreams to generic 'digital media devices'. This device could be permanently connected to the internet (could be an anytime wireless connection like GPRS (General Packet Radio Service), Bluetooth, could be a cable of some kind). The device contains an agent. The agent is programmable with a user profile, which samples the datastreams and presents content according to expressed preferences and context.

Indeed, it is possible to imagine relatively sophisticated functionality for such an agent: for example, it could schedule entire programmes, for example playlists, news, local information (e.g. weather report on the hour, travel updates every ten minutes), and so on. The agent could also negotiate with the radio station, for example, over the number of adverts per song in lieu of direct charges, but more interestingly over content, e.g. auctions for new content of interest to the user. Thus the agent could have specific responsibility for both service and content adaptation, with particular reference to context. Moreover, the agent ensures that what gets played is only what the owner of this 'digital media device' is entitled to, but there could be a different policy for each agent/device. Thus the management of rights is decentralised.

3.4 Decentralised Production & Rights

For the final scenario, assume a sufficiently large user base that just wants some content (e.g. music, although any other information type, e.g. help files, works equally well). Then with peer-to-peer networking and agent-enabled 'digital media devices', it is possible to eliminate the radio station and the intermediary rights holder (the producers) as profit centres. Content creators and consumers are then aggregated, through the agents functioning on these device, into a loosely affiliated user community. The consumer gets all the content free at the point of access. The creator injects content into the network. Assuming that the creator does want to see some return on their investment, then one possible arrangement to support this relies on:

- *Recommendation*, in the form of word of mouth and tipping points;
- *Reputation*, in the form of 'shareware' attitudes and self-regulation mechanisms (e.g. tit-for-tat),
- *Mass Customization*, by every contract for content being separately negotiated and each article of the contract associated at the very edge of the system, i.e. with the content itself.

3.5   Analysis of the Scenarios

In this section we analyse the implications raised by these scenarios in terms of the requirements of the open agent society to achieve mass user support. The implications concern each of the characteristics of the open agent society referred to earlier, but we also consider some technological assumptions.

Information Trading In all the scenarios, there was a contract, more or less explicitly, being negotiated between two (or more) agents. The contracts themselves are fully executed in a digital environment. The validity of the transaction and the exercising of the rights are, however, underwritten by a number of implicit social and legal relations, i.e. information is a social construct [7]. Furthermore, what is traded is not just the data, but more importantly, a legal position to exploit a copyrighted work (while noting that the exclusive right of making copies is clearly inappropriate in a digital environment).

For example, the dataset {40,11,6} is just data. It becomes information if one knows that these three numbers respectively represent someone's age, the insurance category of his car, and the number of points on his licence. An insurance company agent has the right to use disclosed profile information to compute insurance premiums, but no right to communicate it to the applicant's bank manager or car sales agents. Similarly, digitised audio and video files are just sequences of voltage variations, which can be endlessly cached in networks and copied on hard disks. Arguably, these acts are inconsequential: it is only when the appropriate software is applied to the data that a significant event (in a legal or financial sense) occurs. The significance is whether there was a right to apply the software to the data or not.

Therefore information trading focuses on which actions *count as* establishing certain social, legal or normative positions, and which other acts are, as a consequence, permitted, legal, empowered, and so on.

Respect for Rights Privacy (e.g. of profile information) and protection (e.g. of intellectual property rights) are essential for achieving consumer confidence and critical mass. However, we believe that unbreakable content protection, is unachievable, and the situation is comparable to encryption. That is, what is required is a level of content protection such that the cost of breaking the scheme is more than the value of breaking it.

As part of achieving such consumer confidence, critical mass and content protection, the broadcasters and service providers have to add value, and be perceived (by content creators and consumers) as adding value. Currently, certain organizations are perceived as exploiting the content creators (through unfavourable contracts and royalties) and the general public (through overpriced goods and other marketing practices). (Whether this is true or not is not the issue: the fact is, the *perception* exists.) And while it exists, the hacker who unlocks encryption technologies will be revered as a hero rather than reviled as a pirate.

When invasions of privacy, misuse of rights, or lack of added value do occur, users lose trust in the technology, and/or lose trust in the organisation that introduced or sponsored the technology [5]. The result is large-scale opt-out by users, or imposition of simplistic regulations that stop the distribution of such data altogether (which simply encourages some users to seek new ways of circumventing the regulations). There is therefore a need for mutually trusted mechanisms that adequately protect privacy and rights while allowing the exchange of multimedia content that is beneficial to the originators, broadcasters and users. Regrettably, this mutual trust is currently far from being realised.

Accountability Peer-to-peer systems have the potential to create universal, nearly instantaneous word-of-mouth recommendations between like-minded individuals. If the content creator makes music which is recommended, and the feedback is positive, then the agents will pass the recommendation on. The number of agents involved in the system is such that positive recommendations, from agents with a sufficiently high reputation, will spread very quickly to large numbers. If this number is sufficiently large, then there is a chance that the content will 'tip', to use the term of [13]. This point is when a word of mouth recommendation snowballs, and something of low popularity suddenly becomes in mass demand. If the people behind the demand do apply shareware attitudes, then they will pay for the privilege or right to access the content. Not paying or poor recommendation leads to damaged reputation, which, combined with an appropriate filtering system, leads to a form of social exclusion (rather than formal exclusion). The system is then largely self-regulating.

Technological Assumptions We conclude this section with an indication that considerable amount of technological foundations are required to realise this scenario. In particular, we assume a complete, viable e-commerce infrastructure, including digital signatures, TTP (trusted third parties), PKI (public key infrastructure, MPI (micro payments infrastructure), and so on.

There is considerable existing technology for digital rights management, e.g. XrML [33] and DOI [10]. XrML (eXtensible rights Markup Language) provides a method for securely specifying and managing rights associated with all kinds of resources, including digital content and services. DOI (Digital Object Identifier) is a system for identifying and exchanging intellectual property in the digital environment. It provides a framework for managing intellectual content and enabling automated copyright management for all types of media.

In addition, A number of content adaptation technologies have been developed. The IETF standard CC/PP (Composite Capabilities/Preference Profile) [8] aims to customize the representation of Web content on mobile devices, by defining a hardware profile representing the capabilities of the user device. SLP (Service Location Protocol) [31] provides a protocol for finding services depending on the location of a user device in a mobile environment. iPlanet [24] is a portal server for web services, and customizes content for users who are managed by the server.

4   Technology Integration

Given the existence of the technology briefly mentioned in the previous section, we review here the set of platforms and technologies, whose planned integration forms the basis for our implementation of open agent societies for mass user support.

4.1   Virtual Private Community

In the field trial experiments described above, a new technology was developed, called VPC (Virtual Private Community) [16, 17]. VPC facilitates information change and exchange, depending on user profiles but without disclosure of their attributes. VPC enables services to be described as a rule base. VPC platforms that run on a user device (e.g., a PDA) manage user profiles securely, and deduce appropriate services for users according to specific service descriptions and user attributes.

In VPC, each unit of information is an agent, that can manage itself, controls access rights and interacts with other agents autonomously. Agents in VPC are activated according to users' attributes, including location. VPC also supports collaboration among agents in an ad hoc network under mobile environments. The p2p services are defined as policy packages that consist of conditional rules to activate agents according to users, agent definitions called roles, and contents for the services.

VPC enables information in peer-to-peer services to act as an agent. VPC provides a mechanism that defines an agent behavior, authenticates users, and executes agents. Agents communicate with each other through communities that are created by agents who have accepted the policy packages. Services are offered by interaction among agents in communities. For example, in a music retail service, a policy package contains two agents, an authorized agent who can play the complete music file, and a trial agent which can play only part of the music file. Users who have purchased the music file can listen to the music through authorized agents.

4.2   KODAMA Agent Platform

In a KODAMA system, agents are the basic entities from which the system can be abstracted, organized and composed [34] (see Figure 2).

Agents are basically required to act, at run-time, to achieve both their individual and collective objectives in a worldwide network computing environment such as the Internet. The emphasis on interaction (both agent-to-agent and agent-to-user) also makes multi-agent systems suitable for developing applications for the next-generation web in which agents can help present and manage web resources in an autonomous or semi-autonomous way.

All agents in KODAMA systems are categorized into various agent communities, which in turn are linked together to form a DAG structure (see Figure 2).

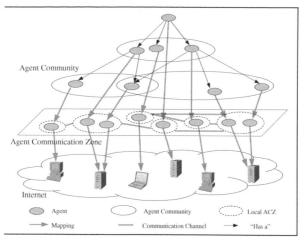

Fig. 2. An overview of the KODAMA system

On the other hand, for building such an agent system directly on top of a distributed network is not feasible, since the network itself is full of latencies and overheads.

In order to solve this problem, KODAMA deploys the agent middleware for the network communication. We call it Agent Communication Zone (ACZ). ACZ is designed to enable agent interactions in an open, worldwide computing environment where both agents and data are distributed and unpredictable. Agents are peer entities, which may reside anywhere and talk with anyone at anytime. To relieve agents from the management of network issues, once agent messages are passed from agents to ACZ, they should be delivered to their destination without further interaction with agents. In order to systematically regulate the low-level network communication processes among instances of ACZ, a new network protocol, called agent platform protocol (APP)[30], has been designed and implemented.

The relations among agents, agent middleware and networks is summarized by a multi-tier model. Typically, all agents speak one or more languages, each of which is an agent communication language (ACL). This layer is a logical world consisting of agents only. Next comes the *agent middleware* layer (or ACZ layer), which plays a vital role in connecting the logical world with the physical world of networks. As a matter of fact, ACZ must be installed on every machine which might have KODAMA agents. Those individually installed ACZs are called *local ACZs* and their host machines are called *agent host machines*. Within one multi-agent system, all instances of agent middleware (e.g. all local ACZs) usually use one specified network protocol, called APP, to interact with each other.

The lowest layer is the *transport* layer in which the transport service is practically realized, and considered as a physical world. There is a de facto standard for the transport layer on the Internet, namely TCP/IP.

This three-tier abstraction model embodies everything that a typical process of agent communication may involve.

4.3   The Go! Programming Language

We intend to implement our agents in a new, multi-paradigm rule based programming language called Go![9]. This has declarative component comprising function and relation rules and an imperative component comprising action rules. Go! also supports object oriented programming using a notation based on McCabe's L&O[21] extension of Prolog. The function and relation rules are used for agent knowledge representation, and the action rules are used for programming agent behaviours. The high integrity of Go! makes it appropriate for representation and reasoning with digital rights.

Go! is also multi-threaded, a feature we consider essential for implementing agents. Threads execute action procedures, calling functions and querying relations as need be. Threads can communicate and coordinate either using asynchronous messages or by using shared dynamic relations acting as Linda [6] memory stores. A thread can suspend waiting for another thread to add or delete some tuple from the shared dynamic relation. To support message communication, each thread has its own buffer of messages it has not yet read, which are ordered in the buffer by time of arrival.

Functions are defined using sequences of function rules of the form:

$$f(A_1,..,A_k)::Test \; => \; Exp$$

where the guard $Test$ is omitted if not required.

Relation definitions comprise sequences of Prolog-style :- relation rules (viz. clauses) with some modifications – such as permitting expressions as well as data terms, and no cut. We can also define relations using *iff* rules.

The locus of action in Go! is a *thread*; each Go! thread executes a procedure. Procedures are defined using non-declarative *action* rules of the form:

$$a(A_1,..,A_k)::Test \; -> \; Action_1;...;Action_n$$

As with equations, the first action rule that matches some call, and whose test is satisfied, is used; once an action rule has been selected there is no backtracking on the choice of rule.

The permissible actions of an action rule include: message dispatch and receipt, I/O, updating of dynamic relations, the calling of a procedure, and the spawning of any action, or sequence of actions, to create a new action thread.

The message send action: $Msg \; >> \; To$ sends the message Msg to the thread identified by the handle To.

To look for any one of several messages, and to act appropriately when one is found, the conditional receive:

$$(\; Ptn_1 \; << \; From_1 \; -> \; Actions_1 \; | \; ...| \; Ptn_n \; << \; From_n \; -> \; Actions_n \;)$$

can be used. When executed, the message buffer of the thread is searched to find the first message that will *fire* one of these alternate message receive rules. The matched message is removed from the message buffer and corresponding actions are executed. Messages that don't match are left in the message buffer for a later message receive to pick up.

The message receive action suspends if matching message is found, causing the thread to suspend. The thread resumes only when a matching message is received. This is the message receive semantics of `Erlang`[1] and `April`[22].

As an example of the use of action rules let us consider programming the top level of an agent with a mission: this is to achieve some fixed goal by the repeated execution of an appropriate action. The two action rule procedure:

```
performMission()::Goal -> {}.
performMission() -> doNextStep; performMission().
```

captures the essence of this goal directed activity. ({} is the empty action.) This procedure would be executed by one thread within an agent whilst another concurrently executing thread is monitoring its environment, constantly updating the agent's beliefs about the environment; these beliefs being queried by *Goal*, and by *doNextStep*. `performMission` is tail recursive procedure and will be executed as an iteration by the Go! engine.

The declarative part of a Go!program can be accessed from action rules in a number of ways:

- Any expression can invoke functions.
- An action rule guard – $(A_1, .., A_k) :: Q$ – can extend the argument matching with a query Q.
- If Q is a query, $\{Q\}$, indicating a single solution to Q, can appear as an 'action' in an action rule body.
- We can use a set expression $\{Trm \mid\mid Q\}$ to find all solutions to some query. This is Go!'s `findall`.
- We can use Go!'s *forall* action. $(Q \ *> \ A)$ iterates the action A over all solutions to query Q.

As an example of the use of *>:

```
(is_a_task(Task),I_cant_do(Task),
cando(Ag,Task)*>request(Task)>>Ag)
```

might be used to send a `request` message for each current sub-task that the agent cannot itself do to some agent it believes can do the task.

4.4   Norm-Governed Interaction

A particular outcome of the EU ALFEBIITE project (IST-1999-10298) was to establish the logical and computational foundations of socially-organized, norm-governed, open distributed (multi-agent) systems. In particular, the project has developed [2, 4, 3]:

- A theoretical framework for the analysis of (social) constraints that govern the behaviour of components in open, norm-governed systems. Such analysis provides an explicit representation of institutional powers, permissions and obligations, and sanctions for 'unacceptable behaviour';
- Formal specifications of such normative concepts using two action description languages from Computer Science, namely extensions of the C+ language [12], and the event calculus [19];
- A computational framework, serving largely as a design tool, supporting executable specification of C+ and/or event calculus descriptions, facilitating prediction, postdiction and planning queries.

The theoretical framework facilitates the analysis and specification of institutional activities in information trading economies. By *institutional*, me mean institutional facts [27] and institutional powers [18], which allow that the performance of certain acts, in particular communicative ones, count as establishing certain facts as true according to the rules of the institution. We generalise this notion by treating certain actions as both initiating and terminating certain normative positions, for example permissions, obligations and indeed institutional powers themselves: see for example [2, 4].

A particular kind of institutional power is the notion of counts-as-in-context [18], which grants that the performance of certain actions by empowered agents, will count as, in the context of an institution or society S, as S itself seeing to that certain institutional facts are true. Introducing $\mathcal{E}_A$ as the relativised (to agents) sees-to-it-that operator and $\Rightarrow_S$ as the relativised (to institutions) counts-as operator, then we write:

$$_S\mathbf{Pow}_a\rho \stackrel{def}{=} \mathcal{E}_A\phi \Rightarrow_S \mathcal{E}_S\psi$$

to denote that a is empowered in/by S to perform action that will count, in S, just as if S saw to it that ψ itself. We say that a has the power ρ.

This is the basic concept, but it turns out that institutional powers are more commonly dynamic or transient, there fore we have to have a formalism that facilitates representation and reasoning of the effects of actions in terms of what facts are initiated or terminated, and under what conditions. Looking ahead, then, to an Event Calculus [19] implementation, such as that in [2], we will specify powers as above, but *codify* powers as Prolog like rules. Note this move is a first approximation to be compatible with existing agent implementations, although we are reducing the modal notion of count as, as formalised in [18] to a simple implication.

Therefore, given the axiom:

$$holdsat(\psi, t_1) \leftarrow$$
$$happens(a : \phi, t_0) \wedge$$
$$initiates(a : \phi, \psi, t_0) \wedge$$
$$t_0 < t_1$$

we can state how institutional facts are initiated or terminated. The domain-independent axiom above states that ϕ holds at time t_1, if agent a performs action ϕ at time t_0, ϕ initiates ψ, and based on some ordering of time points, t_0 is before (earlier than) t_1. In the cases in which we are interested, ϕ initiates ψ if the corresponding institutional power holds, i.e.:

$$initiates(a : \phi, \psi, t_0) \leftarrow$$
$$holdsat(_S\mathbf{Pow}_a\rho, t_0)$$

Correspondingly, we can terminate institutional facts:

$$holdsat(\neg\psi, t_1) \leftarrow$$
$$happens(a : \phi, t_0) \wedge$$
$$terminates(a : \phi, \psi, t_0) \wedge$$
$$t_0 < t_1$$

given:

$$terminates(a : \phi, \psi, t_0) \leftarrow$$
$$holdsat(_S\mathbf{Pow}_a\rho', t_0)$$

where here the institutional power ρ' is specified as:

$$_S\mathbf{Pow}_a\rho' \overset{def}{=} \mathcal{E}_A\phi \Rightarrow_S \mathcal{E}_S\neg\psi$$

5   Research Programme

5.1   Research Plan

The norm-governed approach to specifying open agent societies therefore provides:

- mechanisms for automated self-organization and self-management of components, in particular the introduction of new services;
- precise, formal specifications of the conditions which allow applications to arrange bespoke network services;
- infrastructure to support ad hoc collaborations between groups of agents, in particular for authorizing members of the group;
- normative concepts that arise when addressing issues of trust and security (e.g. from database access control and file sharing to control of service invocation).

Furthermore, while the emphasis is on automation between autonomous components, the appropriate visualisation and explanation of normative and institutional relations is also a sound basis for human interaction and collaboration.

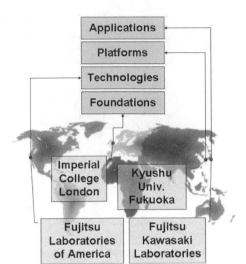

Fig. 3. Research Programme

From this starting point, we aim to work from the theoretical specification of open systems to a physical implementation deployed in practical applications. It is our plan to seek a route from theory to practice founded on an innovative combination of scientific and engineering methodologies as outlined in Section 4. We propose to specify and design open agent societies using the theoretical framework, appropriately enriched to analyse further normative relations required for a particular agent community; to implement this framework in agents programmed in Go!, organise the secure distribution of such agents using the KODAMA framework, and test the resulting system through the implementation, deployment and evaluation of practical instantiations of the agent community as a VPC.

Figure 3 presents an illustration of our overall research programme: an Anglo-Japanese collaboration involving the fusion of a number of base platforms and technologies based on which we aim to develop application scenarios of the kind identified in section 3. In particular, we take a vertical slice through the 'levels' of R&D: foundations, technologies, platforms and applications, and seek to integrate them as outlined above. Imperial College London are developing the scientific foundations for open agent societies, Fujitsu Laboratories of America are leading development of the technology (the programming language Go!), Kyushu University are developing the platform (KODAMA), and Fujitsu Kawasaki Laboratories are leading development of the applications.

5.2   An Example

In this final subsection, we consider, by way of an example, how the integration of the technologies described in section 4, following the research plan above, serves to:

- contribute to mass user and society services;
- address issues raised in the discussion of the scenarios in section 3; and
- provide mass users' utility over mere personal information services.

For our example, consider a music (file) sharing community S. Essentially, we can use some form of role-assignment protocol which can be used to allocate to certain agents a role they will occupy in a certain Virtual Private Community. For example, following [2], each of these roles will be associated with a set of preconditions which the agent must satisfy in order to occupy that role, and a set of constraints that describe the behaviour of the agent while occupying that role (with respect to what is 'meaningful', 'valid' or 'legal').

So, following the original example of [17], let us assume three levels of membership, l_0 for non-member, l_1 for trial member, and l_2 for full member. A non-member may apply to become a trial member, and a trial member can apply for full membership. A non-member has no permission (right) to play any of the music files, a trial member can play samples, and a full member has unlimited playing rights. A membership secretary is responsible for processing applications and assigning member levels. All of these are in a sense roles in the community, and confer certain institutional powers. Assume communicative acts apply, assign and revoke: let j and k be specific agents (and A be a variable over agents) and let e.g. j : assign(k, ϕ) denote agent j communicating to k the message assign with content ϕ. Then we can specify the institutional powers associated with the roles as follows, where the act counts as, according to the rules of community S, initiating and terminating new institutional facts, from which we can infer new powers, permissions and obligations.

There are three powers in this simple example, ρ_1, ρ_2 and ρ_3, specified by:

$$_S\mathbf{Pow}_k\rho_1(A, L) \stackrel{def}{=} \mathcal{E}_k\mathsf{assign}(A, L) \Rightarrow_S$$
$$\mathcal{E}_S\, member(A, L, S)$$

$$_S\mathbf{Pow}_k\rho_2(A, L) \stackrel{def}{=} \mathcal{E}_k\mathsf{revoke}(A, L) \Rightarrow_S$$
$$\mathcal{E}_S\neg member(A, L, S)$$

$$_S\mathbf{Pow}_A\rho_3(L) \stackrel{def}{=} \mathcal{E}_A\mathsf{apply}(k, L, S) \Rightarrow_S$$
$$\mathcal{E}_S\, application(A, L, S)$$

The aim here is to give agent k the power to assign and revoke membership 'levels', where different levels of membership will provide different permissions (here k is the membership secretary). However, this power is not total: we would not want k arbitrarily assigning membership to all and sundry. Therefore this power will only be enabled by an application, specifically to k, and that is the third power.

This analysis is codified as axioms:

$$initiates(k : \mathsf{assign}(A, L), member(A, L), t) \leftarrow$$
$$holdsat(_S\mathbf{Pow}_k\rho_1, t)$$
$$terminates(k : \mathsf{revoke}(A, L), member(A, L), t) \leftarrow$$
$$holdsat(_S\mathbf{Pow}_k\rho_2, t)$$
$$initiates(A : \mathsf{apply}(A, L, S), application(A, L), t) \leftarrow$$
$$holdsat(_S\mathbf{Pow}_A\rho_3, t)$$

We then require the following implications which hold at all time points t:

$$holdsat((application(A, L, S) \rightarrow {}_S\mathbf{Pow}_k\rho_1(A, L)), t)$$
$$holdsat(((c_1(A, L) \wedge \ldots \wedge c_n(A, L)) \rightarrow {}_S\mathbf{Per}_k\rho_1(A, L)), t)$$
$$holdsat((member(A, l_1, S) \rightarrow {}_S\mathbf{Per}_A sample\_play), t)$$
$$holdsat((member(A, l_2, S) \rightarrow {}_S\mathbf{Per}_A full\_play), t)$$
$$holdsat((_S\mathbf{Per}_A\rho_3(l_1)), t)$$
$$holdsat((member(A, l_1, S) \rightarrow {}_S\mathbf{Per}_A\rho_3(l_2)), t)$$

The first formula ensures that an application by any agent gives k the power to assign that agent to the requested level. Note that while k may have the power, it may may not have the permission to exercise that power unless A also satisfies the conditions $c_1, \ldots, c_n$. If an agent becomes a member at level l_1, then it has sample playing permission, and at level l_2 it has full playing permission. Every agent has the power to apply for membership at level l_1; becoming a member at this level then gives the power to make applications at the higher level.

Finally, we have not yet said anything about k's power of revocation. Again, this is not a power which k should have at all times: k should only be empowered to revoke membership if an agent has done something 'wrong', as it were. We will say that an agent is sanctioned in such case. One possible sanction could be caused by an agent attempting a full play without permission (i.e. it is only a level l_1 member). Then k may have the power to revoke A's membership, which will be terminated. Thus we have:

$$initiates(A : full\_play, sanctioned(A), t) \leftarrow$$
$$\neg holdsat(_S\mathbf{Per}_A full\_play, t)$$
$$holdsat((sanctioned(A) \rightarrow {}_S\mathbf{Pow}_k\rho_1(A, l_1)), t)$$

We have now specified a (simple) system of norm-governed interaction. This could be used in either the Society Visualiser developed in [ ], using Event

Calculus implementations directly, or by using an alternative action description language such as C/C+ ([12] and corresponding tool CCalc [23, 20]), or even by developing new action languages altogether [29]. In either of these cases, our next step is to encode such specifications in Go!, either using Prolog features of the language itself, or by using other tools (e.g. CCalc) as separate services. These Go! agents can then be incorporated as components in the KODAMA agent platform and architecture, as indicated above, which in turn is used to implement Virtual Private Communities.

It is our conjecture – which remains to be validated by further research and development – that this approach provides the foundations for developing and deploying open-ended applications, where content-production and right management are completely decentralised (as per the scenario described in section 3.4).

Furthermore, this approach to digital right managements addresses other issues raised with respect to this scenario, in particular the issue of information trading. Social constraints, formalised in electronic societies and represented by deontic concepts and/or normative positions of the kind described above, can be used to implement socially-organized, norm-governed, open distributed multi-agent systems. It is then our second conjecture, that this will be the basis for other system properties that, in other research, we have referred to as supra-functional requirements (i.e. system requirements that are not functional or non-functional, for example, in our case, to "create loyalty" [32]). In information trading applications, we are now thinking in terms of user trust and satisfaction, based on qualities like privacy, accountability and respect for rights; and other benefits of emergent behaviour stemming from recommendation and reputation systems. It is this outcome, if realised, that contributes to mass user or society support, by maximising the mass of the users' utility, profit or expectation, and of the society as a whole, way beyond that which could be derived by mere personal information services.

6   Summary & Conclusions

We detect considerable technology push and application pull in what is coming to be called *pervasive computing*. The technology push is provided by a combination of advances in high bandwidth wireless networks, low power high performance computing devices, and significant developments in sensor technology. The application pull is coming from tools for 'professional' digital production of content by individuals and bottom-up, community-based sharing of information. These applications involve large scale communities of users, and we have argued that alongside the decentralisation of production, a decentralisation of digital rights management is also required.

This paper has then identified a set of platforms and technologies whose integration is aimed at providing support for large scale electronic communities through individual digital rights management. This localisation of rights with content and the use of agent technology to individually manage those rights is fully in keeping with the 'intelligence at the edge' paradigm of peer-to-peer computing, and, we believe, lays the foundations for mass user support in pervasive computing applications which involve information trading economies within societies of agents.

We have outlined a research programme developing, integrating and applying these technologies. However, it should be clear that we are at the first stages of this programme: the intention of the current article is primarily to articulate a position statement which stimulates discussion within and enables feedback from the community.

Acknowledgements

This work has been partially supported by the EU FET ALFEBIITE Project (IST-1999-10298), the British Council/Monbusho, and the UK Royal Society. We gratefully acknowledge the support that has made this collaboration possible. Thanks to the anonymous reviewers for their useful comments.

References

[1] J. Armstrong, R. Virding, and M. Williams. *Concurrent Programming in Erlang*. Prentice-Hall International, 1993. 165

[2] A. Artikis, J. Pitt, and M. Sergot. Animated specifications of computational societies. In C. Castelfranchi and L. Johnson, editors, *Proceedings AAMAS'02*, pages 1053–1062. ACM Press, 2002. 157, 165, 166, 169, 170

[3] A. Artikis, M. Sergot, and J. Pitt. An executable specification of an argumentation protocol. In *Proceedings of Conference on Artificial Intelligence and Law (ICAIL)*. ACM Press, 2003. 165

[4] A. Artikis, M. Sergot, and J. Pitt. Specifying electronic societies with the causal calculator. In F. Giunchiglia, J. Odell, and G. Weiss, editors, *Proceedings AOSE'03*, volume LNCS2585, page to appear. Springer-Verlag, 2003. 165, 166

[5] D. Brin. *The Transparent Society*. Addison-Wesley, 1998. 161

[6] N. Carriero and D. Gelernter. Linda in context. *Communications of the ACM*, 32(4):444–458, 1989. 164

[7] C. Castelfranchi. The social nature of information and the role of trust. In M. Klusch and F. Zambonelli, editors, *Proceedings Cooperative Information Agents V*. Springer-Verlag, 2001. 157, 160

[8] CC/PP. Composite capability/preference profiles (cc/pp). http://www.w3.org/TR/NOTE-CCPP, 1999. 161

[9] K.L. Clark and F.G. McCabe. Go! – a high integrity logic programming language. Technical report, Available from authors, 2002. 164

[10] DOI. Digital object identifier system. www.doi.org. 161

[11] FIPA. FIPA'97 specification part 1: Agent platform. FIPA (Foundation for Intelligent Physical Agents), http://www.fipa.org, 1997. 157

[12] E. Giunchiglia and V. Lifschitz. An action language based on causal explanation: Preliminary report. In *Proceedings AAAI*, pages 623–630. 1998. 166, 171

[13] M. Gladwell. *The Tipping Point*. Little, Brown, 2000. 161

[14] C. Hewitt. Open information systems: Semantics for distributed artificial intelligence. *Artificial Intelligence*, 47(1–3):79–106, 1991. 157

[15] T. Iwao, Y. Wada, M. Okada, and M. Amamiya. Experiments with virtual private community (vpc) framework. In *CIA'02*, volume LNCS2446. Springer, 2002. 155

[16] T. Iwao, Y. Wada, S. Yamasaki, M. Shioucji, M. Okada, and M. Amamiya. A framework for the next generation of e-commerce by peer-to-peer contact: Virtual private community. In *WETICE'01*, pages 340–341. IEEE, 2001. 162

[17] T. Iwao, Y. Wada, S. Yamasaki, M. Shioucji, M. Okada, and M. Amamiya. Collaboration among agents in a logical network of peer-to-peer services. In *SAINT'02*, pages 6–7. IEEE, 2002. 162, 169

[18] A. Jones and M. Sergot. A formal characterisation of institutionalized power. *Journal of the Interest Group in Pure and Applied Logics*, 4(3):429–455, 1996. 166

[19] R. Kowalski and M. Sergot. A logic-based calculus of events. *New Generation Computing*, 4(1):67–96, 1986. 166

[20] V. Lifschitz. Missionaries and cannibals in the causal calculator. In A. Cohn, F. Giunchiglia, and B. Selman, editors, *Proceedings Conference on Principles of Knowledge Representation and Reasoning)*, pages 85–96. Morgan Kaufmann, 2000. 171

[21] F.G. McCabe. *L&O: Logic and Objects*. Prentice-Hall International, 1992. 164

[22] F.G. McCabe and K.L. Clark. April - Agent PRocess Interaction Language. In N. Jennings and M. Wooldridge, editors, *Intelligent Agents, LNAI, 890*. Springer-Verlag, 1995. 165

[23] N. McCain. Causality in commonsense reasoning about actions. Ph.D. Thesis, University of Texas at Austin, 1997. 171

[24] Sun MicroSystems. iplanet. http://sdc.sun.co.jp/iplanet/product.html. 161

[25] K. Popper. *The Open Society and its Enemies: Volume 1: The Spell of Plato*. Routledge (5th Edition), 1962. 157

[26] G. Sartor and J. Bing (eds.). Legal transfer. EU ALFEBIITE Project Deliverable D9, 2003. 157

[27] J. Searle. *Speech Acts: An Essay in the Philosophy of Language*. Cambridge University Press, 1969. 157, 166

[28] J. Searle. *Mind, Language and Society: Philosophy in the Real World*. Basic Books, 1999. 157

[29] M. Sergot. The language $(\mathcal{C}/\mathcal{C}+)^{++}$. In J. Pitt, editor, *The Open Agent Society*. Wiley, 2003. 171

[30] K. Takahashi, G. Zhong, D. Matsuno, S. Amamiya, T. Mine, and M. Amamiya. Agent platform protocol: A network protocol for global multi-agent systems. In *LNAI*. Springer-Verlag, to appear (2003). 163

[31] J. Veizades, E. Guttman, C. Perkins, and S. Kaplan. Service location protocol. IETF RFC 2165, 1997. 161

[32] M. Witkowski, B. Neville, and J. Pitt. Agent mediated retailing in the connected local community. *Interacting with Computers*, 15:5–32, 2003. 171

[33] XrML. Extensible rights mark-up language. www.xrml.org. 161

[34] G. Zhong, S. Amamiya, K. Takahashi, T. Mine, and M. Amamiya. The design and application of kodama system. *IEICE Transaactions INF.&SYS.*, E85-D(4):637–646, 2002. 162

Fairy Wing: Distributed Information Service with RFID Tags

Eiji Murakami and Takao Terano

Graduate School of Systems Management, University of Tsukuba, Tokyo
3-29-1, Otsuka, Bunkyo-ku, Tokyo 112-0012, Japan
{murakami,terano}@gssm.otsuka.tsukuba.ac.jp

Abstract. Information recommendation in E-commerce applications often uses a social filtering method to cluster similar users based on their profiles, characteristics or attitudes on specific subjects. This paper describes Fairy Wing: a distributed information service system, which utilizes Radio Frequency Identification (RFID) tags as portable media for user-computer interaction with inexperienced users. The characteristics of the proposed system are summarized as follows: (1) The system is installed on small PCs with a reasonable RFID reader/writer and works with/without computer networks (2) It is effective in distributed computer environments even for a small number of users. (3) It gradually accumulates users' profiles from individual behaviors then generates recommendations and advice for each user. A prototype system has been implemented and validated on user navigation in a shopping mall.

1 Introduction

Social filtering is a way of clustering similar users based on profiles, characteristics or attitudes on specific subjects [1]. The techniques are often used in E-commerce applications to recommend appropriate consumer goods to a specified groups of customers [2]. The techniques involve recommendation of items liked by other similar users. Thus, to implement the methods, we analyze ratings of items by users to classify the users into groups, so that users in a particular group share similar interests. Then, a user is recommended items which similar users have rated highly and he/she has not looked at.

Examples of Collaborative-filtering recommendation are found in the systems: GroupLends [3] and Firefly [4]. Social filtering deals with any kind of contents, because the system need not analyze contents to generate recommendations. There are, however, shortcomings which are summarized in [2]; we need to have enough users and enough rating information compared with the number of items[5]. When the number of users is small, recommended items will become only a small part of the total items [6].

To utilize the benefits and to overcome the difficulty, this paper describes a PC-based distributed agent system [7]. The system utilizes Radio Frequency Identification (RFID) tags and/or smart IC cards [8] as portable media for user-computer interaction and data assistants for inexperienced users.

K. Kurumatani et al. (Eds.): MAMUS 2003, LNAI 3012, pp. 174-189, 2004.
© Springer-Verlag Berlin Heidelberg 2004

The performance of recent RFID tags and/or smart IC cards is equal to the performance of micro-computer kits about twenty years ago, thus, we use RFID tags and/or IC cards as a medium for human-computer interaction to implement a social filtering system [9]. The idea is implemented in Fairy Wing, another mobile computing system for community computing in a digital city [10]. The system aims at supporting personal information management and information services [11].
This paper describes a simplified version of Fairy Wing for practical use and the implementation of the prototype information service system in a shopping mall.

2 Background

In this section, we will describe the background, motivation, and objectives of our work from the viewpoint of social requirements, RFID Tags and/or smart IC cards, and software technology on agent-based systems.

2.1 Social Requirement

In a shopping mall or tourist area customers often require up-to-date information and shop managers would like to establish good relationships with customers. To cope with these problems, we examine the following three issues:

Issue 1: The first issue is the user skills needed and the cost of computer equipment. Even recently available small personal data assistants are too difficult and too expensive for people who are not familiar with PCs. Although the virtual space of the WWW means we have no logical boundaries to limit us, we have physical and mental restrictions among people and cities. Barriers are much greater than those in physical towns because we cannot directly touch, speak, or hear other people who are not connected with computers and networks. Skills and money are required for computers to fulfill their function.

Issue 2: The second issue is the management of a large amount of information on people and the town. In order to make things run smoothly, large databases must be maintained. There are two categories of database. The first one covers city resources; this must be frequently updated as new things are introduced. Of course, catalog and logistical information on commercial goods must also be kept up to date. The second category covers personal information which must be provided, collected and managed. The cost of maintaining information will become too high, even if it is controlled by local government.

Issue 3: The third issue is the problem of security and privacy. It is repeatedly reported that companies participating in electronic commerce pay a high cost to maintain customer databases, however, security holes still occur. As stated in [12], there is a delicate balance between protecting the privacy of citizens and facilitating the sharing of information. Therefore, for a good community to develop in a city [13], some kind of user-centered information control mechanism is essential.

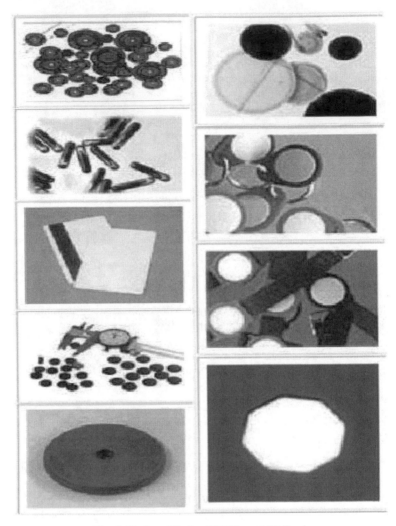

Fig. 1. Various Kinds of RFIDs and IC Cards

In summary, systems to support communities must cope with: (1) cost and ease-of-use, (2) information management, and (3) security and privacy. To meet the requirements, it is desirable to develop distributed cooperative systems [14] to support personal information management, information services, and dynamic social filtering.

2.2 RFIDs and Smart IC Cards

To date, it is reported that over one billion smart cards have been issued. Recently, RFID tags have also shown the capacity to maintain a limited amount of information. The main purposes of such new devices have been limited to e-cash, including advanced credit card or debit card systems, storing personal information such as health care, e-tickets for traveling in everyday life, and address tags for mailing.

However, research and development work is too concentrated on security issues and has not attempted to focus on utilizing the potential of the devices as computers, when they have the same capacity as the micro computers of twenty years ago.

The current costs of the IC card and/or RFID tags and the reader/writer are respectively about 10-20 US$ and 100-200 US$. Thus, from both computational and cost-based viewpoints, the performance of the small devices is between that of conventional magnetic cards and conventional personal data assistants. It is reasonable to deploy these devices for inexperienced users and to use PCs with the reader/writers.

Fig.1 shows the devices we used to implement the prototype system.

2.3 Field of Application

The main conventional applications of RFID and Smart IC Card cover such areas: 1) use as an electronic commuter pass in transportation such as trains and buses, 2) use as a sophisticated financial card instead of a usual electromagnetic card as ATM cards of banks and credit cards in financial markets, 3) use as an electronic expense sheet instead of paper expense sheet used in business transaction, 4) use as an electronic tag to guarantee the quality of a product by clarifying its marketing channel.

Research and development of RFIDs and Smart IC Cards have depended on their applications. The device to deal with pecuniary exchange such as electronic money requires an advanced security function. The device used as electronic money is generally expensive since it is equipped with such a security function. On the other hand, when a security function is unnecessary and when the memory installed in the device is small, the device will become low cost. The application utilizing such a cheap device has an advantage for both sides who operate the application and who eventually utilize the application. Low-price and low-end device without a security function will be widely used due to the increase of the memory capacity and the further price-reduction in the future. For example, Hitachi Inc. has presented a new tag with less than 10 yen cost per device in December, 2003.

A practical Suica system East Japan Railway Company, which possesses both functions as a commuter pass and electronic money [15], has gained two million users in approximately two months from the beginning of its service in November, 2001 in Tokyo, and the number of the users has been increasing since then.

The device with an electronic money function such as Suica is equipped with the firewall feature and excels at security. However, the device does not have flexibility, and the application design has restrictions. On the other hand, a cheap device is inferior in terms of its security, but it has lesser restrictions in using the device. Thus, a flexible application can be designed. If the device without a security function were equipped with an electronic money function, it would be required to develop strategies, so that a crime, an operational error, a trouble of the system would not cause the change in the value of the electronic money. Since the strategies inevitably become large-scale, the flexibility which inheres in the device would be lost.

Both expensive and cheap devices have different application areas to utilize their unique characteristics.

2.4 Coping with the Issues of Information Services via Small Devices

Using the functions of the small devices, we can overcome the issues discussed above. The system consists of personal information in the small devices, information services in PCs with and/or without networks, and pointers to the resources of a city. We assume that there exist ubiquitous information terminals in the physical towns and that sufficient information for daily life is available [16].

About **Issue 1:** our approach is that (1) we provide the target place with holders' personal information within the small devices, and (2) fully distributed systems are developed to compensate for the defects of current PDAs and information terminals by integrating both personal and public information. Current PDAs are more flexible than PCs, because they are fully personalized for the holders. On the other hand, information terminals in a city can have much more powerful user interfaces than those of current PDAs with a small display and narrow communication channels. Using the personal information in the small devices, according to the context, situation and wishes of the users, we can manage the functions of the information services.

About **Issue 2:** our systems will work without central personal information databases and any specific information control mechanisms in the center. End users are responsible for their personal information and usages. Fairies contain sufficient personal information to access the services of the digital cities. Thus, users or device-holders can actively control the availability or privacy of their personal information. For example, users mask any personal information depending on the features of target applications [17]. Fairies will also contain footprints or recent access records to the applications. This footprint information can be used as bookmarks to get corresponding information services. The information can be used as the key to directly access the desired information on stand-alone type information terminals. This reduces the development cost of information services. For example, users can access the appropriate information while moving around the targeted place.

About **Issue 3:** our policy is that holder centered control mechanisms are essential. Fairies containing personal information are fully distributed. Thus, compared with centralized personal database systems, complex management tasks for personal information are avoided. Users must be responsible for their own information. It would be a desirable feature for the activities to be governed in a bottom-up manner. As the personal information is contained in Fairies, under the holders' control, it can be dynamically integrated into the information terminals. This enables users to support community formation tasks via social filtering. Conventional filtering algorithms usually assume that very large amounts of data are available in the analysis and, therefore, the algorithm must be kept simple in order to handle the large amount of data in a reasonable time. As Fairy-based systems will dynamically analyze small amounts of the data on user access information, we can implement sophisticated algorithms.

3   Fairy Wing: Yet Another Mobile Computing System

This section describes the architecture of Fairy Wing and the feasibility of the systems.

3.1 System Components and How They Work

The proposed system consists of (1) Smart Cards and/or RFIDs with Fairies for storing and managing personal information, (2) Ubiquitous information terminals with device readers/writers, and (3) Distributed information space [18], which does not necessarily assume the existence of centralized data warehouses or communication networks. Fig.2 shows the conceptual architecture of Fairy Wing. In subsequent sections, we will describe the features of each component.

Fig. 2. General Architecture of the Fairy Wing System

3.1.1   Fairy Wing Devices

Fairy Wing Cards or RFIDs are flexible, easy-to-use, and cheap mobile terminals corresponding to conventional PDAs. The small devices contain (1) the security information, or the pin number of the holder, (2) personal information, which can be masked per data item by users in order to conceal or reveal individual information, (3) the user's footprints which maintain past records of activities in a digital city, and (4) local information, which must be transferred among information terminals.

If necessary, each Fairy can transfer information to conventional personal data assistant systems or to a user's own PC. Furthermore, the design of the equipment with Fairies can be in any shape or form; for example, it can be like a notebook page, a leaflet, a button, and/or any wearable style. All information in the cards is under control of the device holder, thus, he or she must be responsible for managing and maintaining it. When a device-holder loses his or her device, immediately he or she can distribute the information that the device is no longer valid for the applications. This is easily done by accessing the ubiquitous information terminals. All the user need do is to give the information about the specific card ID to the applications. Then the information will immediately be widely distributed.

3.1.2   Information Terminals

Users interact with the ubiquitous information terminals, which should be equipped with easy-to-use and look-and-feel interfaces for inexperienced users (for example, touch screens and voice information guidance are desirable). The terminals have a reader/writer for the devices. Users start the session by inserting their devices in the reader/writer. When Fairy Wings are inserted into the terminals, the terminal will show the most appropriate information to the user based on the stored information in the terminal and the footprints on the Fairy Wing.

The information terminals are basically client systems connected with total information servers in the targeted area. However, they are not necessarily networked, if the terminals have enough information for the current users. This is because the Fairies contain footprint information, so that the information providing task can be performed in stand-alone type terminals. This capability will reduce the cost of system deployment.

3.1.3   Information Space

Users of Fairy-Wing connect to the information services based on the information of Fairies and information terminals. Fairy Wings are used both in virtual and physical information spaces. For example, in the virtual space shown in a private PC, users can explore digital city malls based on personal information and can buy favorite things, based on the concepts of relationship marketing. They also unite the user community based on the filtering mechanisms [19]. On the other hand, in the physical space, the user will have appropriate information or recommendations from the digital city via information terminals and/or private PCs, based on the footprint information.

3.2 Discussion on the Applicability of Fairy Wing

The unique characteristics of Fairy Wing lie in the fact that all private information is contained only in users' own Fairies and not in central control and maintenance mechanisms. In summary, the development of Fairy Wing will benefit users in the following ways:

(1)   Users are responsible for their own privacy, thus, they can be active in concealing and revealing private information.
(2)   The target place provides citizens with appropriate information based on content and context. As the information controls depend on the information of Fairies, the recommendation information can be available even if the information terminals are not connected with computer networks.
(3)   The application systems at each information terminal can be developed separately, because Fairies can maintain both static and dynamic personal information.

(4)   Complex user management systems are not necessary in the central server systems, thus, system development and maintenance will become easier.

(5)   Collaborating filtering systems can be supplied in each information terminal; therefore, interfacing with a specific terminal, users can form communities with the same interests or subjects.

4   A Prototype Information Service

To assess the feasibility of Fairy Wing, we have developed a prototype system to navigate visitors in a shopping mall of a Japanese city. For rapid and simpler implementation, we decided to remove the organizational learning mechanism [20] among users from the previous version described in [21]. However, as described above, the system is intended to realize (1) cost-effective and ease-of-use environments, (2) distributed information management, and (3) holder-centered security and privacy controls.

The hardware devices used in the prototype are shown is Fig.3. The system consists of (1) a few PCs for user registration, which are used to issue and initialize the devices with personal information, and (2) an adequate number of PCs for information terminals at shops in the mall with an IC card reader/writer.

Fig. 3. Hardware Devices for the Prototype (from left to right: coin type RFID, stand-alone PCs, servers, network)

4.1 Issues of the Task Domain

Hitherto, in the field of city planning, the slumism of old towns is a serious issue. There are several reasons for the slumism; one of the reasons is that, as the commercial district of the old town has lost its customers, because most of them go to the shopping center in the suburb area convenient for car drivers, and as a result,   the number of people who visit the old town has decreased. This has caused the loss of the vitality.

Ibusuki City, Kagoshima Prefecture, is the experimental location for the proposed application.   Ibusuki is a sightseeing spot with three million tourists every year. However, the tourists' purpose is to go to hot spring resorts outside the old town, and they do not visit there. Thus, we will consider the information service to facilitate the vitalization of the commercial district of the old town.

Using RFID tags, we have developed a system to facilitate consumer purchasing in the commercial district of the old town. This system is characterized by the function as an electronic coupon to enhance buying motivation, and consumers will accumulate rewards with each purchase. The accumulated rewards are exchanged, as regional currency, for delivery of the products, nursing service, and other services within the commercial district of the old town. Moreover, it is possible to flexibly give preferential treatment to the consumers who make a number of purchases in a short term by giving bonus rewards in order to encourage them to purchase.

Regarding the scale of the system, it is assumed that total ten thousand RFID tags are distributed and that ten thousand people utilize them in a particular area. To carry outfirst step experiments, we have focused on the event related to the training camp of the France team for the World Cup Soccer 2002 in Ibusuki City.   The event was held in June 2002. The prototype information service system with electronic coupons has been implemented for the purpose.

Fig.4 shows a demonstration displays.

The prototype was designed to demonstrate the performance of such information services at a shopping mall in Ibusuki City, Japan, during the 2002, Soccer World Cup. The duration from initial design and demonstration was only two months. Using the system architecture of the previous version, implementation was successful.

End user interfaces are implemented as additional functions of a current web browser, therefore, if users are familiar with web surfing, they can easily enjoy the prototype system.

Fig. 4. Prototype Demonstration at a Shopping Mall

4.2 Contents of Information Service Carried Out in Old Town

Fig.5 indicates the geographic information of the old town which is the experimental location. This is the area with a radius of approximately three kilometers with a large park in the center and the seashore on the right of the map. Since this area is flat, people can move a place to another in the map within approximately 45 minutes at the longest.

The Central Park functions as the event site in commemoration of the World Cup Soccer and has the head office in June 2002. The system operates the information service for the vitalization of the commercial district in the old town. That is, it is an electronic coupon system, issues coupons at the administration head office located in the Central Park, and distributes the coupons to the users. For the duration of the event, if users purchase in the commercial establishment located within the area indicated in Fig.5, the rewards depending on the amount of the purchase are accumulated on this electronic coupon. When the number of the rewards reaches to a certain number, the user can exchange for other multiple services operated in the particular commercial district. Fig.6 indicates the system administration model of the electronic coupons.

4.3 The Electronic Coupon System to Operate the Information Service

The electronic coupons are used in the area with a radius of three kilometers indicated in Fig.5. We assume that the people who possess the electronic coupons make their way only on foot in the area. The system is designed to satisfy the following purposes.

1)   When recording the number of rewards on the electronic coupons at the purchase, the recommended information as a place to visit next is presented, and the information to encourages the purchaser to move to another place is provided.
2)   This information includes the one which directly and/or indirectly encourages consumers to make another purchase at another location.

At the purchase in an outlet, the consumers who possess the electronic coupons place the RFID which is, in fact, the electronic coupon, onto the RFID Reader and Writer indicated in Fig.3. The system communicates with this device, adds the rewards, and shows the following information on the TFT display.

1)   The number of rewards after the accumulation and the reminder of the service which can be exchanged for the number of the rewards.
2)   The information which encourages to consumers to move.

Fig.7 shows information terminal of this system.
The purpose to encourage the consumers to move is important for the following reasons. The area indicated in Fig.5 is thinly populated potentially. In order to vitalize this area utilizing this small population effectively, the encouragement of the movement of the consumers plays an important role. The movement and eventual interaction between people can vitalize the region and eventually vitalize the commercial activities. The system actively delivers and allows the TFT display to

show not only the information which directly or indirectly leads the consumers to a purchase, but also the local information which is unrelated to a purchase.

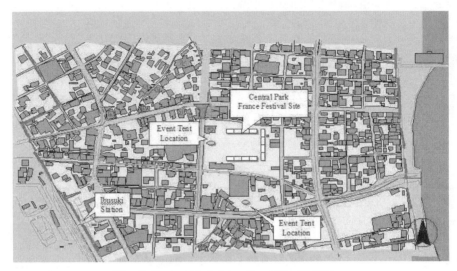

Fig. 5. Geographic Information of the Old Town

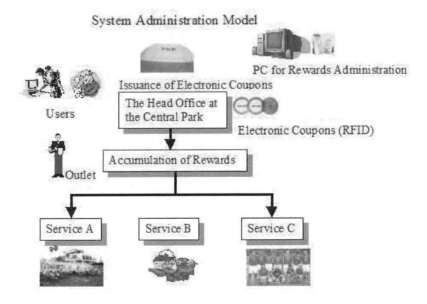

Fig. 6. Abstraction of Electronic Coupon System

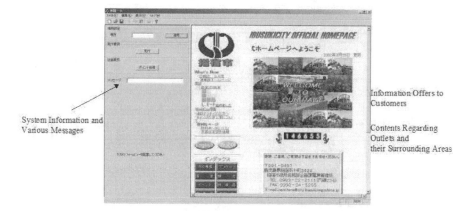

System Information and Various Messages

Information Offers to Customers

Contents Regarding Outlets and their Surrounding Areas

Fig. 7. Information Terminal of Electronic Coupon System

We cogitated about the rewards added. The accumulated rewards can be exchanged for the service provided in the area. However, the rewards are not the official currency. Rather, since they have characteristics as local currency, the rewards are not only added in a fixed rule all the time; Entertainment-like fascinating aspect such as bonus rewards which are added during a particular period and probabilistic uncertainty is considered.

4.4 Inference Methods for Showing the Information

This time, since the system must immediately be developed and delivered, we do not use the organizational learning mechanism in [21]. We only implement the inference method to recommend the next place to visit to the users utilizing their footprint in order to encourage them to continue moving.

The system possesses the fundamental information such as the one in Fig.5. This is geographic information and that of the place of outlets. In addition, this is able to utilize the footprint of the users of the electronic coupons. The system provides the information about which outlet the consumers visited and added rewards to the coupons and about what types of information the system showed as recommendation in the past. This information is stored on the RFID the users possess. The system reading this information makes it possible to obtain the information in the individual level. When the types of the recommended information can be recognized as the only ID, the system can figure out which spot on the geographic information in Fig.5 the recommended information is about. That is, the recommended information can be utilized as the geographic information.

The RFID memory space is small, only 112 bytes. Thus, it is required to infer and generate the recommendation information for the RFID holders utilizing the limited information. As the whole fundamental information the system has, all outlets are indicated with green nodes as in Fig.8. As the information in the individual levels, the outlets are connected with the directed lines following the sequences in which the rewards are added. Moreover, the red nodes indicate the outlets related to the recommended place provided as the recommendation in the past. The system assumes that the individuals already know the locations indicated with the red nodes or those which are connected with the directed lines. That is, such locations are excluded from the sites the system recommends in the future.

The electronic coupon system set at each outlet possesses a unique ID for the machine. Utilizing the ID and the geographic information in Fig.5 makes it possible to figure out the location of the machine itself. The geographic information of each outlet in the Fig.5 is converted to such information as in Fig.8 and stored on the RFID individuals possess. As described above, the locations the individuals already know are excluded, and those which they do not know are recommended. The locations to recommend here should satisfy the following:

1)   The closest location from the current position.
2)   The locations which the individual does not know.

The following operation is needed to search the locations which satisfy these conditions.

a)   In order to hold the distance information, grid which is interchangeable with the geographic information in Fig.5 is formed on the RFID memory, and the nodes which indicate outlets are placed on the grid [22].
b)   The users can obtain the geographic information of the candidate site utilizing beam search [23] at the current position.

Although multiple candidate sites might be obtained, the one firstly found is designated as the end of the search, because the electronic coupon system does not possess sufficient information to choose one from the multiple candidate site as a best recommendation.

4.5 Electronic Coupon System and Data Mining

It is necessary to understand the present conditions of the whole region in order to vitalize the commercial district of the old town. When the users eventually exchange the accumulated rewards for service, the system provides the method to retrieve the users' footprint from the RFID and store it on the system as their log. When issuing an electronic coupon, creating an ID which can recognize the individual in the user's RFID enables the system to learn how the identified user has moved within the area and what recommended information the user has received [24].

Fig.9 indicates an example of the user's footprint information stored on the RFID. It consists of the user's ID, time when the rewards are added, outlet ID, and recommended information ID. If the footprint for each user is indicated in one line of the tabular data, it is possible to show the all users' footprint with one table. Such data can be acquired with the method as in [25]. Utilizing the ID of the outlet at which the user purchases and the recommended information ID provided as the next candidate site makes it possible to learn whether the user follows the electronic coupon system's recommendation. Based on the geographic information, the present electronic coupon system recommends the closest spot from the current place as the next candidate site. When a pattern in the users' movement is found through the method in [25], it is possible to generate an increasingly appropriate recommendation based on the pattern. The system generating the next recommendation based on the information which the system has recommended and the movement which the user has actually taken enhances the appropriateness of the inference of the system. Moreover, since the global picture of the commercial district in the old town becomes clearer, it will become possible to contrive a scheme for the vitalization.

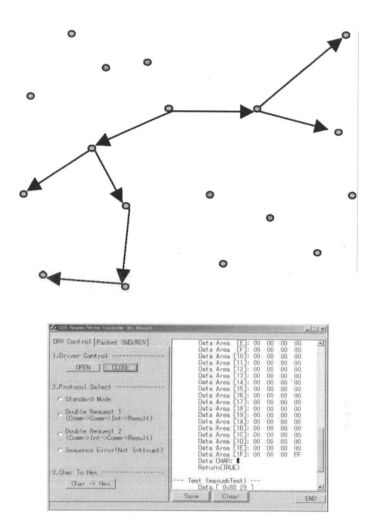

Fig. 8. User's Geographic Footprint (up) and its Stored Memory Reside on RFID (112byte memory space) (down)

Fig. 9. User's Footprint for Data Mining

4.6 Discussion

The proposed Fairy Wing architecture is applicable to various task domains, which feature user-centered participants, user-centered information management, user-centered information navigation, advanced information services and easy-to-maintain distribution [26]. Candidates for this application include relationship marketing support inter-communities/companies, visitor information assistance at exhibition centers, healthcare information services, and collaborative education support.

The implementation techniques are at a reasonable level for rapid development and easy maintenance. The assumptions we have made are not demanding; they are summarized as follows: (1) the existence of ubiquitous information terminals, (2) users' continuing interest in the information services, (3) a small amount of personal information required to run the system, and (4) an adequate number of participants entering the system at the same time.

5   Concluding Remarks

This paper has proposed Fairy Wing: another mobile computing system for community computing in a digital city. The system is characterized by the concept of smart IC cards and aims at supporting personal information management, information services, and dynamic collaborative filtering. We have discussed the advantages of the system and architectural issues. We believe the proposed system architecture is effective in various applications, which will provide wide coverage physically, virtually, and temporally. We also think the Fairy concept will lead to the development of a popular device for expanding advanced agent systems.

References

[1]   Shardanand, U., P. Maes, Social Information Filtering: Algorithms for Automating 'Word of Mouth'. Proceedings of the CHI-95, ACM Press (1995)
[2]   Resnick, P., Varian, H.R.: Recommender Systems. Commnications of the ACM, Vol. 40, No.3, (1997)56-58
[3]   Resnick, P., Iacovou, N., Suchak, M. et al.: GroupLends: An Open Architecture for Collaborative Filtering of Netnews. Proceedings of the Conference on Conputer Supported Cooperative Work, (1994)175-186
[4]   NetPerceptions Inc., Recommendation Engine White Paper.
       http://www.netperceptions.om/iterature/conent/recommendatio
       n.pdf, (2003)
[5]   Ishida, T. (ed.): Community Computing - Collaboration over Global Information Networks. John-Wiley & Sons (1998)
[6]   Ishida, T. (ed.): Community Computing and Support Systems - Social Interaction in Networked Communities. Springer-Verlag Lecture Notes in Computer Science, Vol. 1519 (1998)
[7]   Weiss, G. (ed.): Multiagent Systems – A Modern Approach to Distributed Artificial Intelligence. MIT Press (1999)
[8]   Dreifus, H., Monk, J. T. : Smart Cards – A Guide to Building and Managing Smart Card Applications. John-Wiley & Sons (1998)

[9]   Van den Besselaar, P. and Beckers, D.: Demographics and Sociographics of the Digital
        City, In Ishida, T. (ed.): Community Computing and Support Systems, Lecture Notes in
        Computer Science, Vol. 1519, Springer-Verlag, (1998) 109-125
[10]   T. Terano, T. Nishimura, E. Murakami, Y. Ishino: Fairy in a Smart IC Card: Interfacing
        People, Town, and Digital City. in T. Ishida and K. Isbister Eds, Digital Cities:
        Experiences, Technologies and Future Perspectives, Lecture Notes in Computer Science
        1765, Springer-Verlag, (2000) 378-390
[11]   Ishida, T., Akahani, J., Hiramatsu, K., Isbister, K., Lisowski, S., Nakanishi, H.,
        Okamoto, M., Miyazaki, Y., Tsutsuguchi, K.: Digital City Kyoto: Towards A Social
        Information Infrastructure, Cooperative Information Agents III. Lecture Notes in
        Artificial Intelligence, Vol. 1652, Springer-Verlag, (1999)23-35
[12]   Vigna, G. (ed.): Mobile Agents and Security. Lecture Notes in Computer Science, Vol.
        1419, Springer-Verlag (1998)
[13]   Terano, T., Kurahashi, S., Minami, U.: TRURL: Artificial World for Social Interaction
        Studies. Proc. 6th Int. Conf. on Artificial Life (ALIFE VI), (1998) 326-335
[14]   Jennings, N. R., Wooldridge, M. J. : Agent Technology - Foundations, Applications, and
        Markets. Springer-Verlag, (1998)
[15]   www.jreast.co.jp
[16]   Mitchell, W. J.: Designing the Digital City. in T. Ishida and K. Isbister Eds, Digital
        Cities: Experiences, Technologies and Future Perspectives, Lecture Notes in Computer
        Science 1765, Springer-Verlag, (2000)1-6
[17]   Lau, T., Etzioni, O., Weld, D. S.: Privacy Interfaces for Information Management.
        Communications of ACM, Vol.42, No. 10, (1999)89-94
[18]   Bradshaw, J. M., (ed.): Software Agents. AAAI/MIT Press (1997)
[19]   Prietula, M. J., Carley, K. M. and Gasser, L. (eds.): Simulating Organizations:
        Computational Models of Institutions and Groups. CA: Morgan Kaufman (1998)
[20]   Takadama, K., Terano, T., Shimohara, K., Hori, K., Nakasuka, S.: Making
        Organizational Learning Operational: Implication from Learning Classifier System. J.
        Computational and Mathematical Organization Theory, Vol. 5, No. 3, (1999) 229-252
[21]   Murakami, E., Terano, T.: Collaborative Filtering for a Distributed Smart IC Card
        System. In Yuan, S.-T., Yokoo, M.. (eds.): Intelligent Agents: Specification, Modeling,
        and Applications (PRIMA 2001 Proceedings), Lecture Notes in Artificial Intelligence,
        LNAI 2132, (2001)183-197
[22]   Russel, S., Norvig, P.: Artificial Intelligence A Modern Approach. Prentice Hall (1995)
[23]   Mitchell, T. M. : Machine Learning, McGraw-Hill Series in Computer Science (1997)
[24]   Fayyad, U. M., Piatetsky-Shapiro, G., Smyth, P., and Uthurusamy, R. (eds.): Advances
        in Knowledge Discovery and Data Mining. AAAI/MIT Press (1996)
[25]   25. Agrawal, R., Mannila, H. ,Srikant, R, Toivonen, H., Verkamo, A. I. : Fast Discovery
        of Association Rules, Advances in Knowledge Discovery and Data Mining, The MIT
        Press (1996)
[26]   26. Aiba, H., Terano, T.: A Computational Model for Distributed Knowledge Systems
        with Learning Mechanisms. Expert Systems with Applications Vol. 10, (1996) 417-427

CONSORTS: A Multiagent Architecture for Service Coordination in Ubiquitous Computing

Akio Sashima, Noriaki Izumi, and Koichi Kurumatani

Cyber Assist Research Center (CARC)
National Institute of Advanced Industrial Science and Technology (AIST)
Aomi 2-41-6, Koto-ku, Tokyo, 135-0064 Japan
sashima@carc.aist.go.jp
niz@ni.aist.go.jp
k.kurumatani@aist.go.jp
http://www.consorts.org/

Abstract. One of the fundamental issues of Ubiquitous Computing is concerned with the coordination gaps between devices, services, and users. When numerous devices, various information services, and users who have different intentions are physically co-located in a environment, how can we coordinate the services and devices to assist a particular user in receiving a particular service so as to maximize the user's' satisfaction there? In order to solve this human-centered service coordination issue, we have been developing a multiagent architecture for Ubiquitous Computing, called CONSORTS (Coordination System of Real world Transaction Services). In this paper, we first outline some coordination gaps in Ubiquitous Computing, and describe three design concepts of the CONSORTS to bridge the gaps: *physically-grounding*, *cognitive resource managements*, and *location-mediated service coordination*. Then, we show the outline of CONSORTS architecture, and two applications of CONSORTS, context-aware information assist systems in museums and wireless-LAN based location system on AgentCities Networks.

1 Introduction

Recently, a computing framework that mainly concentrates handling real world information and physical objects, such as Ubiquitous Computing [1], Intelligent Room [2], and Ambient Intelligence [3], have been received much interest in both research and application.

Ubiquitous Computing, which we focus on in this paper, enables computers to provide various information assists by using real world information. In the framework, numbers of sensor devices and computers are invisibly integrated in environments. The sensor devices may also include tiny, portable devices carried or worn by the users. The computers interact with the users by the sensor devices, not by conventional human interface devices such as keyboards and mice. For example, context-aware information assist systems, a typical application of the Ubiquitous Computing, aim to recognize users' contexts (e.g. locations, profiles and current activities), based on the sensor data, and provide proper information according to the users' context.

K. Kurumatani et al. (Eds.): MAMUS 2003, LNAI 3012, pp. 190-216, 2004.

Although the Ubiquitous Computing is a promising framework of the intelligent services like context-aware information assists, it is still has many research issues. One of the fundamental issues is concerned with coordination among devices, services, and users. When numerous devices (e.g. terminals, RF-IDs, cameras, information appliances etc.), various information services that use the devices (e.g. navigations, guides, information retrievals, controlling devices, etc.), and users who have different intentions are physically co-located in a Ubiquitous Computing environment, how can we coordinate the services and devices to assist a particular user in receiving a particular service so as to maximize the user's satisfaction? In other words, how can we dynamically coordinate the surrounding heterogeneous services and devices to be integrated into a consistent human-centered service according to a user's intention?

In this research, to solve this human-centered coordination issue in Ubiquitous Computing, we focus on a research activity on the Internet, the Semantic Web [4]. The research goal of Semantic Web is to establish the methodology to manage a rich diversity of web-contents that explode on the Internet by adding "meta-data", meta-information of the web-contents. RDF (Resource Description Framework) [5] and RDFS (RDF Schema) [6] are such meta-data developed on top of XML. The RDF/RDFS can represent semantic networks which stand for an ontology [12] that defines concepts in a domain. Since the meta-data have well-defined meanings based on the ontology, "Semantic Web agents", autonomous computer programs that read the meta-data, can understand logical meanings of web-contents with meta-data. For example, the agents semantically infer identification between "my father's father" and "my grand father" based on ontology about family. Thus, with the deep understanding of the web-contents, Semantic Web agents choose proper contents out of numerous contents on the Internet behalf of users, coordinate the contents for the users, and assist the users in accessing the contents.

Inspired by this ability of the Semantic Web agents that handle the meaning of the resources on the Internet, we have been developing a multiagent architecture called CONSORTS (Coordination System of Realworld Transaction Services) [7][8][9]. Although we have developed some variations of CONSORTS according to their application domains, we describe first version of CONSORTS, called CONSORTS ver.1, in this paper. The main feature of CONSORTS ver.1 is handling the meaning of the resources in Ubiquitous Computing environments. Using standardized agent communication language, called FIPA-ACL [10], and standard ontology for Ubiquitous Computing environments, CONSORTS agents can manage devices, services, and users in Ubiquitous Computing, and coordinate the services and the devices so as to assist the users in human-centered manner.

In this paper, we first outline some research issues related to the human-centered coordination in Ubiquitous Computing. Secondly, we describe three essential requirements for the agents to solve the issues. Thirdly, we propose a multiagent architecture, called CONSORTS ver.1, which satisfy the above requirements. The CONSORTS agents use standardized agent communication and ontological description of Ubiquitous Computing environments to understand the meanings of the resources. Finally, we show two different applications of CONSORTS ver.1, context-aware information assist systems in museums and wireless-LAN based location systems on AgentCities Networks [11], and confirm the flexibility of the architecture.

2   Human-Centered Coordination in Ubiquitous Computing

In the chapter 1, we have addressed a question: how can we dynamically coordinate the surrounding heterogeneous services and devices to be integrated into a consistent human-centered service according to a user's intention? In order to answer the question, in this chapter, we address two coordination gaps in Ubiquitous Computing, gaps between services and gaps between user intentions and services,

2.1 Gaps between Services

There exist some cooperation gaps between the independent services. Most of current Ubiquitous Computing researches do not take care about cooperation between services, and ignore knowledge sharing among the services. Each of isolated services has ad hoc original data representation cannot shared with other services. In addition, the data of the services are not accessible to other services; there are no standard communication protocol and data format, such as HTTP and HTML on the Internet. Thus, it is difficult to share the data with other services. If the data could be sharable, numerous cooperative services are possible. For example, if cooking assist service can know what the user purchased at a supermarket today, the service can suggest a reasonable menu based on the purchased ingredients. For another example, if information search service at home knows paintings that the user looked at in a museum today, the user can search the information about the paintings without knowing titles of the paintings.

Similarly, most of Ubiquitous Computing services are designed for a specific device, which has a certain communication speed, memory capacity and sensing accuracy. Thus, it is difficult to share the data in the services that presuppose different devices. For example, the location service that presupposes RF-ID-sensor-data cannot be applied the location service that presupposes Infra-red sensor data or GPS-data. There exist representation gaps between the device-oriented services so as to realize human-centered service coordination.

2.2 Gaps between User Intentions and Services

The Ubiquitous Computing services decide which service should be provided to a user according to the user's intention. However it is difficult to capture correct users' intentions because intentions are inner statuses in human beings. Thus, there exist gaps between captured user intentions and services provided.

In addition, if the user's intentions are correctly captured, the services may not be easily accessible from the users because appropriate services must be chose out of various information services (e.g. navigations, guides, information retrievals, controlling devices, etc.) physically co-located there. Thus, there exist gaps between users' intentions and choosing matched services.

3   A Multiagent Architecture that Bridge the Gaps in Ubiquitous Computing

In order to realize the multiagent architecture that bridges the coordination gaps in Ubiquitous Computing which we have addressed in chapter 2, we propose three design concepts to realize the architecture, that is, "*physically-grounding*", "*cognitive resource managements*", and "*location-mediated coordination*." In this chapter, we argue that these concepts are important to bridge the coordination gaps in the Ubiquitous Computing, and describe how the concepts bridge the gaps.

3.1 Bridging Gaps between Services

The key to bridge the gap between services is "knowledge sharing." To share knowledge between services, we need a common description of knowledge and a communication protocol between services. The diversity of the access methods to the services and the devices should be wrapped by such a description and a protocol so that each of services can freely access other services, devices, and legacy applications.

For such a sharing mechanism, we propose a multiagent approach that the services consist of various kinds of autonomous agents so as to share the knowledge each other. Each agent knows about their own services, such as a service agent knowing about exhibitions in a museum, and communicates with other agents based on a common format of the knowledge description like FIPA Agent Communication Language [10]. FIPA Agent Communication Language (FIPA-ACL) is a current standard of the agent communication language. Using such standardized communication format, knowledge sharing between services can be realized.

In addition, a diversity of the access interfaces of the devices is eliminated by the standardized multiagent architecture. By wrapping the service APIs by the agent commutation languages like FIPA-ACL, the APIs can be standardized. Thus standardized multiagent architecture can make possible to knowledge sharing between heterogeneous services and devices, and bridge the cooperation gap between various services.

3.2 Bridging Gaps between User Intentions and Services

The keys to bridging gaps between user intentions and services are "capturing user intentions", "describing user intentions" and "choosing matched services." In this research, we propose new concepts to capturing user contexts, called *physically-grounding* [8][9] and *cognitive resource managements,* and another new concept to choosing matched services, called *location-mediated coordination.*

The *physically-grounding* is a design concept of the multiagent architecture that aims to be tightly coupled with the physical world. Through the various agents that can access the real world, such as device wrapper agents, the physically-grounding agents are aware of user status and environmental status in the real world that requires capturing the user intention correctly.

However, in order to capture the user context in human-centered manner, the agents must recognize cognitive meaning of the real world, not only physical information, because human beings cognitively interpret the real world as resources of their daily activities. To handle this kind of cognitive meaning of the world, all information should be described by *Ontologies* [12]. We call this kind of ontology-based information managements in the real world *cognitive resource managements* and apply them to the issue.

In order to resolve another issue: choosing matched services in Ubiquitous Computing, we propose *location-mediated coordination*, a natural extension of *middle-agent* based service coordination framework on the Internet [17][18][19]. In contrast with middle agents on the Internet, physical constraints of the real world are critical for quality of choosing matched services in Ubiquitous Computing environment. We suppose the most of user's current intention is relate to the user's physical location. For example, museum guide systems provide guide information of an exhibition to a user who located near the exhibition because the most of users require the guide information of the nearest exhibition. Thus, by considering the physical places where service providers and the service requesters are located, the middle agents choose matched services. If a service is semantically matched to a request but the service resource is far removed from the requesting user, the service should not be provided in the context of Ubiquitous Computing; the nearer service resource to the user is often better than any other services. The location-mediated coordination framework can solve this kind of matchmaking issues based on the semantics of the locations.

4   Design Concepts of Multiagent Architecture in Ubiquitous Computing

In this chapter, we describe three design concepts physically-grounding, cognitive resource managements, and location-mediated coordination to realize the multiagent architecture that bridges the coordination gaps in Ubiquitous Computing.

4.1 Physically-Grounding

Most of software agent researches focus on the problem how the system effectively serves the user who operates a computer terminal connected to the Internet [13][14]. They usually interact with the user by explicit symbolic information. However, in the Ubiquitous Computing environment, there are no conventional human interface devices, such as keyboard and mouse, in the ubiquitous environment. In order to provide the user with proper information in the current situation, the agents should focus on not only explicit information of the user interaction, but also on implicit context information in the real world (user location, activity, and physical state of environment, etc.). For example, the agents must notice subtle behavior of the user or slight changes of the environmental states to understand the user's intention. In other words, the agents in a digital world should be aware of such context information in the real world. We call the awareness of (and control if possible) the physical environment by the agents "physically-grounding."

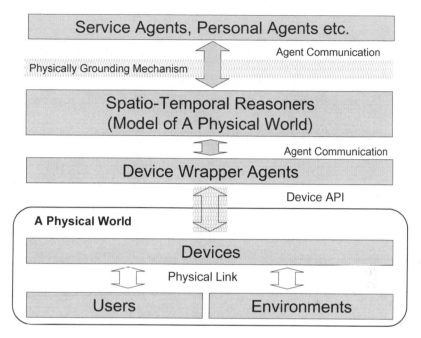

Fig. 1. Physically-Grounding Mechanism of Agents

In this research, we propose a multiagent architecture with "spatio-temporal reasoners" and "device wrapper agents" as the system architecture of the physically-grounding agents. A spatio-temporal reasoner manages "spatio-temporal inference engine" and "spatial information repository". The repository manages the device-oriented raw geometric information of the ubiquitous computing environments, such as location of users and raw data from sensor devices. Device wrapper agents manage and control devices, such as sensors and information appliances, in the environment. We illustrate the concept of physically-grounding in Fig. 1. The spatio-temporal reasoner receives physical information from the device wrapper agents, manages the spatiotemporal model, and sends consistent physical information to the other agents that request the information. As the requested agents are aware of some aspects of physical environments based on the messages from the spatio-temporal reasoners, the physical information can be shared by all agents on the architecture. In addition, as the devices can be controlled by device wrapper agents according to the other agents' requests, the function of devices can be shared by all agents on the architecture. Thus, the physically-grounding agents are realized on multiagent architecture with spatio-temporal reasoners.

4.2 Cognitive Resource Managements

Physically-grounding agents can virtually share physical information of the Ubiquitous Computing environments. However, in order to realize human-centered coordination, they must recognize cognitive meaning of the world because human beings cognitively interpret the real world as resources of their daily activities. For example, to provide some information supports based on the user's location, the agents should understand user's location like "the user is in a museum now", rather than "the user is at Longitude: 140.38.54 E, Latitude: 35.77.44 N at Mon Jan 13 12:47:06 2003 JST". If the agents also understand the meanings of "museum," the agents can provide information services related to the museum.

To realize these kinds of cognitive modeling of the world, all information should be described by ontologies by the agents. In this research, the meaning of Ontology is *a specification of a conceptualization* [12]. Ontology for the Ubiquitous Computing is a description of the concepts and relationships that relate to the Ubiquitous Computing (e.g. Sensor Ontology, Spatial Ontology, and Service Ontology, etc.). We call such ontology-based information management in the real world "cognitive resource managements."

In this research, we apply this concept to the spatial information repository of the spatio-temporal reasoner. We have described that the repository manages the device-oriented raw geometric information of the ubiquitous computing environments. In addition to the device-oriented geometric information, the repository also manages cognitive tree-representation of the environment; In short, spatio-temporal reasoner can manage both the tree-representation and the device-oriented geometric representation, and translate from the geometric representation into the tree-representation, and vice versa. (See Fig. 2.) Tentatively, .the translation is a deterministic mapping process between raw representations and ontological representation that we have defined beforehand.

The ontological tree-based representation is based on the human understanding of spatial concept generally called mereological thinking [15], reasoning about part-of relation. The representation consists of part-of relations among 3-dimentional spatial regions in the real world. Although we formularize the ubiquitous computing environments as a tree-structure of spatio-temporal regions based on Bittner [16], in this paper, we only deal with a tree-structure of spatial regions. A tree structure of spatial regions is denoted by G: $G=(R,\subseteq)$ where $R:(r\in R)$ denotes a set of spatio-temporal regions, $\subseteq$ denotes a part-of relation between two regions. The regions in G have following natures.

1) $\exists r_i : r_i \subseteq r_i$

2) $\exists r_i, r_j : r_i \subseteq r_j \wedge r_j \subseteq r_i \rightarrow r_j = r_i$

3) $\exists r_i, r_j, r_k : r_i \subseteq r_j \wedge r_j \subseteq r_k \rightarrow r_i \subseteq r_k$

where r_i, r_j, r_k is a region.

Spatio-Temporal Reasoner

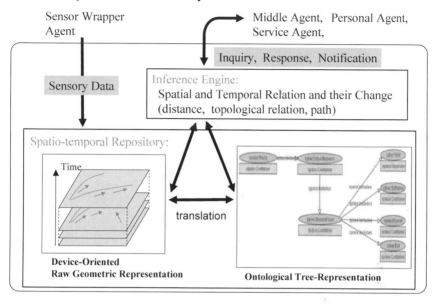

Fig. 2. Data representations of Spatio-Temporal Reasoner

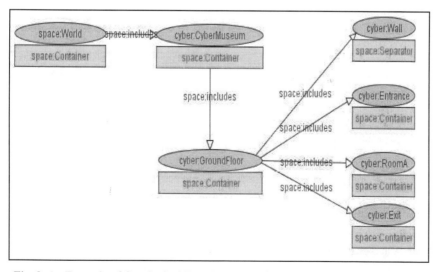

Fig. 3. An Example of Ontological Tree-Representation (A Description of a Museum)

Based on the above formalization, we define the relation of spatial regions, and their property in the spatial ontology which we have developed to describe the Ubiquitous Computing environments as a tree-representation. An example of ontological tree-representation (a structure of a museum) which we have developed is shown in Fig. 3. *Space:inculdes* relations in the figure are the relations denoted by ⊆ in above logical expressions. Handling spatial data on this representation, the spatio-temporal reasoner realizes cognitive resource managements and physically grounding.

4.3 Location-Mediated Service Coordination

In a Ubiquitous Computing environment, a lot of service agents are usually co-located because a service agent must be specialized for a service (e.g. navigation, guide, advertising, information retrieval, controlling devices, etc.) in order to keep their functional independence. Therefore, as we enrich the environment with various services, service agents will increase. When more than one service agent can simultaneously provide services to a user, the agents must coordinate each other to appropriately provide the service for the user then and there. How can the software agents coordinate with each other in order to realize such human-centered service coordination?

One possible answer is that the service agents should be orchestrated by *middle agents* [17][18][19]. In general, *middle agent* matches service provider agent to service requester agent, initiates their communication, and mediates the flow of information between them. However, conventional middle agent frameworks do not deal with the information of location where service provider agent and service requester agent communicate with each other. As we described before, the place of interaction is important in the context of Ubiquitous Computing. If the service and request is completely matched and physical distance between the requesting user and the service resource is long, the match making service is nonsense. In the context of Ubiquitous Computing, the middle agent must be aware of the place of the interaction.

In order to realize the service coordination being aware of the physical locations of the interaction, we introduce *location-aware middle agent* into the multiagent architecture with *spatio-temporal reasoner*. While spatio-temporal reasoner manage the location information, and execute reasoning about spatio-temporal relation, the location-aware middle agents concentrate the matching process,. Using the facility of the spatio-temporal reasoner, the middle agents extend the internet-based coordination framework to the location-mediated coordination framework for Ubiquitous Computing.

Because the descriptions of locations are separately managed in the spatio-temporal reasoner, no modification to service contents is required if the location of the service is changed. Content developers can concentrate the contents of service without considering the service locations; Service manager in the venue, such as museums, manage the location information related to the services contents.

4.4 Outline of the Location-Mediated Service Coordination

In order to realize the location-mediated service coordination, we have introduced a new type of agents, *location-aware middle agents*. Using the spatio-temporal reasoner and location-aware middle agents, we extend the conventional middle agent framework to realize the location-mediated coordination in the Ubiquitous Computing. The location-mediated coordination process consists of following agents:

- **Service Provider Agent (Service Agents)**: the agent that provides some types of service, such as problem solving, mediating Semantic Web services;
- **Service Requester Agent (Personal Agents)**: the agent that needs provider agents to perform some services for them;
- **Location-Aware Middle Agent**: the agent that helps locate other agents along with Spatio-Temporal Reasoner;
- **Spatio-Temporal Reasoner**: the agent that manages physical locations of Service Providers and Service Requesters, and reason about their spatial relation in cognitive way.

The coordination is as follows (See Fig. 4):

1) provider agents advertise their capabilities and physical service areas to middle agents;
2) middle agents store these advertisements, and inform their service areas to spatio-temporal reasoners;
3) spatio-temporal reasoners store these service areas;
4) a requester asks some middle agents whether they know providers with desired capabilities;
5) the middle agents ask some spatio-temporal reasoners whether the stored service areas cover the requester's location or not, and get the results, a subset of the stored service areas;
6) taking account of the results, the middle agent matches the request with the stored advertisements, and returns the result, a subset of the stored advertisements.

This process is a natural extension of matching process proposed by Sycara et al. [17]. By integrating above agents with ordinal web agents on the Internet, we can extend application areas of Web agents (and Web Services) to Ubiquitous Computing environment. Various mechanisms to determine a matched service can be implemented in the location-aware middle agents. In this research, as a first version of location-based matching process, we adopt a simple calculation mechanism, calculating matching degree by *part-of* relations, which we will describe in chapter 5.

200   Akio Sashima et al.

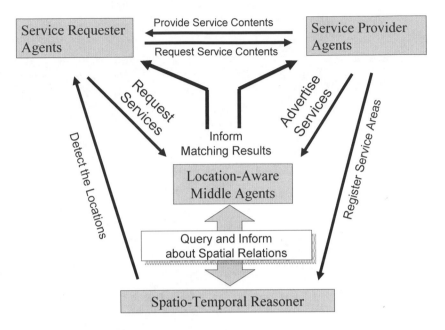

Fig. 4. Location-Mediated Service Coordination

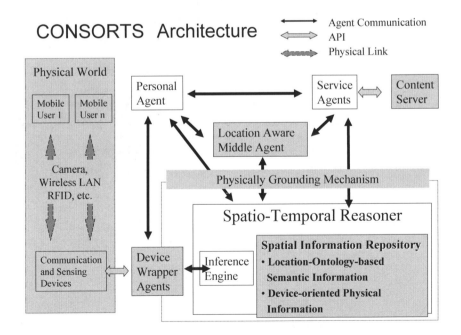

Fig. 5. Outline of CONSORTS Architecture (Ver.1)

5   CONSORTS Architecture

Under the three design concepts: physically-grounding; cognitive resource managements; location-mediated coordination, we have been developing a multiagent architecture called CONSORTS ver.1 (Coordination System of Realworld Transaction Services) so as to realize the human-centered coordination in Ubiquitous Computing. Using standardized agent communication language, called FIPA-ACL [10], and standard ontology framework of the Semantic Web, This version of CONSORTS agents can manage devices, services, and users in Ubiquitous Computing, and coordinate the services and the devices so as to assist the users in human-centered manner.

In this chapter, we describe how the three concepts are realized within the CONSORTS architecture. We first describe the outline of the whole system architecture of the CONSORTS architecture.

5.1 Outline of the CONSORTS Architecture

Fig. 5 shows an outline of CONSORTS Architecture that consists of following type of agents.

Services Agents. Service agents provide services, such as tour guide, navigation, and information presentation. Services agents realize the flexible service by using semantic information through the content servers. The content servers are resources on the Internet, especially Semantic Web and Web Services.

Personal Agents. Personal agents request service behalf of a user. The agents communicate with Device wrapper agents, and manage them as user interface devices.

Location-Aware Middle Agents. Location-aware Middle Agents manage to interaction to mediate between agents and a user. The agent sends the request to the middle agents, and controls the interaction between service agents and the user.

Spatio-Temporal Reasoners. Spatio-Temporal Reasoners manage physical locations of users, services, agents, and objects. STR reasons about their spatial relation in cognitive way. The agents manage both device-oriented physical information in the real world and cognitively comprehensive information in the digital world. Physically-grounding and cognitive resource managements are realized by the Spatio-Temporal Reasoners

Device Wrapper Agents. Device Wrapper Agents hide the diversity of physical device and legacy application from other agents. For example, Device Wrapper Agents wrap the raw information, which is derived from legacy devices, with the standardized agent communication language.

5.2 Implementations of CONSORTS

We have implemented the CONSORTS (Ver.1) using Java (JDK 1.4) and JADE 3.0[20]. JADE is a software framework to develop the agent system that conforms to FIPA specifications. FIPA Agent Communication Language (ACL) is a current standard of the agent communication language. Thus, CONSORTS agents can freely communicate with other FIPA-agents developed by other researchers on the AgentCities network [11]. AgentCities network is an open research test bed for the experiments for world-wide agent networks. We adopt FIPA-ACL to make the CONSORTS work on such world-wide agent networks. Using such standardized communication language and global agent networks that are open to the Internet resources, the CONSORTS can mediate the agents handling the information in the Ubiquitous Computing and the agents handling the information on the Semantic Web (see Fig. 6).

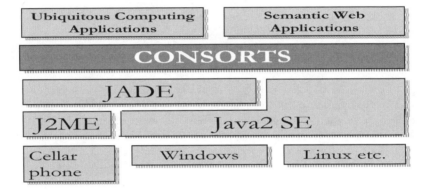

Fig. 6. Implementations Layers of CONSORTS

List 1. An Example of FIPA-ACL Messages

```
(inform
    :sender      device-wrapper-agent1
    :receiver    spatio-temporal-reasoner1
    :content     (located
                    John (Location (x 120) (y 100)))
    :in-reply-to message1
    :language    fipa-sl
    :ontology    carc-location1
)
```

5.3 Agent Communications

All messages of the agent communication are described with FIPA-ACL (Foundation for Intelligent Physical Agents Agent Communication Language)[10]. Artificial intelligence researchers have already proposed some Agent Communication Languages (ACL), such as Foundation for Intelligent Physical Agent ACL (FIPA-

ACL) and Knowledge Query Manipulation Language (KQML) [21]. In this research, considering interoperability of agent communication, we adopt FIPA-ACL as communication language of the agents. FIPA-ACL is one of standard agent communication language, which is based on speech-act theory. A lot of agent communication software and tools for FIPA-ACL have been developed. A FIPA ACL message consists of a header, the "communicative act" (e.g. "inform", "request", "propose", etc.).

The message content is described with FIPA-SL. List 1 shows a message which represents "Personal Agent request to Museum Service Agent to provide the service named Mona Lisa (showing information about the painting of the Mona Lisa)." This message flows at arrow-line [6] in Fig. 9. Although we have already implemented RDF (Resource Description Framework) based descriptions as a content part of the message, we adopt FIPA-SL as the content language in current implementation because of FIPA-SL's excellent interoperability with other agent platform.

FIPA-ACL can choose a content language and ontology in the message, such as `fipa-sl` (Semantic Language) and `carc-location1` in List 1. For example, the meaning of *John* is defined in the ontology named `carc-location1`in List 1. It may be defined as the name of a man. Since the agent can use the definition, the agent may also infer that "*A man is located on (120, 100)*". This kind of inference mechanism enables the agents to share the meaning of context information with each other.

5.4 Ontology of CONSORTS

The message content is described with FIPA-SL. We adopt FIPA-SL as the content language in current implementation. The meanings of the content part are defined by JADE ontologies, a set of concepts, their relationships and their attributes. The JADE parser can convert a content part into a set of Java objects predefined as JADE ontology classes. Using JADE ontologies, JADE agents use the same words in the content with the same meaning. Although we have already implemented RDF (Resource Description Framework) based descriptions as a content part of the message, we adopt JADE ontology in current implementation because of its excellent interoperability. Using Protégé [22], an ontology editor that can handle various formats of ontology, and Bean Generator [23], a plug-in to of Protégé, we can create JADE ontology classes by conversions of RDF/RDFS.

5.5 Location-Mediated Matching Process Based on Part-of Relations

Various mechanisms to determine a matched service can be implemented in the location-aware middle agents. In this research, as a first version of location-based matching process, we adopt a simple calculation mechanism, calculating matching degree by *part-of* relations. A combination between the service provider and the requester that has the highest matching degree is a matched service for the request.

The matching process calculates the matching degrees based on part-of relations of the tree. An environment is represented by tree representation. Each of services has a service area associated to a node of the tree. At first, the agent identifies the all node of the tree the requester is located at. Then, the agent picks up all services associated to the nodes, and calculates matching degrees of the service.

The matching degrees of the service areas are discrete values corresponding to the path lengths from root node to the nodes of the service areas on a *part-of* relation tree. In the tree representation in Fig. 3, if the user is located at "*Entrance*", the matching degree is 2. In other words matching degree of narrower region has high value (e.g. g(*Room A*) >g(*Ground Floor*) in Fig. 3).

6   Applications

Two prototype application systems of the CONSORTS are shown in this chapter. To show the relevance of the CONSORTS, the applications are claimed in the interoperation of Web-based information and physical (or the real world's) information. In the following two applications, we try to show the three significant roles of CONSORTS agents:

A)   connecting agents each other based on ACLs,
B)   interacting heterogeneous agents mutually based on ontologies,
C)   and coordinating with sensory information and web resources on the Internet.

6.1 Context-Aware Information Assist Systems in Museums

Based on the CONSORTS architecture, we have implemented context-aware information assist systems in museums. In this system, the agents are aware of the spatial relations between users and paintings in a museum, and provide some services to the users based on the relations. For example, when a user is located near a painting, the user can receive the information of the painting via the user's portable display device from the agents. If the user needs more information of the painting, the user should push the "tell me" button of the portable device. The CONSORTS agents notice the user's request, make a search query about the painting with the necessary information they've already had, e.g. the painting's name and user's preference, and access the Web Services [24] on the Internet, e.g. Google Web Services [25], behalf of the user.

This service is implemented on the procedure of *matching degrees by part-of relation.* The agent identifies the locations where the users are located, and pick up all services associated to the locations, and determine the best service for the user. In this application, we provide two services: a) providing nearest painting's information which is available near paintings, and b) providing user's own location in the room. Thus, if the user is near a painting, service a) should be provided, otherwise service b).

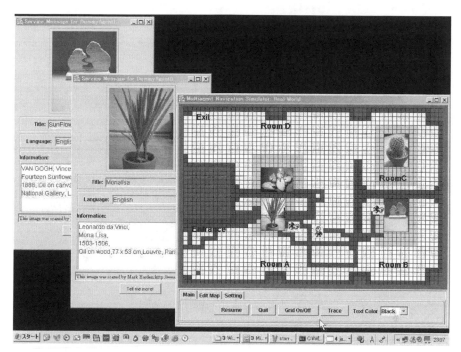

Fig. 7. A Snapshot of the Context-aware Information Assist Systems in Museums

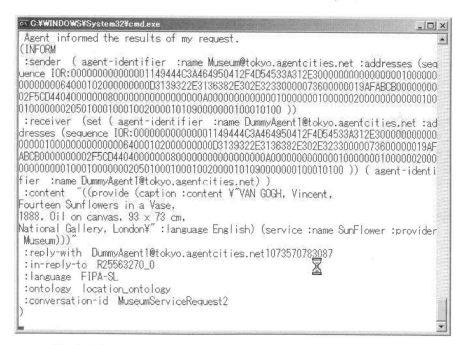

Fig. 8. A Snapshot of the Monitor Window of the Agents' Communications

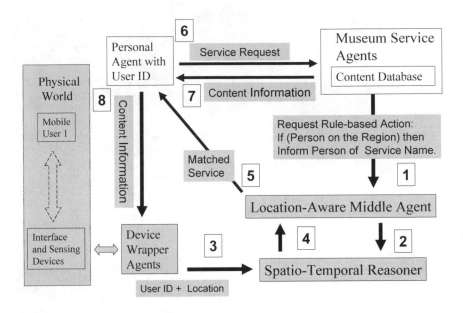

Fig. 9. Message Flows in the Assist Systems in Museums

Fig. 7 shows a snapshot of the monitor display of the system. This application is accessible on our website (http://consorts.carc.jp/). In the figure, you can see a museum map in a main window in lower right side of the figure, two information windows with a picture in left side of the figure. In the map, human icons represent current locations of the users; each zone surrounding a picture represents service zones of the museum service agents; each line after the users represents users' trajectories. The information windows correspond to the screen of users' portable devices. In this demonstration, the users randomly roam in the museum. If a user enters the service zone, an information window with a "tell me" button in pops up. When the user push the "tell me" button, the user can see the picture's information resulting from the Internet search service in a new window. In this program, we use Google Web service API for the Internet search service. Currently, users, users' behaviors, and a museum in the system are simulated.

Fig. 8 shows a snapshot of the monitor window of the agents' communications. The messages in the window are FIPA-ACL messages. The museum agent tells some information about a requested picture.

The cordination process is as follows. Fig. 9 outlines the agent communication in the museum system.

List 2. A MessageA message at [1] in Fig. 9

```
(REQUEST
:sender              MuseumAgent
:receiver            RoomAMiddleAgent
:content   "((associate
                 (service  :name Monalisa
                      :provider MuseumAgent)
                 (region   :name MonalisaArea
                      :x0 4 :y0 0 :x1 13 :y1 8)))"
:language  FIPA-SL
:ontology  carc-location1
)
```

List 3. A MessageA message at [3] in Fig. 9

```
(INFORM
:sender              RoomADeviceWrapper
:receiver            RoomAMiddleAgent
:content   "((located
                 (person :name PersonalAgent1)
                 (location :x 1 :y 6)))"
:language  FIPA-SL
:ontology  location_ontology
)
```

List 4. A MessageA message at [6] in Fig. 9

```
(REQUEST
   :sender           PersonalAgent
   :receiver         MuseumAgent
   :content          "((action  (agent-identifier
                          :name      MuseumAgent)
                   (provide
                   (person  :name      PersonalAgent)
                   (service :name      Monalisa
                        :provider  MuseumAgent)))"
   :language         fipa-sl
   :ontology         carc-location1
)
```

List 5. A Message at [7] in Fig. 9

```
(INFORM
      :sender    MuseumAgent
      :receiver  PersonalAgent
      :content   "((provide
                    (caption
                      :content "Leonardo da Vinci,
                                Mona Lisa, 1503-1506"
                       :language English)
                    (service
                      :name Monalisa
                      :provider MuseumAgent)))"
      :language  fipa-sl
      :ontology  location-ontology1
 )
```

List 6. A Request Message to the GoogleAgent

```
(REQUEST
      :sender    PersonalAgent
      :receiver  GoogleAgent
      :content   "((action
                    (agent-identifier
                                :name GoogleAgent)
                    (search :keyword monalisa
                      :account xxxxxxxxxxxxxxx)))"
      :language  fipa-sl
      :ontology  google-api-ontology
      :protocol  fipa-request
      :conversation-id GoogleReq0
 )
```

List 7. A Message from the GoogleAgent

```
(INFORM
      :sender    GoogleAgent
      :receiver  PersonalAgent
      :content   "((googled (sequence
                    (result
                    :title \"DaVinci Leonardo,... \"
                    :url http://foo.bar.com/Artists/
                    :snippet \"… \"
                    :summary \"\")
                    (result ….) 46))"
      :reply-with PersonalAgent
```

```
:in-reply-to R12750007_0
:language fipa-sl
:ontology google-api-ontology
:protocol fipa-request
:conversation-id GoogleReq0
)
```

1) First, the service agent requests the middle agent to continuously infer whether users are located on a service region associated with a service name ([1] in Fig. 9). List 2 shows a message from a museum service agent to a middle agent. The meaning of message includes a definition of the service area: a rectangle region described by (*x0, y0, x1, y1*) on the 2D sensor space; named *MonalisaArea*.

2) The middle agent requests the Spatio-Temporal Reasoner to register a service region described in the rule, and to request to inform when users are located on the area ([2] in Fig. 9).

3) On the other hand, the device wrapper agent informs the spatio-temporal reasoner where a user with unique id is located ([3] in Fig. 9). List 3 shows an example of such a message between a sensor wrapper agent and a spatio-temporal reasoner in "Room A". The message shows A user with "Personal Agent 1" is located at (1, 6) on the sensor space. In this application, we assume service areas and user's locations are described using the same coordinate space.

4) When the spatio-temporal reasoner notice a user is located on a service region, the reasoner informs the middle agent of the user id and the name of the area ([4] in Fig. 9).

5) The middle agents tell the personal agents of the user available service name ([5] in Fig. 9).

6) Then, the personal agent requests a service based on the name, and receive a service content from the service agent ([6] [7] in Fig. 9). List 4 and List 5 show messages between a museum service agent and a personal agent at such a request and inform interaction.

7) Finally, the personal agent requests the device wrapper agent to show the service content on a user's portable display device ([8] in Fig. 9).

8) Additionally, if a user needs more information about the received contents, the personal agent behalf of the user can request "Google Web Service Agent" to search the resources on the Internet by using the keyword of the received contents (see List 6 and List 7).

Fig. 10 is a summary of the ontologies that we have defined to represents the messages between the agents in this application. We have defined 5concepts describing objects in museums and 6 predicates for describing relations between objects. List 8 shows some example programs of concept definitions for this application (*Person*, *Region*, and *Service*) .

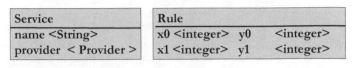

- **5 Concepts**
  - Person, Location, Rule, Service, Caption

Service	Rule		
name <String>	x0 <integer>	y0	<integer>
provider < Provider >	x1 <integer>	y1	<integer>

- **6 Predicates**
  - Associate, Located, Available, NotAvailable, Consume, Provide,

Associate	Located	Available
service <Service>	location <Location>	person <Person>
Rule < Rule >	person < Person >	service < Service >

• Except for Google Search Ontology

Fig. 10. Ontology for the Information Assist Systems in Museums

List 8. Example Programs of Concept Definitions using JADE Ontology

```
ConceptSchema personSchema
 = new ConceptSchema(PERSON);
          personSchema.add(NAME, stringSchema);
          add(personSchema, Person.class);
          add(placeSchema, Place.class);
          add(locationSchema, Location.class);


ConceptSchema regionSchema
 = new ConceptSchema(REGION);
          regionSchema.add(NAME, stringSchema);
          regionSchema.add(X0, integerSchema);
          regionSchema.add(Y0, integerSchema);
          regionSchema.add(X1, integerSchema);
          regionSchema.add(Y1, integerSchema);
          add(regionSchema, Region.class);


ConceptSchema serviceSchema
      = new ConceptSchema(SERVICE);
          serviceSchema.add(NAME, stringSchema);
          serviceSchema.add(PROVIDER, stringSchema);
          add(serviceSchema, Service.class);
```

In the system, we have confirmed the simplest framework of the location-mediated coordination by applying the CONSORTS agents to the context-aware information systems. Using the agent-based coordination framework, we have built the context-aware information systems very rapidly. If you define new service agents and its ontology, you can add new services to the system by defining the service agents and their ontologies.

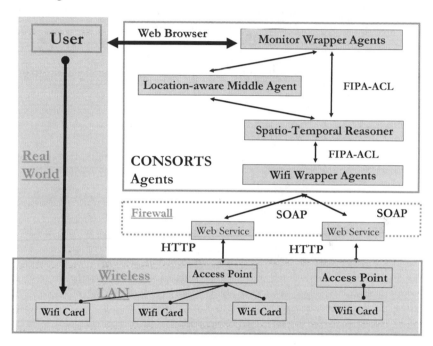

Fig. 11. Outline of Wireless-LAN based Location System

6.2 Wireless-LAN Based Location Systems

To implement "real" application in the Ubiquitous Computing, we need physical devices to detect users' locations. Because we design the device wrapper agent to hide the diversity of the devices API, we can easily integrate the physical devices into the system on the CONSORTS.

Based on the CONSORTS ver.1 architecture, we have implemented Wireless-LAN (IEEE 802.11b) based location system. In the system, the agents are aware of users' locations by watching the status of the wireless-LAN stations. When a note PC or PDA with a user connects with one of the stations, the system detects the connected WiFi card, and stores a MAC address of the card with a physical location of the station. Because a MAC address is globally unique, the system can track the location of the card (with the user) globally.

Fig. 11shows an outline of the location system. In the system, Web services, which provide location information like sensor devices, are integrated with a FIPA-Agent platform, and the information is shared with FIPA-agents. In the system, WiFi-wrapper agents access WiFi access points, and collect information of connected WiFi cards. Collected information is managed by spatio-temporal reasoner in the system.

Fig. 12 is a summary of the ontologies that we have defined to represents the messages between the agents in this application. We have defined 4concepts describing objects of the location system and 2 predicates for describing operations of the system.

We have confirmed the functionality with real wireless-LAN stations that located on various cities (e.g. Barcelona, Tokyo, etc.) in the world using AgentCities Network. Fig. 13 shows a snapshot of the monitor window of the location system in that experiment.

In this experiment, we have shown the potential of the CONSORTS agents to the field where the system needs to access and unify the device-oriented information services covering all over the world.

- **4 Concepts**
  - WifiLocation, Location, Station, Card

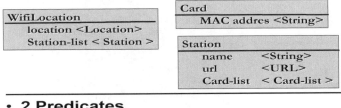

- **2 Predicates**
  - Register, ChkRegistered

Fig. 12. Ontology for the Wireless-LAN based Location System

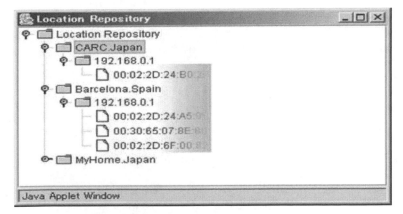

Fig. 13. Snapshot of the Monitor Wrapper Agent

7   Related Work

Numbers of researches on context-aware information assists [26][27][28][29] have been proposed under the vision of Ubiquitous Computing. The Olivetti Active Badge [27] system transmits a unique infrared signal to inform the user's current location every 10 seconds. Based on the information, the system allows the user to re-route incoming calls to the phone nearby. Active Badge is a primitive example of location-based information assist. Xerox PARCTAB [28] system consists of palm-sized mobile computers that can access local area network through infrared transceivers and can inform current location using a unique id. Since these systems are device-oriented prototype systems, they lack the flexible adaptability to the contents and the service domain. Cyberguide [29] is a collection of intelligent tour guides that provide information with tourists based on knowledge of their position and orientation. Because it cannot manage the personal information, it has difficulty to deal with sophisticated user interaction.

Some researchers have applied agent technology to the context-aware information assist services. Using the agent technology, they achieve the flexibility and more sophisticated interaction with users. C-Map [30] is a tour guidance system which provides information to visitors at exhibitions based on location and individual interests. The interface agents manage personal information and realize natural interaction with the user. Agent Augmented Reality [31] is an attempt to use agent technologies for the augmentation of our real world environment. The research realizes personal information assist using mobile agent technology. These systems realize the context-aware information assist by simple cooperation of the agents. However, they seem to have difficulty in sharing the context information among various kinds of services because the context information lacks the basis of well-defined ontological meanings. Thus, it is difficult for them to achieve dynamic intelligent cooperation among the agents based on deep understanding of the context information.

CoolAgent [32] is a context-aware software agent system. The agents can share the context information described by RDF that can be an ontology description framework for the Semantic Web. However, CoolAgent system does not provide the implementations framework of ubiquitous agents, such as location-aware middle agent. In this paper, we formally describe the design pattern of the coordination of ubiquitous agents.

Finally, there exist some researches for middle agents [17][18][19]. As we described before, the work in this paper is extension of their works in Ubiquitous Computing. Hence, their results, such as integration of DAML-S [33], must be useful for our future research.

8   Future Work

In Chapter 2, we have addressed the gaps between users' intentions and services in the Ubiquitous Computing. However we have presupposed that a user's intentions and behaviors do not affect other users' intentions and behaviors. As we design the services not for a single user but for multi users, we confront another gap about user intentions, that is, a gap between mass users' intentions and limited service resources. In order to maintain the performance of the whole system under the limited service resources, the system must consider the way of providing information to users because serious conflict among users about the resource allocation may happen. In that situation, the whole service performance will decrease. In other words, intentions of each user may cause serious conflicts of accessing the limited service resources. For example, navigation systems for emergency evacuation by a fire must consider the strategy of telling evacuees how to evacuate the building safely. If the systems simultaneously tell all users about physically shorted path to the exit, they may flood into the path, and get caught in the crush.

In order to bridge the gaps between mass users' intentions and limited service resources, We are planning to introduce the concept of "Social Coordination" [7][9]. "Social Coordination" aim to resolve the conflict with multi users' requirements and to implicitly modify the providing information for each user in order to maintain the performance of the whole system. We are implementing the facility using market mechanism, called "user intention market" [34].

9   Conclusion

We have shown a multiagent architecture called CONSORTS that aims to realize the human-centered coordination in Ubiquitous Computing. Using standardized agent communication language, called FIPA-ACL, and standard ontology for Ubiquitous Computing, CONSORTS agents can manage devices, services, and users in Ubiquitous Computing, and coordinate the services and the devices based on the locations. In contrast with the Semantic Web agents understand meanings of web-resources on the Internet, the CONSORTS agents focus on understanding cognitive meanings of real-world resources in the Ubiquitous Computing environments.

We have shown two applications of CONSORTS, intelligent information assist systems in museums and wireless-LAN based location systems. Based on the standardized open agent systems that can access and unify the real world information covering all over the world, we can make world-wide applications, and create new application by revising the cooperation scheme of the agents. These applications have shown the potential of the CONSORTS agents that bridge the coordination gaps in the Ubiquitous Computing.

References

[1]   Weiser, M.: The Computer for the 21st Century. Scientific American (1991) 94–104
[2]   Coen, M.H.: Design Principles for Intelligent Environments. In Proceedings of the Conference on Artificial Intelligence (1998) 547–554
[3]   ISTAG: Ambient Intelligence: from vision to reality. `ftp://ftp.cordis.lu/pub/ist/docs/istag-ist2003_draft_consolidated_report.pdf`, (2003)
[4]   Berners-Lee, T., Hendler, J., Lassila, O.: The Semantic Web. Scientific American (2001)

[5]   Resource Description Framework (RDF). http://www.w3.org/RDF/ (2002)
[6]   RDF Vocabulary Description Language 1.0: RDF Schema. http://www.w3.org/TR/rdf-schema/ (2002)
[7]   Kurumatani, K.: Social Coordination with Architecture for Ubiquitous Agents - CONSORTS. In Proceedings of International Conference on Intelligent Agents, Web Technologies and Internet Commerce (CDROM) (2003)
[8]   Sashima, A., Kurumatani, K., Izumi, N.: Physically-Grounding Agents in Ubiquitous Computing. In Proceedings of Joint Agent Workshop and Symposium 2002 (2002) 196–203
[9]   Kurumatani, K.: Social Coordination in Architecture for Physically-Grounding Agents. In Proceedings of Landscape Frontier International Symposium 2002 (2002) 57–62
[10]   The Foundation for Intelligent Physical Agents (FIPA), http://www.fipa.org/ (2002)
[11]   AgentCities Web, http://www.agentcities.org/ (2003)
[12]   Guarino, N.: Formal Ontology and Information Systems. In Proceedings of Formal Ontology in Information Systems (1998) 3–15
[13]   Jennings, N. R.: An agent-based approach for building complex software systems. Communications of the ACM, 44 (4) (2002) 35–41
[14]   Maes, P.: Agents that Reduce Work and Information Overload. Communications of the ACM, 37 (7) (1994) 31–40
[15]   Varzi, C., Casati, R.: Parts and Places. The Structures of Spatial Representation, MIT Press, Cambridge, MA, and London (1999)
[16]   Bittner, T.: Reasoning About Qualitative Spatio-Temporal Relations at Multiple Levels of Granularity. In Proceedings of the 15th European Conference on Artificial Intelligence, IOS Press, Amsterdam (2002) 317–321
[17]   Sycara, K., Decker, K., Williamson, M.: Middle-Agents for the Internet. In Proceedings of the 15th International Joint Conference of Artificial Intelligence (1997) 578–583
[18]   Paolucci, M., Kawamura, T., Payne, T.R., Sycara, K.: Semantic Matching of Web Services Capabilities. In Proceedings of the 1st International Semantic Web Conference (2002) 333–347
[19]   Sycara, K., Klusch, M., Widoff, S., Lu, J.: Dynamic Service Matchmaking among Agents in Open Information Environments. SIGMOD Record (ACM Special Interests Group on Management of Data), 28(1) (1999) 47–53
[20]   Java Agent DEvelopment Framework (JADE). http://sharon.cselt.it/projects/jade/ (2002)
[21]   Finin, T., Labrou, Y., Meyeld. J.: KQML as an Agent Communication Language. In Bradshaw, J.M. (eds.): Software Agents, MIT Press (1997) 291–316
[22]   Noy, N.F., Sintek, M., Decker, S., Crubezy, M., Fergerson, R.W., Musen, M.A.: Creating Semantic Web Contents with Protégé–2000. IEEE Intelligent Systems 16(2) (2001)60–71
[23]   beanGenerator. http://gaper.swi.psy.uva.nl/beangenerator/content/main.php (2003)
[24]   Web Services Activity. http://www.w3.org/2002/ws/ (2002)
[25]   Google Web APIs. http://www.google.com/apis/ (2003)
[26]   Schilit, B., Adams, N., Want. R.: Context-aware Computing Applications. In IEEE Workshop on Mobile Computing Systems and Applications (1994) 85–90
[27]   Way, R., Hopper, A., Falcao, V., Gibbons. J.: The Active Badge Location System. ACM Transactions on Information System, 10(1) (1992) 91–102
[28]   Want, R., Schilit, B.N., Adams, N.I., Gold, R., Peterson, K., Goldberg, D., Ellis, J.R., Weiser, M.: An Overview of the ParcTab Ubiquitous Computing Experiment. In Imielinski, T., Korth, H.F. (eds.): Mobile Computing. Kluwer Academic Publishers, (1996)

[29]   Long, S., Kooper, R., Abowd, G. D., Atkeson, C.G.: Rapid Prototyping of Mobile Context-aware Applications: the Cyberguide Case Study. In Proceedings of First International Symposium on Handheld and Ubiquitous Computing, Springer Verlag (1999) 52–66

[30]   Sumi, Y., Mase, K.: Toward a Real-world Knowledge Medium: Building a Guidance System for Exhibition Tours, New Generation Computing, 17(4) (1999) 407–416

[31]   Nagao, K., Rekimoto, J.: Agent Augmented Reality: A Software Agent Meets the Real World. In Proceedings of the Second International Conference on Multi-Agent Systems (1996) 228–235

[32]   Chen, H., Tolia, S.: Steps Towards Creating a Context-aware Agent System. TR-HPL-2001–231, HP Labs (2001)

[33]   DAML Service. http://www.daml.org/services/ (2002)

[34]   Kurumatani, K.: User Intention Market for Multi-Agent Navigation - An Artificial Intelligent Problem in Engineering and Economic Context. In Proceedings of The AAAI-02 Workshop on Multi-Agent Modeling and Simulation of Economic Systems (2002)1–4

Author Index

Lecture Notes in Artificial Intelligence (LNAI)

Printed in the United States
By Bookmasters